# Contents

## Physics 2b — Electricity and the Atom

## Physics 3a — Medical Applications of Physics

## Phys... and Electromagnetism

## Practice Exams

Published by CGP

From original material by Richard Parsons.

Editors:
Ellen Bowness, Helena Hayes, Felicity Inkpen, Edmund Robinson,
Hayley Thompson, Julie Wakeling, Sarah Williams.

Contributors:
Paddy Gannon, Gemma Hallam, Judith Hayes, Barbara Mascetti, Pat Szczesniak.

ISBN: 978 1 84762 662 2

With thanks to Michael Birch, Ian Francis, Karen Wells and Dawn Wright for the proofreading.
With thanks to Jan Greenway for the copyright research.

Data used to construct stopping distance diagram on page 84 from the Highway Code. ©
Crown Copyright re-produced under the terms of the Click-Use licence.

With thanks to iStockphoto.com for use of the images on page 143.

Groovy website: www.cgpbooks.co.uk

Printed by Elanders Ltd, Newcastle upon Tyne.
Jolly bits of clipart from CorelDRAW®

## The Scientific Process

You need to know a few things about how the world of science works. First up is the <u>scientific process</u> — how a scientist's <u>idea</u> turns into a <u>widely accepted theory</u>.

### Scientists come up with **hypotheses** — then **test** them

*About 500 years ago, we still thought the Solar System looked like this.*

1) Scientists try to <u>explain</u> things. Everything.

2) They start by <u>observing</u> something they don't understand — it could be anything, e.g. planets in the sky, a person suffering from an illness, what matter is made of... anything.

3) Then, they come up with a <u>hypothesis</u> — a <u>possible explanation</u> for what they've observed.

4) The next step is to <u>test</u> whether the hypothesis might be <u>right or not</u> — this involves <u>gathering evidence</u> (i.e. <u>data</u> from <u>investigations</u>).

5) The scientist uses the hypothesis to make a <u>prediction</u> — a statement based on the hypothesis that can be <u>tested</u>. They then <u>carry out an investigation</u>.

6) If data from experiments or studies <u>backs up the prediction</u>, you're one step closer to figuring out if the hypothesis is true.

*Investigations include lab experiments and studies.*

### Other scientists will **test** the hypothesis too

1) <u>Other</u> scientists will use the hypothesis to make their <u>own predictions</u>, and carry out their <u>own experiments</u> or studies.

2) They'll also try to <u>reproduce</u> the original investigations to check the results.

3) And if <u>all the experiments</u> in the world back up the hypothesis, then scientists start to think it's <u>true</u>.

4) However, if a scientist somewhere in the world does an experiment that <u>doesn't</u> fit with the hypothesis (and other scientists can <u>reproduce</u> these results), then the hypothesis is in trouble.

5) When this happens, scientists have to come up with a new hypothesis (maybe a <u>modification</u> of the old hypothesis, or maybe a completely <u>new</u> one).

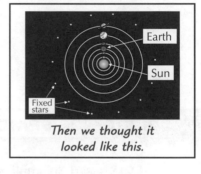

*Then we thought it looked like this.*

### If **evidence** supports a hypothesis, it's **accepted** — **for now**

1) If pretty much every scientist in the world believes a hypothesis to be true because experiments back it up, then it usually goes in the <u>textbooks</u> for students to learn.

*Now we think it's more like this.*

2) Accepted hypotheses are often referred to as <u>theories</u>.

3) Our <u>currently accepted</u> theories are the ones that have survived this 'trial by evidence' — they've been tested many, many times over the years and survived (while the less good ones have been ditched).

4) However... they never, <u>never</u> become hard and fast, totally indisputable <u>fact</u>. You can never know... it'd only take <u>one</u> odd, totally inexplicable result, and the hypothesising and testing would start all over again.

### If you expect me to believe it, then show me the evidence

If scientists think something is true, they need to produce evidence to convince others — it's all part of <u>testing a hypothesis</u>. One hypothesis might survive these tests, while others won't — it's how things progress. And along the way some hypotheses will be disproved — i.e. shown not to be true.

# Your Data's Got To be Good

Evidence is the key to science — but not all evidence is equally good.
The way evidence is gathered can have a big effect on how trustworthy it is.

## Lab experiments and studies are better than rumour

1) Results from experiments in laboratories are great. A lab is the easiest place to control variables so that they're all kept constant (except for the one you're investigating). This makes it easier to carry out a FAIR TEST.

*See page 7 for more about fair tests and variables.*

2) For things that you can't investigate in the lab (e.g. climate) you conduct scientific studies. As many of the variables as possible are controlled, to make it a fair test.

3) Old wives' tales, rumours, hearsay, "what someone said", and so on, should be taken with a pinch of salt. Without any evidence they're NOT scientific — they're just opinions.

## The bigger the sample size the better

1) Data based on small samples isn't as good as data based on large samples.

2) A sample should be representative of the whole population (i.e. it should share as many of the various characteristics in the population as possible) — a small sample can't do that as well.

3) The bigger the sample size the better, but scientists have to be realistic when choosing how big.

4) For example, if you were studying how lifestyle affects people's weight it'd be great to study everyone in the UK (a huge sample), but it'd take ages and cost loads. Studying a thousand people is more realistic.

## When it comes to samples, bigger means better

A census is a study which takes into account the entire population — great for collecting loads of data, and properly representative of the whole population, but very difficult and expensive to carry out. A census is conducted in the UK every ten years and is used by the government to plan for the future, but it isn't cheap — the costs of the 2011 census were estimated to be at around £500 million.

# Your Data's Got To be Good

## Evidence needs to be **reliable (repeatable** and **reproducible)**

Evidence is only <u>reliable</u> if it can be <u>repeated</u> (during an experiment) AND <u>other scientists can reproduce it too</u> (in other experiments). If it's not reliable, you can't believe it.

> RELIABLE means that the data can be <u>repeated, and reproduced by others</u>.

> <u>EXAMPLE: COLD FUSION</u>
>
> In 1989, two scientists claimed that they'd produced '<u>cold fusion</u>' (the energy source of the Sun — but without the big temperatures). It was huge news — if true, it would have meant cheap and abundant energy for the world... forever. However, other scientists just <u>couldn't reproduce the results</u> — so the results <u>weren't reliable</u>. And until they are, 'cold fusion' isn't going to be accepted as <u>fact</u>.

## Evidence also needs to be **valid**

> VALID means that the data is <u>reliable</u> AND <u>answers the original question</u>.

> <u>EXAMPLE: DO POWER LINES CAUSE CANCER?</u>
> Some studies have found that children who live near <u>overhead power lines</u> are more likely to develop <u>cancer</u>. What they'd actually found was a <u>correlation</u> (relationship) between the variables "<u>presence of power lines</u>" and "<u>incidence of cancer</u>" — they found that as one changed, so did the other.
>
>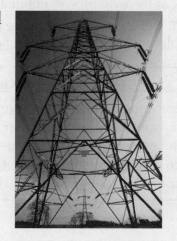
>
> But this evidence is <u>not enough</u> to say that the power lines <u>cause</u> cancer, as other explanations might be possible. For example, power lines are often near <u>busy roads</u>, so the areas tested could contain <u>different levels</u> of <u>pollution</u> from traffic. So these studies don't show a definite link and so don't <u>answer the original question</u>.

---

## RRRR — Remember, Reliable means Repeatable and Reproducible

By now you should have realised how <u>important</u> trustworthy <u>evidence</u> is. Unfortunately, you need to know loads more about fair tests and experiments — see page 7 for more on that.

# Bias and Issues Created by Science

Even the world of science isn't without its problems. <u>Bias</u> can get the better of even the most accomplished scientists — which is why it's important for you to <u>recognise</u> it when it rears its ugly head.

## Scientific *evidence* can be *presented* in a *biased way*

1) People who want to make a point can sometimes <u>present data</u> in a <u>biased way</u>, e.g. they overemphasise a relationship in the data. (Sometimes <u>without knowing</u> they're doing it.)

2) And there are all sorts of reasons <u>why</u> people might <u>want</u> to do this — for example...

- They want to keep the <u>organisation</u> or <u>company</u> that's <u>funding the research</u> happy. (If the results aren't what they'd like they might not give them any more money to fund further research.)
- <u>Governments</u> might want to persuade voters, other governments, journalists, etc.
- <u>Companies</u> might want to show off their products or make impressive safety claims.
- <u>Environmental campaigners</u> might want to persuade people to behave differently.

## Things can affect *how seriously evidence is taken*

1) If an investigation is done by a team of <u>highly-regarded scientists</u> it's sometimes taken <u>more seriously</u> than evidence from <u>less well known scientists</u>.

2) But having experience, authority or a fancy qualification <u>doesn't</u> necessarily mean the evidence is <u>good</u> — the only way to tell is to look at the evidence scientifically (e.g. is it reliable, valid, etc.).

3) Also, some evidence might be <u>ignored</u> if it could create <u>political problems</u>, or <u>emphasised</u> if it <u>helps a particular cause</u>.

<u>EXAMPLE: GLOBAL WARMING</u>

Some governments were <u>pretty slow</u> to accept the fact that human activities are causing <u>global warming</u>, despite all the <u>evidence</u>. This is because accepting it means they've got to <u>do something about it</u>, which <u>costs money</u> and could <u>hurt their economy</u>. This could <u>lose</u> them a lot of <u>votes</u>.

## Trust me — I've got a BSc and a PhD

It's easy to believe people in authority, but you have to ignore that fact and look at the evidence. Spotting biased evidence can be difficult — ask yourself 'Does the scientist (or the person writing about it) stand to gain something (or lose something)?' If they do, it's possible that it could be biased.

# Bias and Issues Created by Science

No area of science is without issues of some kind — whether it's the matter of finding the money to <u>fund research</u>, <u>environmental problems</u> or even <u>ethical issues</u>, there's always plenty of room for <u>controversy</u>.

## *Scientific developments are great, but they can raise issues*

Scientific <u>knowledge is increased</u> by doing experiments. And this knowledge leads to <u>scientific developments</u>, e.g. new technologies or new advice. These developments can create <u>issues</u> though. For example:

**Economic issues:** Society <u>can't</u> always <u>afford</u> to do things scientists recommend (e.g. investing heavily in alternative energy sources) without <u>cutting back elsewhere</u>.

**Social issues:** Decisions based on scientific evidence affect <u>people</u> — e.g. should fossil fuels be taxed more highly (to invest in alternative energy)? Should alcohol be banned (to prevent health problems)? <u>Would the effect on people's lifestyles be acceptable...</u>

**Environmental issues:** <u>Nuclear power stations</u> can provide us with a reliable source of <u>electricity</u>, but disposing of the <u>waste</u> can lead to <u>environmental issues</u>.

**Ethical issues:** There are a lot of things that scientific developments have made possible, but <u>should we do them</u>? E.g. develop better nuclear weapons.

## *Where science goes, controversy follows*

<u>Nuclear energy</u> is one area of science that raises a lot of issues — <u>economic</u> (is it too expensive? Is it a viable energy option?), <u>social</u> (will it affect people living nearby?), <u>environmental</u> (will nuclear waste pollute the surrounding area?) and <u>ethical</u> (should we use the technology to develop weapons?).

# Science Has Limits

Science can give us amazing things — cures for diseases, space travel, heated toilet seats...
But science has its limitations — there are questions that it just can't answer.

## Some questions are **unanswered** by science — so far

1) We don't understand everything. And we never will. We'll find out more,
   for sure — as more hypotheses are suggested, and more experiments are done.
   But there'll always be things we don't know.

   > EXAMPLES:
   > - Today we don't know as much as we'd like about the impacts of global warming.
   >   How much will sea level rise? And to what extent will weather patterns change?
   > - We also don't know anywhere near as much as we'd like about the Universe.
   >   Are there other life forms out there? And what is the Universe made of?

2) These are complicated questions. At the moment scientists don't all agree on the
   answers because there isn't enough reliable and valid evidence.

3) But eventually, we probably will be able to answer these questions once and for all...
   All we need is more evidence.

4) But by then there'll be loads of new questions to answer.

## Other questions are **unanswerable** by science

1) Then there's the other type... questions that all the experiments in the world won't help us answer
   — the "Should we be doing this at all?" type questions. There are always two sides...

2) Take space exploration. It's possible to do it — but does that mean we should?

3) Different people have different opinions.

For example...
Some people say it's a good idea... it increases our knowledge about the
Universe, we develop new technologies that can be useful on Earth too,
it inspires young people to take an interest in science, etc.

Other people say it's a bad idea... the vast sums of money it costs should
be spent on more urgent problems, like providing clean drinking water
and curing diseases in poor countries. Others say that we should
concentrate research efforts on understanding our own planet better first.

4) The question of whether something is morally or ethically right or wrong can't be answered by
   more experiments — there is no "right" or "wrong" answer.

5) The best we can do is get a consensus from society — a judgement that most people are more or
   less happy to live by. Science can provide more information to help people make this judgement,
   and the judgement might change over time. But in the end it's up to people and their conscience.

---

## Science doesn't have all the answers

Science can't tell you whether you should or shouldn't do something. That kind of thing is up to you
and society to decide. There are tons of questions that science might be able to answer in the future
— like how much sea level might rise due to global warming, or what the Universe is made of.

# Designing Investigations

You need to know a lot about <u>investigations</u> for your <u>controlled assessment</u> and <u>all your exams</u>. Investigations include <u>experiments</u> and <u>studies</u>. The next nine pages take you from start to finish. Enjoy.

## Investigations *produce evidence* to *support* or *disprove* a *hypothesis*

1) Scientists <u>observe</u> things and come up with <u>hypotheses</u> to explain them (see page 1).

2) To figure out whether a hypothesis might be correct or not you need to do an <u>investigation</u> to gather some <u>evidence</u>.

3) The first step is to use the hypothesis to come up with a <u>prediction</u> — a statement about what you <u>think will happen</u> that you can <u>test</u>.

4) For example, if your <u>hypothesis</u> is:

> "Tooth cavities are caused by eating too much sugary food."

Then your <u>prediction</u> might be:

> "People who eat more sugary food will have more tooth cavities."

*Sometimes the words 'hypothesis' and 'prediction' are used interchangeably.*

5) Investigations are used to see if there are <u>patterns</u> or <u>relationships</u> <u>between two variables</u>. For example, to see if there's a pattern or relationship between the variables 'having tooth cavities' and 'consumption of sugary food'.

*See page 3 for more on reliability and validity.*

6) The investigation has to be a <u>FAIR TEST</u> to make sure the evidence is <u>reliable</u> and <u>valid</u>...

## To make an investigation a *fair test* you have to *control the variables*

1) In a lab experiment you usually <u>change one variable</u> and <u>measure</u> how it affects the <u>other variable</u>.

> EXAMPLE: you might change only the angle of a slope and measure how it affects the time taken for a toy car to travel down it.

2) To make it a fair test <u>everything else</u> that could affect the results should <u>stay the same</u> (otherwise you can't tell if the thing you're changing is causing the results or not — the data won't be reliable or valid).

> EXAMPLE continued: you need to keep the slope length the same, otherwise you won't know if any change in the time taken is caused by the change in angle, or the change in length.

3) The variable you CHANGE is called the INDEPENDENT variable.

4) The variable you MEASURE is called the DEPENDENT variable.

5) The variables that you KEEP THE SAME are called CONTROL variables.

> EXAMPLE continued:
> Independent variable = angle of slope
> Dependent variable = time taken
> Control variable = length of slope

# Designing Investigations

Before you start collecting data, it's useful to know the sort of results you might get so you can design your experiment to be as good as it can be. That's why scientists use <u>trial runs</u> and <u>preliminary experiments</u>.

## Trial runs *help decide the* range *and* interval *of* variable values

1) It's a good idea to do a <u>trial run</u> first — a <u>quick version</u> of your experiment.

SLOPE EXAMPLE FROM PREVIOUS PAGE CONTINUED:

- You might do trial runs at 20, 40, 60 and 80°. If the time taken is too short to accurately measure at 80°, you might narrow the range to 20-60°.

- If using 20° intervals gives you a big change in time taken you might decide to use 10° intervals, e.g. 20, 30, 40, 50°...

2) Trial runs are used to figure out the <u>range</u> of variable values used in the proper experiment (the upper and lower limit). For example, if you <u>can't</u> accurately measure the change in the dependent variable at the upper values in the trial run, you might <u>narrow</u> the range in the proper experiment.

3) And trial runs can be used to figure out the <u>interval</u> (gaps) between the values too. The intervals can't be too small (otherwise the experiment would take ages), or too big (otherwise you might miss something).

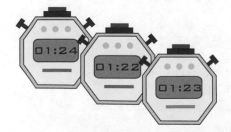

4) Trial runs can also help you figure out <u>how many times</u> the experiment has to be <u>repeated</u> to get reliable results. E.g. if you repeat it three times and the <u>results</u> are all <u>similar</u>, then three repeats is enough.

## You won't get a trial run at the exam, so get learning

Always use trial runs to help you <u>plan</u> your investigation so you can make it as <u>effective as possible</u>. A trial run can give you an idea of <u>what kind of values you're looking for</u>.

# Designing Investigations

Not all investigations can be conducted within the laboratory. Sometimes there are <u>extra variables</u> that you can't control. That doesn't mean you can ignore them though — it means it's time for a <u>control group</u>.

## It can be *hard* to *control the variables* in a *study*

1) It's important that a study is a <u>fair test</u>, just like a lab experiment.

2) It's a lot trickier to control the variables in a study than it is in a lab experiment though (see page 7). Sometimes you can't control them all, but you can use a <u>control group</u> to help.

3) This is a group of whatever you're studying (people, plants, lemmings, etc.) that's kept under the <u>same conditions</u> as the group in the experiment, but doesn't have anything done to it.

> EXAMPLE: PESTICIDES
>
> If you're studying the effect of pesticides on crop growth,
> pesticide is applied to one field but <u>not to another field</u> (the control field).
>
>
> Both fields are planted with the <u>same crop</u>, and are in the <u>same area</u> (so they get the same weather conditions). The control field is there to try and account for variables like the weather, which don't stay the same all the time, but could <u>affect the results</u>.

## Investigations can be *hazardous*

1) A <u>hazard</u> is something that can <u>potentially cause harm</u>. Hazards include:

- <u>Microorganisms</u>, e.g. some bacteria can make you ill.
- <u>Chemicals</u>, e.g. sulfuric acid can burn your skin and alcohols catch fire easily.
- <u>Fire</u>, e.g. an unattended Bunsen burner is a fire hazard.
- <u>Electricity</u>, e.g. faulty electrical equipment could give you a shock.

2) Scientists need to <u>manage the risk</u> of hazards by doing things to reduce them. For example:

*You can find out about potential hazards by looking in textbooks, doing some internet research, or asking your teacher.*

- If you're working with <u>sulfuric acid</u>, always wear gloves and safety goggles. This will reduce the risk of the acid coming into contact with your skin and eyes.
- If you're using a <u>Bunsen burner</u>, stand it on a heat proof mat. This will reduce the risk of starting a fire.

# Collecting Data

After designing an investigation you'll need to get your hands mucky and <u>collect some data</u>.

## Your data should be *reliable*, *accurate* and *precise*

1) To <u>improve</u> reliability you need to <u>repeat</u> the readings and calculate the <u>mean</u> (average). You need to repeat each reading at least <u>three times</u>.

2) To make sure your results are reliable you can cross check them by taking a <u>second set of readings</u> with <u>another instrument</u> (or a <u>different observer</u>).

3) Checking your results match with <u>secondary sources</u>, e.g. other studies, also increases the reliability of your data.

4) Your data also needs to be <u>ACCURATE</u>. Really accurate results are those that are <u>really close</u> to the <u>true answer</u>.

5) Your data also needs to be <u>PRECISE</u>. Precise results are ones where the data is <u>all really close</u> to the mean (i.e. not spread out).

| Repeat | Data set 1 | Data set 2 |
|--------|-----------|-----------|
| 1 | 12 | 11 |
| 2 | 14 | 17 |
| 3 | 13 | 14 |
| Mean | 13 | 14 |

*Data set 1 is more precise than data set 2.*

## Your *equipment* has to be *right for the job*

1) The measuring equipment you use has to be <u>sensitive enough</u> to measure the changes you're looking for.

> For example, if you need to measure changes of 1 ml you need to use a measuring cylinder that can measure in 1 ml steps — it'd be no good trying with one that only measures 10 ml steps.

2) The <u>smallest change</u> a measuring instrument can <u>detect</u> is called its <u>RESOLUTION</u>.

> E.g. some mass balances have a resolution of 1 g, some have a resolution of 0.1 g, and some are even more sensitive.

3) Also, equipment needs to be <u>calibrated</u> so that your data is <u>more accurate</u>.

> E.g. mass balances need to be set to zero before you start weighing things.

## For good data, remember RAP — Reliable, Accurate and Precise

Weirdly, data can be really <u>precise</u> but <u>not very accurate</u>, e.g. a fancy piece of lab equipment might give results that are precise, but if it's not calibrated properly those results won't be accurate. Likewise, data can be accurate <u>without</u> being precise. For example, an experiment might tell you that the speed of sound in air is in the range of 300 m/s to 350 m/s. This is accurate (because it's true) but it's not at all precise.

# Collecting Data

All experimental data have some errors in them. A good scientist doesn't ignore errors, but instead finds out why they are there and tries to minimise them.

## You need to look out for errors and anomalous results

1) The results of your experiment will always vary a bit because of random errors — tiny differences caused by things like human errors in measuring.

2) You can reduce their effect by taking many readings and calculating the mean.

3) If the same error is made every time, it's called a systematic error. For example, if you measured from the very end of your ruler instead of from the 0 cm mark every time, all your measurements would be a bit small.

4) Just to make things more complicated, if a systematic error is caused by using equipment that isn't calibrated properly it's called a zero error. For example, if a mass balance always reads 1 gram before you put anything on it, all your measurements will be 1 gram too heavy.

5) You can compensate for some systematic errors if you know about them though, e.g. if your mass balance always reads 1 gram before you put anything on it you can subtract 1 gram from all your results.

6) Sometimes you get a result that doesn't seem to fit in with the rest at all. These results are called anomalous results.

7) You should investigate them and try to work out what happened. If you can work out what happened (e.g. you measured something totally wrong) you can ignore them when processing your results.

| Park | Number of pigeons | Number of litter bins |
|------|-------------------|----------------------|
| A | 28 | 4 |
| B | 42 | 2 |
| C | 1127 | 0 |

## Avoid zero errors — always calibrate your equipment

It's not enough just to identify which results are anomalous — you should provide a reason for why they are there. Otherwise, they might not be anomalous results at all, they could just a be a result that you are missing due to bias in your experiment. One scientist's anomaly could be another's discovery.

# Processing and Presenting Data

After you've collected your data you'll have <u>lots of info</u> that you have to <u>make some kind of sense of</u>. You need to <u>process</u> and <u>present</u> it so you can look for <u>patterns</u> and <u>relationships</u> in it.

## Data needs to be organised

1) Tables are dead useful for <u>organising data</u>.

2) When you draw a table <u>use a ruler</u>, make sure <u>each column</u> has a <u>heading</u> (including the <u>units</u>) and keep it neat and tidy.

3) Annoyingly, tables aren't very useful for showing <u>patterns</u> or <u>relationships</u> in data. You need to use some kind of graph for that.

## You might have to process your data

1) When you've done repeats of an experiment you should always calculate the <u>mean</u> (average). To do this <u>ADD TOGETHER</u> all the data values and <u>DIVIDE</u> by the total number of values in the sample.

2) You might also need to calculate the <u>range</u> (how spread out the data is). To do this find the <u>LARGEST</u> number and <u>SUBTRACT</u> the <u>SMALLEST</u> number from it.

*Ignore anomalous results when calculating these.*

EXAMPLE

| Test tube | Repeat 1 (g) | Repeat 2 (g) | Repeat 3 (g) | Mean (g) | Range (g) |
|-----------|-------------|-------------|-------------|----------|-----------|
| A | 28 | 37 | 32 | (28 + 37 + 32) ÷ 3 = 32.3 | 37 − 28 = 9 |
| B | 47 | 51 | 60 | (47 + 51 + 60) ÷ 3 = 52.7 | 60 − 47 = 13 |
| C | 68 | 72 | 70 | (68 + 72 + 70) ÷ 3 = 70.0 | 72 − 68 = 4 |

## If your data comes in categories, present it in a bar chart

1) If the independent variable is <u>categoric</u> (comes in distinct categories, e.g. blood types, metals) you should use a <u>bar chart</u> to display the data.

2) You also use them if the independent variable is <u>discrete</u> (the data can be counted in chunks, where there's no in-between value, e.g. number of people is discrete because you can't have half a person).

3) There are some <u>golden rules</u> you need to follow for <u>drawing</u> bar charts:

If you've got more than one set of data <u>include a key</u>.

Remember to include the <u>units</u>.

Ice Cream Sales in Malmesbury and Chippenham

Label both axes.

Draw it nice and <u>big</u> (covering at least a third of the graph paper).

Leave a <u>gap between</u> different categories.

## Bar charts — perfect for discrete variables

The stuff on this page might all seem a bit basic, but it's <u>easy marks</u> in the exams. Examiners are a bit picky when it comes to bar charts — if you don't draw them properly they won't be happy. Also, <u>double check</u> any mean or range <u>calculations</u> you do, just to be sure they're correct.

# Presenting Data

## If your data is *continuous*, plot a *line graph*

1) If the independent variable is <u>continuous</u> (numerical data that can have any value within a range, e.g. length, volume, temperature) you should use a <u>line graph</u> to display the data.

2) Here are the <u>rules</u> for <u>drawing</u> line graphs:

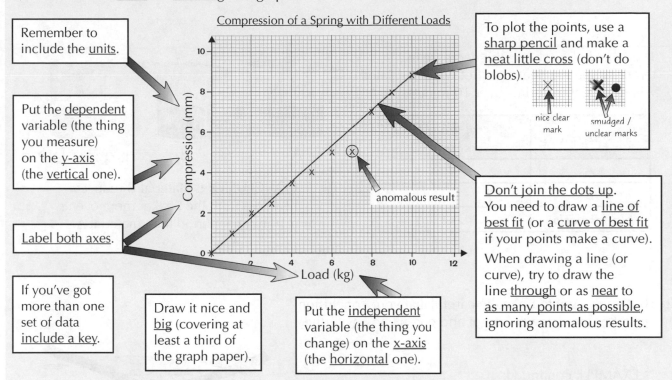

Compression of a Spring with Different Loads

Remember to include the <u>units</u>.

Put the <u>dependent</u> variable (the thing you measure) on the <u>y-axis</u> (the <u>vertical</u> one).

<u>Label both axes</u>.

If you've got more than one set of data <u>include a key</u>.

Draw it nice and <u>big</u> (covering at least a third of the graph paper).

Put the <u>independent</u> variable (the thing you change) on the <u>x-axis</u> (the <u>horizontal</u> one).

anomalous result

To plot the points, use a <u>sharp pencil</u> and make a <u>neat little cross</u> (don't do blobs).

nice clear mark

smudged / unclear marks

<u>Don't join the dots up</u>. You need to draw a <u>line of best fit</u> (or a <u>curve of best fit</u> if your points make a curve).

When drawing a line (or curve), try to draw the line <u>through</u> or as <u>near</u> to <u>as many points as possible</u>, ignoring anomalous results.

3) Line graphs are used to <u>show the relationship</u> between two variables (just like other graphs).

4) Data can show <u>three</u> different types of correlation (relationship):

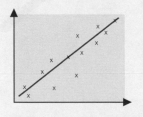

<u>POSITIVE correlation</u> — as one variable <u>increases</u> the other <u>increases</u>.

<u>NEGATIVE correlation</u> — as one variable <u>increases</u> the other <u>decreases</u>.

<u>NO correlation</u> — there's <u>no relationship</u> between the two variables.

5) You need to be able to describe the following relationships on line graphs too:

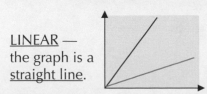

<u>LINEAR</u> — the graph is a <u>straight line</u>.

<u>DIRECTLY PROPORTIONAL</u> — the graph is a <u>straight line</u> where both variables increase (or decrease) in the <u>same ratio</u>.

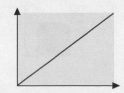

---

## There's a positive correlation between revision and boredom

...but there's also a positive correlation between <u>revision</u> and getting a <u>better mark in the exam</u>. Cover the page and write down the <u>rules</u> you need to remember when <u>drawing graphs</u>.

# Drawing Conclusions

So you've made a hypothesis, done your experiment, collected your data and made some very nice graphs. Congratulations — you've made it to the <u>final step</u> of a gruelling investigation — <u>drawing conclusions</u>.

## You can *only conclude* what the data shows and *NO MORE*

1) Drawing conclusions might seem pretty straightforward — you just <u>look at your data</u> and <u>say what pattern or relationship you see</u> between the dependent and independent variables.

EXAMPLE:
The table below shows the decrease in temperature of a beaker of hot water insulated with different materials over 10 minutes.

| Material | Mean temperature decrease (°C) |
|----------|-------------------------------|
| A | 4 |
| B | 2 |
| No insulation | 20 |

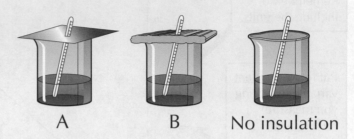

A          B          No insulation

CONCLUSION: Material <u>B</u> reduces heat loss from the beaker more over a <u>10 minute</u> period than material A.

2) But you've got to be really careful that your conclusion <u>matches the data</u> you've got and <u>doesn't go any further</u>.

EXAMPLE continued:
You <u>can't</u> conclude that material B would reduce heat loss by the same amount for <u>any other type of container</u> — the results could be totally different.

3) You also need to be able to <u>use your results</u> to <u>justify your conclusion</u> (i.e. back up your conclusion with some specific data).

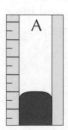 

EXAMPLE continued:
Material B reduced heat loss from the beaker by 2 °C more on average than material A.

---

## *I conclude that this page is a bit dull...*

...although, just because I find it dull doesn't mean that I can conclude it's dull. In the exams you could be given a <u>conclusion</u> and asked <u>whether some data supports it</u> — so make sure you understand <u>how far conclusions can go</u> and don't go any further — it's bad science otherwise.

# Drawing Conclusions

Sometimes, drawing a conclusion is really <u>straightforward</u>. But it can be easy to make a conclusion that <u>seems</u> to be supported by your evidence, but <u>actually isn't</u>. This page explains how to avoid these pitfalls.

## *Correlation DOES NOT mean cause*

1) If two things are correlated (i.e. there's a relationship between them) it <u>doesn't</u> necessarily mean that a change in one variable is <u>causing</u> the change in the other — this is <u>really important, don't forget it</u>.

2) There are <u>three possible reasons</u> for a correlation:

### 1 CHANCE

1) Even though it might seem a bit weird, it's possible that two things show a correlation in a study purely because of <u>chance</u>.

2) For example, one study might find a correlation between people's hair colour and how good they are at frisbee. But other scientists don't get a correlation when they investigate it — the results of the first study are just a fluke.

### 2 LINKED BY A 3rd VARIABLE

1) A lot of the time it may <u>look</u> as if a change in one variable is causing a change in the other, but it <u>isn't</u> — a <u>third variable links</u> the two things.

2) For example, there's a correlation between water temperature and shark attacks. This obviously isn't because warmer water makes sharks crazy. Instead, they're linked by a third variable — the number of people swimming (more people swim when the water's hotter, and with more people in the water you get more shark attacks).

### 3 CAUSE

1) Sometimes a change in one variable does <u>cause</u> a change in the other.

2) For example, there's a correlation between exposure to radiation and thyroid cancer. This is because radiation can cause cancer.

3) You can only conclude that a correlation is due to cause when you've <u>controlled all the variables</u> that could, just could, be affecting the result. (For the radiation example above this would include things like age and exposure to other things that cause cancer).

## *Some correlations are more complicated than they first seem*

If there is one thing to take away from this page it's that <u>correlation does not imply causation</u>. This is a <u>really important</u> idea in science — you could link pretty much anything to anything else if you try hard enough. For example, there's a <u>correlation</u> between the rise in atmospheric $CO_2$ levels and the rise in obesity — which could lead you to conclude that obesity is <u>caused</u> by atmospheric $CO_2$. But it might be that both atmospheric $CO_2$ levels and obesity levels have risen with the <u>number of cars sold</u>.

# Controlled Assessment (ISA) — Section One

Controlled Assessment involves doing an experiment and answering two question papers on it under exam conditions. First up, planning your experiment.

## There are two sections in the Controlled Assessment

### Part one: planning

Before you do the Section 1 question paper you'll be given time to do some research into the topic that's been set — you'll need to develop a hypothesis/prediction and come up with two different methods to test it.

In your research, you should use a variety of different sources (e.g. the internet, textbooks etc.). You'll need to be able to outline both methods and say which one is best (and why it's the best one) and describe your preferred method in detail.

You're allowed to write notes about your two methods on one side of A4 and have them with you for both question papers.

In Section 1, you could be asked things like:

1) What your hypothesis/prediction is.

2) What variables you're going to control (and how you're going to control them).

3) What measurements you're going to take.

4) What range and interval of values you will use for the independent variable.

5) How you'd figure out the range and interval using a trial run (sometimes called a 'preliminary investigation' in the question papers). See page 8 for more.

6) How many times you're going to repeat the experiment — a minimum of three is a good idea.

*There's lots of help on all of these things on pages 7-11.*

7) What equipment you're going to use (and why that equipment is right for the job).

8) How to carry out the experiment, i.e. what you do first, what you do second...

9) What hazards are involved in doing the experiment, and how to reduce them.

10) What table you'll draw to put your results in. See page 12 for how to draw one that examiners will love.

When you've done the planning and completed the first question paper you'll actually do the experiment. Then you'll have to present your data. Make sure you use the right type of graph, and you draw it properly — see pages 12-13 for help.

After that it's onto the Section 2 question paper (see next page).

## When you fail to plan, you're planning to fail

That might be an Everest-sized list of stuff, but it's all important. No need to panic at the sight of it though — as long as you've learnt everything on the previous few pages, you should be fine.

# Controlled Assessment (ISA) — Section Two

Once you've planned your experiment and got some data, it's time to move on to the second part of the controlled assessment — coming up with some <u>conclusions</u>.

## Part two: *drawing conclusions and evaluating*

For the Section 2 question paper you have to do these things for <u>your experiment</u>:

1) <u>Analyse</u> and <u>draw conclusions</u> from your results. For this you need to <u>describe the relationship</u> between the variables in <u>detail</u> — see page 13 for how to do this.

> E.g. 'I found that there is a relationship between eating sugary foods and having tooth cavities. The more sugary foods you eat the more tooth cavities you'll have. For example, my results showed...'.

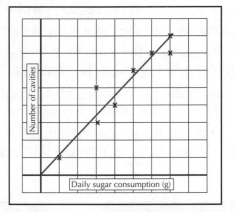

2) Say whether your results <u>back up the hypothesis/prediction</u>, and give reasons <u>why</u> or <u>why not</u>.

> E.g. 'My results did not back up the prediction. The prediction was that eating more sugary food has no effect on the number of tooth cavities you have. But I found the opposite to be true in my investigation'.

3) <u>Evaluate</u> your experiment. For this you need to <u>suggest ways you could improve your experiment</u>.

- Comment on your <u>equipment</u> and <u>method</u>, e.g. could you have used more <u>accurate</u> equipment?

- Make sure you <u>explain how</u> the improvements would give you <u>better data</u> next time.

- <u>Refer to your results</u>. E.g. 'My data wasn't accurate enough because the mass balance I used only measured in 1 g steps. I could use a more sensitive one next time (e.g. a mass balance that measures in 0.5 g steps) to get more accurate data'.

4) You'll also be <u>given some secondary data</u> (data collected by someone else) from an experiment on the same topic and asked to <u>analyse it</u>. This just involves doing what you did for your data with the secondary data, e.g. draw conclusions from it.

## *If that's controlled assessment, I'd hate to see uncontrolled assessment*

Don't panic when you're given some secondary data — just because someone else collected it doesn't mean it's any better than the data you have collected yourself so look at it with an <u>unbiased eye</u>. Remember to check for <u>anomalies</u> and <u>trends</u>, and make sure you only make conclusions based on what the data says and <u>no more</u>.

# Heat Radiation

Heat energy flows away from a hotter object to its <u>cooler surroundings</u>.

## *Heat is **transferred** in **three different ways***

1) <u>Heat energy</u> can be transferred by <u>radiation</u>, <u>conduction</u> or <u>convection</u>.
2) <u>Heat radiation</u> is the transfer of heat energy by <u>infrared (IR) radiation</u> (see below).
3) <u>Conduction and convection</u> involve the transfer of energy by <u>particles</u>.
4) <u>Conduction</u> is the main form of heat transfer in <u>solids</u> (see p.20).
5) <u>Convection</u> is the main form of heat transfer in <u>liquids and gases</u> (see p.21).
6) <u>Infrared radiation</u> can be emitted by <u>solids, liquids and gases</u>.
7) <u>Any</u> object can both <u>absorb</u> and <u>emit</u> infrared radiation,
   whether or not conduction or convection are also taking place.
8) The <u>bigger the temperature difference</u> between a body and its surroundings,
   the <u>faster energy is transferred by heating</u>.

## *Infrared **radiation** — **emission** of **electromagnetic waves***

1) <u>All objects</u> are <u>continually</u> emitting and absorbing <u>infrared radiation</u>.
   Infrared radiation is emitted from the <u>surface</u> of an <u>object</u>.
2) An object that's <u>hotter</u> than its surroundings <u>emits more radiation</u> than it <u>absorbs</u> (as it <u>cools</u> down).
   And an object that's <u>cooler</u> than its surroundings <u>absorbs more radiation</u> than it <u>emits</u> (as it <u>warms</u> up).
3) The <u>hotter</u> an object is, the <u>more</u> radiation it radiates in a <u>given time</u>.
4) You can <u>feel</u> this <u>infrared radiation</u> if you stand near something <u>hot</u> like a fire or if you put your hand just above the bonnet of a recently parked car.

(recently parked car)          (after an hour or so)

## *Radiation **depends** on **surface colour** and **texture***

1) <u>Dark</u>, <u>matt</u> surfaces <u>absorb</u> infrared radiation falling on them much <u>better</u> than <u>light</u>, <u>shiny</u> surfaces, such as <u>gloss white</u> or <u>silver</u>. They also <u>emit much more</u> infrared radiation (at any given temperature).
2) <u>Light</u>, <u>shiny</u> surfaces <u>reflect</u> a lot of the infrared radiation falling on them. E.g. <u>vacuum flasks</u> (see p.26) have <u>silver inner surfaces</u> to keep heat in or out, depending on whether it's storing hot or cold liquid.

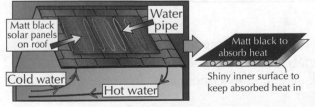

3) <u>Solar hot water panels</u> contain <u>water pipes</u> under a <u>black surface</u> (or black painted pipes under glass).
4) <u>Radiation</u> from the Sun is <u>absorbed</u> by the <u>black surface</u> to <u>heat the water</u> in the pipes.
5) This water can be used for <u>washing</u> or pumped to <u>radiators</u> to heat the building.

---

## *Confusingly, radiators transfer most of their heat by convection*

In the exam, you might be asked about an example of <u>IR radiation</u> that you've not seen before. Just remember that any <u>light</u>, <u>shiny</u> surfaces will <u>reflect</u> IR radiation and <u>dark</u>, <u>matt</u> surfaces will <u>absorb</u> it, and you should be able to figure out what's going on.

# Kinetic Theory

Kinetic theory is simpler than it sounds — it just describes how particles move in solids, liquids and gases. The energy an object (or particle) has because of its movement is called its kinetic energy.

## *Kinetic theory can explain the three states of matter*

The three states of matter are solid (e.g. ice), liquid (e.g. water) and gas (e.g. water vapour). The particles of a particular substance in each state are the same — only the arrangement and energy of the particles are different.

### Solids

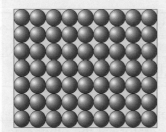

1) Strong forces of attraction hold the particles close together in a fixed, regular arrangement.

2) The particles don't have much energy so they can only vibrate about their fixed positions.

### Liquids

1) There are weaker forces of attraction between the particles.

2) The particles are close together, but can move past each other, and form irregular arrangements.

3) They have more energy than the particles in a solid.

4) They move in random directions at low speeds.

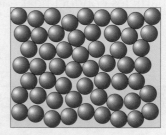

### Gases

1) There are almost no forces of attraction between the particles.

2) The particles have more energy than those in liquids and solids.

3) They are free to move, and travel in random directions and at high speeds.

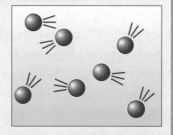

When you heat a substance, you give its particles more kinetic energy (KE) — they vibrate or move faster. This is what eventually causes solids to melt and liquids to boil.

---

## *The higher their kinetic energy, the faster particles can move*

Make sure you learn those diagrams above and you can describe the arrangement and movement of particles in solids, liquids and gases — they could earn you a few easy marks in the exam.

# Heat Conduction

In solids, heat is transferred by conduction.

## Conduction of heat — occurs mainly in solids

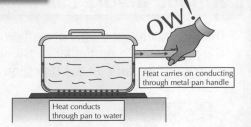

Heat carries on conducting through metal pan handle

Heat conducts through pan to water

CONDUCTION OF HEAT ENERGY is the process where
VIBRATING PARTICLES pass on their EXTRA KINETIC ENERGY to
NEIGHBOURING PARTICLES.

This process continues throughout the solid and gradually some of the extra kinetic energy (or heat) is passed all the way through the solid, causing a rise in temperature at the other side of the solid. And hence an increase in the heat radiating from its surface.

Usually conduction is faster in denser solids, because the particles are closer together and so will collide more often and pass energy between them. Materials that have larger spaces between their particles conduct heat energy much more slowly — these materials are insulators.

## Metals are good conductors because of their free electrons

1) Metals "conduct" so well because the electrons are free to move inside the metal.

2) At the hot end the electrons move faster and collide with other free electrons, transferring energy. These other electrons then pass on their extra energy to other electrons, etc.

3) Because the electrons can move freely, this is obviously a much faster way of transferring the energy through the metal than slowly passing it between jostling neighbouring atoms.

4) This is why heat energy travels so fast through metals.

*Conduction is more efficient through a short, fat rod than through a long, thin rod. It all comes down to how far the electrons have to transfer the energy.*

## So, the better the conductor, the faster heat can be transferred

You'll notice that if a spade has been left in the sun for a while, the metal part will always feel much hotter than the wooden handle. But it isn't hotter — it just conducts the heat into your hand much quicker, so your hand heats up much quicker. In cold weather, the metal part will always feel colder because it takes the heat away from your hand quicker. But remember, it's not colder.

# Convection

Gases and liquids are usually free to move about — and that allows them to transfer heat by convection, which is a much more effective process than conduction.

## Convection of heat — liquids and gases only

CONVECTION occurs when the more energetic particles MOVE from the HOTTER REGION to the COOLER REGION — AND TAKE THEIR HEAT ENERGY WITH THEM.

This is how immersion heaters in kettles and hot water tanks and (unsurprisingly) convector heaters work. Convection simply can't happen in solids because the particles can't move.

## The immersion heater example

In a bit more detail:

1) Heat energy is transferred from the heater coils to the water by conduction (particle collisions).

2) The particles near the coils get more energy, so they start moving around faster.

3) This means there's more distance between them, i.e. the water expands and becomes less dense.

4) This reduction in density means that the hotter water tends to rise above the denser, cooler water.

5) As the hot water rises it displaces (moves) the colder water out of the way, making it sink towards the heater coils.

6) This cold water is then heated by the coils and rises — and so it goes on. You end up with convection currents going up, round and down, circulating the heat energy through the water.

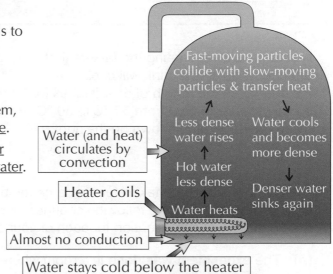

Fast-moving particles collide with slow-moving particles & transfer heat

Less dense water rises — Water cools and becomes more dense

Hot water less dense — Denser water sinks again

Water heats

Water (and heat) circulates by convection

Heater coils

Almost no conduction

Water stays cold below the heater

*Note that convection is most efficient in roundish or squarish containers, because they allow the convection currents to work best. Shallow, wide containers or tall, thin ones just don't work quite so well.*

*Also note that because the hot water rises (because of the lower density) you only get convection currents in the water above the heater. The water below it stays cold because there's almost no conduction.*

CONVECTION CURRENTS are all about CHANGES IN DENSITY.

## The radiator example

Heating a room with a radiator relies on convection currents too.

Hot, less dense air by the radiator rises and denser, cooler air flows to replace it.

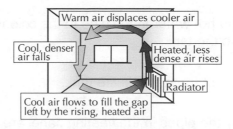

Warm air displaces cooler air

Cool, denser air falls

Heated, less dense air rises

Radiator

Cool air flows to fill the gap left by the rising, heated air

## There's a great experiment with purple crystals to show this

You put some potassium permanganate crystals in the bottom of a beaker of cold water, then heat it gently over a Bunsen flame. The potassium permanganate starts to dissolve and make a bright purple solution that gets moved around the beaker by the convection currents as the water heats.

# Warm-Up and Exam Questions

Here are a few questions for you to try — do the warm-up ones first, then when you think you're ready, have a go at the exam questions. If there's anything you can't do, make sure you go back and check it.

## Warm-Up Questions

1) Give two ways the nature of a surface could be changed so that the surface emits more infrared radiation.
2) Describe the particles in a gas in terms of their arrangement, kinetic energy and movement.
3) Describe the process of heat transfer by conduction.
4) Explain why heated air rises.

## Exam Questions

1   A student is investigating the factors that affect how quickly a drink will cool. He measures the length of time it takes for a cup of water to cool from 60 °C to 30 °C, using the apparatus shown on the right.

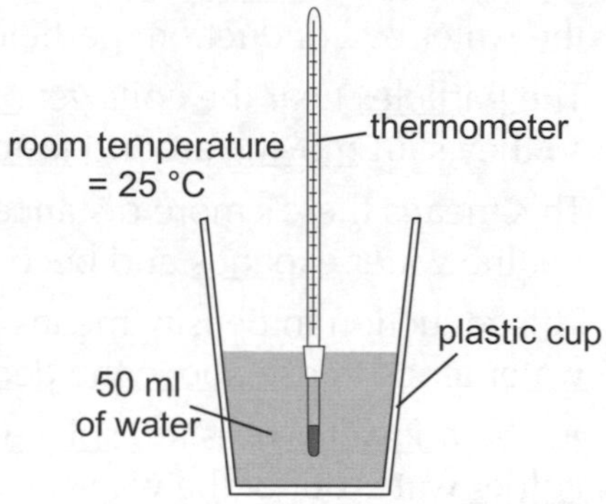

Describe how the time taken for the same temperature change would alter if the following changes were made to the apparatus. Give a reason for each of your answers.

(a)   The experiment was done in a room where the temperature was 15 °C.

*(2 marks)*

(b)   The plastic cup was replaced with an identically sized metal cup.

*(2 marks)*

2   The diagram shows a solar heating panel which is used to heat cold water in a house.

(a)   Describe how heat is transferred:

(i)   from the Sun to the solar heating panel.

*(1 mark)*

(ii)   from the hot water in the pipe to the colder water in the tank.

*(1 mark)*

(iii)   throughout the water in the tank.

*(1 mark)*

(b)   Explain why the pipes in the heating panel are painted black.

*(1 mark)*

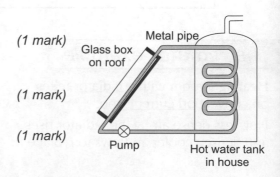

# Condensation and Evaporation

Here are a couple more things about particles in gases and liquids you need to think about.

## Condensation *is when* gas turns to liquid

1) When a <u>gas cools</u>, the particles in the gas <u>slow down</u> and <u>lose kinetic energy</u>. The attractive forces between the particles pull them <u>closer together</u>.

2) If the temperature gets <u>cold enough</u> and the gas particles get <u>close enough together</u> that <u>condensation</u> can take place, the gas becomes a <u>liquid</u>.

3) Water vapour in the air <u>condenses</u> when it comes into contact with <u>cold surfaces</u> e.g. drinks glasses.

4) The <u>steam</u> you see rising from a boiling kettle is actually <u>invisible</u> water vapour <u>condensing</u> to form tiny water droplets as it spreads into cooler air.

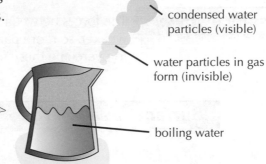

condensed water particles (visible)

water particles in gas form (invisible)

boiling water

## Evaporation *is when* liquid turns to gas

1) <u>Evaporation</u> is when particles <u>escape</u> from a <u>liquid</u>.

2) Particles can <u>evaporate</u> from a liquid at <u>temperatures</u> that are much <u>lower</u> than the liquid's <u>boiling point</u>.

3) Particles <u>near the surface</u> of a liquid can escape and become gas particles if:

> • The particles are travelling in the <u>right direction</u> to escape the liquid.
> • The particles are travelling <u>fast enough</u> (they have enough kinetic energy) to overcome the <u>attractive forces</u> of the <u>other particles</u> in the liquid.

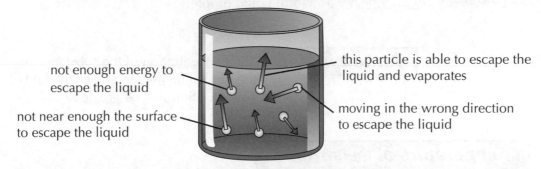

not enough energy to escape the liquid

not near enough the surface to escape the liquid

this particle is able to escape the liquid and evaporates

moving in the wrong direction to escape the liquid

4) The <u>fastest particles</u> (with the most kinetic energy) are <u>most likely</u> to evaporate from the liquid — so when they do, the <u>average speed</u> and <u>kinetic energy</u> of the remaining particles <u>decreases</u>.

5) This decrease in average particle energy means the <u>temperature</u> of the remaining liquid <u>falls</u> — the liquid <u>cools</u>.

6) This <u>cooling effect</u> can be really <u>useful</u>. For example, you <u>sweat</u> when you exercise or get hot. As the water from the sweat on your skin <u>evaporates</u>, it <u>cools</u> you down.

---

## Condensation and evaporation both depend on kinetic energy

If gas particles <u>lose</u> enough <u>kinetic energy</u>, the gas will <u>condense</u> into a liquid. Particles in a liquid need to have a <u>high</u> kinetic energy to be able to <u>evaporate</u>. Remember that when a particle evaporates, it takes its kinetic energy with it — so the <u>average</u> kinetic energy of the particles in the liquid <u>decreases</u>.

# Condensation and Evaporation

The rate of condensation and evaporation depends on a lot of different factors.

## The rate of evaporation will be faster if the...

**Temperature is higher**
At higher temperatures, the average particle energy will be higher, so more particles will have enough energy to escape.

**Density is lower**
The forces between the particles will usually be weaker, so more particles will have enough energy to overcome these forces and escape the liquid.

**Surface area is larger**
More particles will be near enough to the surface to escape the liquid.

**Airflow over the liquid is greater**
1) The lower the concentration of an evaporating substance in the air it's evaporating into, the higher the rate of evaporation.
2) A greater airflow means air above the liquid is replaced more quickly, so the concentration in the air will be lower.

## The rate of condensation will be faster if the...

**Temperature of the gas is lower**
The average particle energy in the gas is lower — so more particles will slow down enough to clump together and form liquid droplets.

**Airflow is less**
The concentration of the substance in the air will be higher, and so the rate of condensation will be greater.

**Temperature of the surface the gas touches is lower.**

**Density is higher**
The forces between the particles will be stronger. Fewer particles will have enough energy to overcome these forces and will instead clump together and form a liquid.

## So temperature isn't the only thing that affects the rates

There are quite a few factors that affect evaporation and condensation rates. Try to picture how each change affects the particles in the liquid or gas, and it'll be easier to work out whether changing a particular condition will increase or decrease the rate of evaporation or condensation.

# Rate of Heat Transfer

There are loads of factors that affect the rate of heat transfer.
Different objects can lose or gain heat much faster than others — even in the same conditions.

## The rate of heat energy transfer depends on many things...

### Surface area and volume

1) Heat energy is radiated from the surface of an object.

2) The bigger the surface area, the more infrared waves that can be emitted from (or absorbed by) the surface — so the quicker the transfer of heat.

> E.g. radiators have large surface areas to maximise the amount of heat they transfer.

3) This is why car and motorbike engines often have 'fins' — they increase the surface area so heat is radiated away quicker. So the engine cools quicker.

Cooling fins on engines increase surface area to speed up cooling.

4) Heat sinks are devices designed to transfer heat away from objects they're in contact with, e.g. computer components.

5) They have fins and a large surface area so they can emit heat as quickly as possible.

6) If two objects at the same temperature have the same surface area but different volumes, the object with the smaller volume will cool more quickly — as a higher proportion of the object will be in contact with its surroundings.

### The type of material

1) Other factors, like the type of material, affect the rate too.

2) Objects made from good conductors (see p.20) transfer heat away more quickly than insulating materials, e.g. plastic.

3) It also matters whether the materials in contact with it are insulators or conductors.

4) If an object is in contact with a conductor, the heat will be conducted away much faster than if it is in contact with a good insulator.

## That's why curling up in the foetal position helps when you're cold

By curling up in a ball, you decrease the surface area of your body that's in contact with the surroundings. Handily, this will lower your rate of heat transfer and help you keep warm. More on the science behind staying the right temperature coming up on the next page.

# Rate of Heat Transfer

Many products are <u>specially designed</u> to <u>control</u> heat transfer. <u>Humans</u> and <u>animals</u> have ways of controlling heat transfer to keep themselves at a comfortable temperature too.

## *Some devices* are designed to *limit heat transfer*

You need to know about <u>heat energy transfers</u> and how products can be designed to <u>reduce</u> them.

### *Example — a vacuum flask*

1) The glass bottle is <u>double-walled</u> with a <u>vacuum</u> between the two walls. This stops <u>all conduction</u> and <u>convection</u> through the <u>sides</u>.

2) The walls either side of the vacuum are <u>silvered</u> to keep heat loss by <u>radiation</u> to a <u>minimum</u>.

3) The bottle is supported using <u>insulating foam</u>. This minimises heat <u>conduction</u> to or from the <u>outer</u> glass bottle.

4) The <u>stopper</u> is made of <u>plastic</u> and filled with <u>cork</u> or <u>foam</u> to reduce any <u>heat conduction</u> through it.

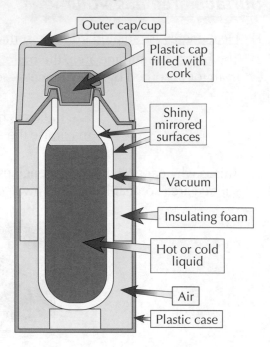

Outer cap/cup

Plastic cap filled with cork

Shiny mirrored surfaces

Vacuum

Insulating foam

Hot or cold liquid

Air

Plastic case

## *Humans* and *animals* have ways of *controlling* heat transfer too

1) In the <u>cold</u>, the hairs on your skin 'stand up' to trap a <u>thicker</u> layer of <u>insulating air</u> around the body. This limits the amount of heat loss by <u>convection</u>. Some animals do the same using <u>fur</u>.

2) When you're <u>too warm</u>, your body diverts more <u>blood</u> to flow near the surface of your skin so that more heat can be lost by <u>radiation</u> — that's why some people go <u>pink</u> when they get hot.

3) Generally, animals in <u>warm</u> climates have <u>larger</u> ears than those in <u>cold</u> climates to help <u>control</u> heat transfer.

### *Example*

<u>Arctic foxes</u> have evolved <u>small ears</u>, with a small surface area to minimise <u>heat loss</u> by <u>radiation</u> and conserve body heat.

<u>Desert foxes</u> on the other hand have <u>huge ears</u> with a large surface area to allow them to <u>lose heat</u> by <u>radiation</u> easily and keep cool.

# Warm-Up and Exam Questions

It's no good learning all the facts in the world if you go to pieces and write nonsense in the exam.
So you'd be wise to practise using all your knowledge to answer some questions.

## Warm-Up Questions

1) What is meant by 'condensation'?
2) Explain how putting a coat on helps keep you warm.
3) Explain how the mirrored surfaces on the inside of a vacuum flask help reduce heat transfer.
4) Give three ways of increasing the rate of condensation of a gas onto a cool surface.

## Exam Questions

1   Animals that live in extreme climates have adapted to control
    their rate of heat transfer.  For example, animals in hot climates
    often have larger ears than those that live in cold climates.

   (a)   Explain how having large ears could be an advantage
         to an animal living in a hot climate.

                                                                        *(2 marks)*

   (b)   In hot conditions, many animals sweat.
         Explain, in terms of particle energies, how sweating will help keep an animal cool.

                                                                        *(3 marks)*

2   Metal heat sinks are often fixed to computer processors to help keep them cool.

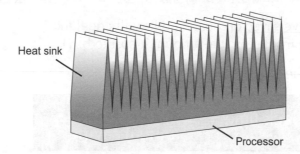

Heat sink

Processor

   (a)   Suggest **two** ways the shape of the heat sink helps transfer heat away quickly from
         the processor.  Give a reason for each of your answers.

                                                                        *(4 marks)*

   (b)   Give **one** other design feature of the heat sink that helps it to do its job.
         Explain your answer.

                                                                        *(2 marks)*

   (c)   Heat sinks are often fitted with fans to cool the air around them.
         Explain how this will affect the rate of heat transfer from the heat sink
         to its surroundings.

                                                                        *(2 marks)*

# Energy Efficiency in the Home

There are lots of things you can do to a building to <u>reduce</u> the amount of <u>energy that escapes</u>. Some are <u>more effective</u> than others, and some are <u>better for your pocket</u> than others. The most obvious examples are in the home, but you could apply this to <u>any situation</u> where you're trying to <u>cut down</u> energy loss.

## *Effectiveness* and *cost-effectiveness* are not the same...

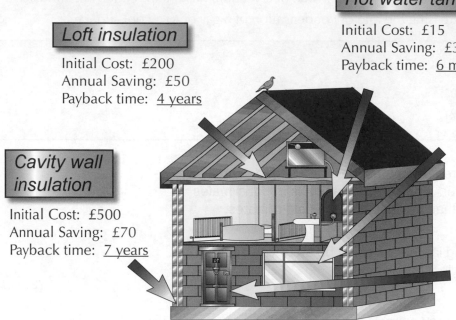

**Hot water tank jacket**

Initial Cost: £15
Annual Saving: £30
Payback time: <u>6 months</u>

**Loft insulation**

Initial Cost: £200
Annual Saving: £50
Payback time: <u>4 years</u>

**Double glazing**

Initial Cost: £3000
Annual Saving: £60
Payback time: <u>50 years</u>

**Cavity wall insulation**

Initial Cost: £500
Annual Saving: £70
Payback time: <u>7 years</u>

**Draught-proofing**

Initial Cost: £100
Annual Saving: £50
Payback time: <u>2 years</u>

1) The <u>most effective</u> methods of insulation are ones that give you the biggest <u>annual saving</u> (they save you the <u>most</u> money <u>each year</u> on your <u>heating bills</u>).

2) Eventually, the <u>money you've saved</u> on heating bills will <u>equal</u> the initial cost of putting in the insulation (the amount it cost to buy).

3) The time it takes is called the <u>payback time</u>.

$$\text{Payback time} = \frac{\text{initial cost}}{\text{annual saving}}$$

4) The <u>most cost-effective</u> methods tend to be the <u>cheapest</u>.

5) They are cost-effective because they have a <u>short payback time</u> — this means the money you save <u>covers</u> the amount you <u>paid</u> really <u>quickly</u>.

## *Make sure you can calculate payback time*

And it's the same with, say, cars. Buying a more fuel-efficient car might sound like a great idea — but if it costs loads more than an older less fuel-efficient car, you might still end up out of pocket. If it's <u>cost-effectiveness</u> you're thinking about, you always have to offset initial cost against annual savings.

# Energy Efficiency in the Home

As well as being able to calculate payback times, you need to know the different methods of <u>heat transfer</u> that are <u>stopped</u> by different types of <u>insulation</u>. Luckily that's what this page is all about.

## Know which **types** of **heat transfer** are involved

<u>DRAUGHT-PROOFING</u> — strips of foam and plastic around doors and windows stop draughts of cold air blowing in, i.e. they reduce heat loss due to <u>convection</u>.

<u>LOFT INSULATION</u> — a thick layer of fibreglass wool laid out across the whole loft floor reduces <u>conduction</u> and <u>radiation</u> into the roof space from the ceiling.

<u>CAVITY WALL INSULATION</u> — foam squirted into the gap between the bricks reduces <u>convection</u>, <u>conduction</u> and <u>radiation</u> across the gap.

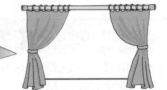

<u>THICK CURTAINS</u> — big bits of cloth over the window to reduce heat loss by <u>conduction</u> and <u>radiation</u>.

<u>HOT WATER TANK JACKET</u> — lagging such as fibreglass wool reduces <u>conduction</u> and <u>radiation</u>.

## *U-values* show *how fast* heat can *transfer* through a material

1) <u>Heat</u> transfers <u>faster</u> through materials with <u>higher U-values</u> than through materials with low U-values.

> The better the insulator (see p.20)
> the lower the U-value.

2) E.g. The U-value of a typical <u>duvet</u> is about <u>0.75 W/m²K</u>, whereas the U-value of <u>loft insulation material</u> is around <u>0.15 W/m²K</u>.

## *The higher the U-value, the poorer the insulator*

So, make sure you know the different types of home insulation on this page, and the types of heat transfer they help to reduce. A lot of methods of insulation work by trapping a <u>layer of air</u> because it's a good insulator — it's great for stopping heating by <u>conduction</u>.

# Specific Heat Capacity

<u>Specific heat capacity</u> is one of those topics that puts people off just because it has a weird name. If you can get over that, it's actually not too bad — it sounds a lot harder than it is.

## *Specific heat capacity — how much energy can be stored*

1) It takes more heat energy to increase the temperature of some materials than others. E.g. you need <u>4200 J</u> to warm 1 kg of <u>water</u> by 1 °C, but only <u>139 J</u> to warm 1 kg of <u>mercury</u> by 1 °C.

2) Materials which need to <u>gain</u> lots of energy to <u>warm up</u> also <u>release</u> loads of energy when they <u>cool down</u> again. They can 'store' a lot of heat.

3) The measure of <u>how much energy</u> a substance can <u>store</u> is called its <u>specific heat capacity</u>.

> <u>Specific heat capacity</u> is the amount of <u>energy</u> needed to raise the temperature of <u>1 kg</u> of a substance by <u>1 °C</u>.

4) Water has a specific heat capacity of <u>4200 J/kg°C</u>.

## *There's a nice formula for specific heat capacity*

You'll have to do calculations involving specific heat capacity. This is the equation to learn:

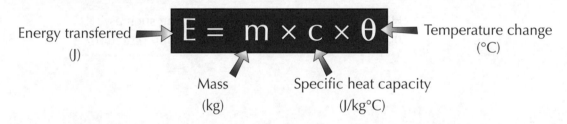

Energy transferred (J) → $E = m \times c \times \theta$ ← Temperature change (°C)

Mass (kg)     Specific heat capacity (J/kg°C)

> <u>EXAMPLE:</u>  How much energy is needed to heat 2 kg of water from 10 °C to 100 °C?
>
> <u>ANSWER:</u>  Energy needed = 2 × 4200 × 90 = <u>756 000 J</u>

If you're <u>not</u> working out the energy, you'll have to rearrange the equation, so a <u>formula triangle</u> will come in dead handy.

You write the bits of the formula in the triangle like this:

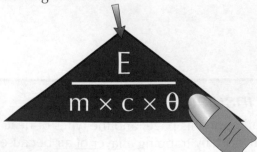

$$\frac{E}{m \times c \times \theta}$$

How to use the formula triangle:
1) You <u>cover up</u> the thing you're trying to find.
2) The parts of the formula you can <u>still see</u> are what it's equal to.
3) E.g. cover up θ and you're left with E ÷ (m × c).
4) So that's how you work it out: θ = E ÷ (m × c).

# Specific Heat Capacity

## *Another specific heat capacity example*

*Remember — you need to convert the mass to kilograms first.*

EXAMPLE: An empty 200 g aluminium kettle cools down from 115 °C to 10 °C, losing 19 068 J of heat energy. What is the specific heat capacity of aluminium?

ANSWER: $SHC = \dfrac{Energy}{Mass \times Temp\ ch} = \dfrac{19\,068}{0.2 \times 105} = \underline{908\ J/kg°C}$

## *Heaters have high heat capacities to store lots of energy*

The <u>materials</u> used in <u>heaters</u> usually have <u>high</u> specific heat capacities so that they can store <u>large amounts</u> of heat energy.

1) <u>Water</u> has a <u>really high</u> specific heat capacity.
2) It's also a <u>liquid</u>, so it can easily be <u>pumped around</u> in pipes — ideal for <u>central heating</u> systems in buildings.

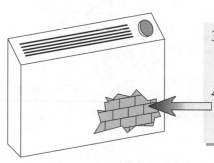

3) Electric <u>storage heaters</u> are designed to store heat energy at night (when electricity is cheaper), and then <u>release</u> it during the day.
4) They store the heat using <u>concrete</u> or <u>bricks</u>, which (surprise surprise) have a <u>high</u> specific heat capacity (around 880 J/kg°C).

5) Some heaters are filled with <u>oil</u>, which has a specific heat capacity of around 2000 J/kg°C. Because this is <u>lower</u> than <u>water's</u> specific heat capacity, oil heating systems are often not as good as water-based systems.
6) Oil does have a <u>higher boiling point</u> though, which usually means oil-filled heaters can safely reach <u>higher temperatures</u> than water-based ones.

## *Most heaters use materials that have a high specific heat capacity*

So, the <u>higher</u> the specific heat capacity, the <u>better</u> the material is at <u>storing heat</u>. Make sure you learn the definition of specific heat capacity on the last page off by heart and that you've got to grips with the formula, and specific heat capacity questions will be a doddle.

# Warm-Up and Exam Questions

Warm-up questions first, then a few exam questions to practise. Make the most of this page by working through everything carefully — it's all useful stuff.

## Warm-Up Questions

1) Give three methods of insulating a house.
2) What is meant by "payback time"?
3) What type of heat transfer does draught-proofing help to reduce?
4) Write down the definition of specific heat capacity.

## Exam Questions

1 A 0.5 kg concrete block is heated from 20 °C to 100 °C. This takes 36 000 J of energy.

(a) Calculate the specific heat capacity of the concrete block.
Clearly show how you work out your answer.

*(4 marks)*

(b) Explain why concrete blocks are often used in heating systems
such as storage heaters.

*(2 marks)*

2 The diagram shows the heat losses from Tom's house. Tom estimates that
£300 of his annual heating bill is wasted on heat lost from the house.

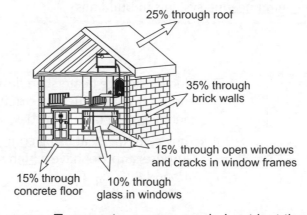

25% through roof

35% through
brick walls

15% through open windows
and cracks in window frames

15% through
concrete floor

10% through
glass in windows

(a) Calculate how much money Tom wastes every year in heat lost through the roof.

*(1 mark)*

(b) Tom decides to insulate the loft and needs to pick from two types of insulation.
Insulation A has a U-value of 0.7 W/m²K, and insulation B has a U-value of
0.6 W/m²K.

Both types of insulation would cost him the same amount to buy and install.

(i) Which type of insulation should Tom buy? Explain your answer.

*(1 mark)*

(ii) The insulation costs him £350, but reduces the amount he spends on
wasted heat to £255 per year. Calculate the payback time for
fitting loft insulation in Tom's house.

*(2 marks)*

# Energy Transfer

Heat is just one type of energy, but there are lots more as well:

## Learn these **nine types** of energy

You should know all of these <u>well enough</u> by now to list them <u>from memory</u>, including the examples:

1) <u>ELECTRICAL</u> Energy........................................ — whenever a <u>current</u> flows.
2) <u>LIGHT</u> Energy.................................................. — from the <u>Sun</u>, <u>light bulbs</u>, etc.
3) <u>SOUND</u> Energy............................................... — from <u>loudspeakers</u> or anything <u>noisy</u>.
4) <u>KINETIC</u> Energy, or <u>MOVEMENT</u> Energy.......... — anything that's <u>moving</u> has it.
5) <u>NUCLEAR</u> Energy............................................ — released only from <u>nuclear reactions</u>.
6) <u>THERMAL</u> Energy or <u>HEAT</u> Energy.................. — <u>flows</u> from <u>hot objects</u> to colder ones.
7) <u>GRAVITATIONAL POTENTIAL</u> Energy............. — possessed by anything which can <u>fall</u>.
8) <u>ELASTIC POTENTIAL</u> Energy........................... — stretched <u>springs</u>, <u>elastic</u>, <u>rubber bands</u>, etc.
9) <u>CHEMICAL</u> Energy.......................................... — possessed by <u>foods</u>, <u>fuels</u>, <u>batteries</u> etc.

## Potential- and **chemical-energy** are forms of **stored energy**

The <u>last three</u> above are forms of <u>stored energy</u> because the energy is not obviously <u>doing</u> anything, it's kind of <u>waiting to happen</u>, i.e. waiting to be turned into one of the <u>other</u> forms.

## You **need** to know the **conservation of energy principle**

There are plenty of different <u>types</u> of energy, but <u>they all obey the principle below</u>:

<u>Energy</u> can be <u>transferred</u> usefully from one form to another, <u>stored</u> or <u>dissipated</u> — but it can never be <u>created or destroyed</u>.

*Dissipated is a fancy way of saying the energy is spread out and lost.*

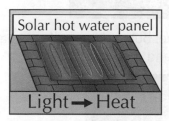

Solar hot water panel

Light → Heat

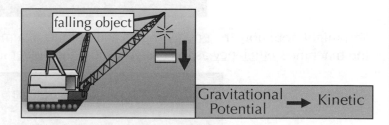

falling object

Gravitational Potential → Kinetic

Another <u>important principle</u> which you need to <u>learn</u> is this one:

Energy is <u>only useful</u> when it can be <u>converted</u> from one form to another.

# Efficiency of Machines

Efficiency is just a measure of how much energy is <u>usefully transferred</u>.

## *Make sure you can work out the main energy transfers of a device*

In the exam, they can ask you about <u>any device</u> or <u>energy transfer system</u> they feel like. If you understand a few different <u>examples</u>, it'll be easier to think through whatever they ask you about in the exam.

### *Examples*

<u>Electrical Devices, e.g. televisions</u>: Electrical energy ⟹ Light, sound and heat energy

<u>Batteries</u>: Chemical energy ⟹ Electrical and heat energy

<u>Electrical Generation, e.g. wind turbines</u>: Kinetic energy ⟹ Electrical and heat energy

<u>Potential Energy, e.g. firing a bow and arrow</u>: Elastic potential energy ⟹ Kinetic and heat energy

## *Most energy transfers involve some losses, often as heat*

Useful devices are only useful because they can transform energy from one form to another.

In doing so, some of the useful input energy is always lost or wasted, often as heat.

The <u>less energy</u> that is '<u>wasted</u>', the <u>more efficient</u> the device is said to be.

The energy flow diagram is pretty much the same for all devices.

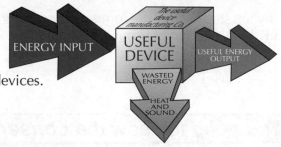

## *It's really simple to calculate the efficiency...*

A <u>machine</u> is a device which turns <u>one type of energy</u> into <u>another</u>.
The <u>efficiency</u> of any device is defined as:

$$\text{Efficiency} = \frac{\text{Useful Energy OUT}}{\text{Total Energy IN}}$$

You might not know the <u>energy</u> inputs and outputs of a machine, but you can <u>still</u> calculate the machine's <u>efficiency</u> as long as you know the <u>power</u> input and output:

$$\text{Efficiency} = \frac{\text{Useful Power OUT}}{\text{Total Power IN}}$$

You can give efficiency as a <u>decimal</u> or you can <u>multiply</u> <u>your answer</u> by 100 to get a <u>percentage</u>, i.e. <u>0.75 or 75%</u>.

As usual, a <u>formula triangle</u> will come handy for rearranging the formulas:

Useful Out

Efficiency × Total In

# Efficiency of Machines

## How to **use** the efficiency **formula** — **nothing to it**

1) You find how much energy is <u>supplied</u> to a machine. (The Total Energy <u>IN</u>.)

2) You find how much <u>useful energy</u> the machine <u>delivers</u>. (The Useful Energy <u>OUT</u>.)
An exam question either tells you this directly or tells you how much it <u>wastes</u> as heat/sound.

3) Either way, you get those <u>two important numbers</u> and then just <u>divide</u> the <u>smaller one</u> by the <u>bigger one</u> to get a value for <u>efficiency</u> somewhere between <u>0 and 1</u> (or <u>0 and 100%</u>). Easy.

4) The other way they might ask it is to tell you the <u>efficiency</u> and the <u>input energy</u> and ask for the <u>energy output</u> — so you need to be able to swap the formula round.

## **Useful energy output isn't** usually **equal** to **total energy input**

For any <u>given example</u> you can talk about the <u>types of energy</u> being <u>input</u> and <u>output</u>, but <u>remember this</u>:

<u>No</u> device is 100% efficient and the <u>wasted energy</u> is
usually <u>spread out</u> as <u>heat</u>.

<u>Electric heaters</u> are the <u>exception</u> to this. They're usually <u>100%</u> <u>efficient</u> because <u>all</u> the electricity is converted to "<u>useful</u>" heat.

Ultimately, <u>all</u> energy <u>ends up as heat energy</u>.
If you use an electric drill, it gives out <u>various types</u> of energy but they all quickly end up as <u>heat</u>.

## We call it **wasted heat** because we **can't do** **anything useful** with it

1) <u>Useful energy</u> is <u>concentrated energy</u>. As you know, <u>the entire energy output</u> by a machine, both useful and wasted, eventually ends up as <u>heat</u>.

2) This heat is <u>transferred</u> to <u>cooler</u> surroundings, which then become <u>warmer</u>. As the heat is <u>transferred</u> to cooler surroundings, the <u>energy</u> becomes <u>less concentrated</u> — it dissipates.

3) The <u>total</u> amount of <u>energy</u> stays the <u>same</u>. The energy is still there, but as it becomes increasingly spread out, it <u>can't be easily used</u> or <u>collected back in</u> again.

## Let there be light — and a bit of wasted heat...

The thing about wasted energy is it's always the same — it always disappears as <u>heat</u> and <u>sound</u>, and even the sound ends up as heat pretty quickly. So when they ask, "Why is the input energy more than the output energy?", the answer is always the same... because some energy is <u>wasted as heat</u>.

# Efficiency of Machines

Efficiency isn't everything — when you're choosing whether to buy a new product, you'll probably want to think about <u>cost-effectiveness</u> too (see p.28).

## You need to think about **cost-effectiveness** and **efficiency**...

### ...when **choosing appliances**

### Example: light bulbs

1) A <u>low-energy</u> bulb is about <u>4 times as efficient</u> as an <u>ordinary</u> light bulb.
2) <u>Energy-efficient</u> light bulbs are more <u>expensive</u> to buy but they <u>last much longer</u>.
3) If an energy-saving light bulb cost £3 and saved £12 of energy a year, its <u>payback time</u> (see p.28) would be <u>3 months</u>.
4) Energy-saving light bulbs are normally <u>more cost-effective</u> than ordinary bulbs.
5) <u>LED light bulbs</u> are even <u>more efficient</u> than <u>low-energy</u> bulbs, and can <u>last even longer</u>.
6) But they are <u>more</u> expensive to buy and <u>don't</u> give out as <u>much light</u> as the other two types of bulb.

### Example: replacing old appliances with newer energy-efficient ones

1) <u>New</u>, <u>efficient</u> appliances are <u>cheaper</u> to run than <u>older</u>, <u>less efficient</u> appliances. But new appliances can be <u>expensive</u> to <u>buy</u>.
2) You've got to work out if it's <u>cost-effective</u> to buy a <u>new appliance</u>.
3) To work out how <u>cost-effective</u> a new appliance will be you need to work out its <u>payback time</u>.

## Sometimes 'waste' energy can actually be useful

1) <u>Heat exchangers</u> reduce the amount of <u>heat energy</u> that is 'lost'.
2) They do this by pumping a <u>cool fluid</u> through the <u>escaping heat</u>.

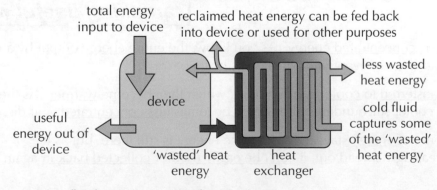

3) The temperature of this <u>fluid</u> rises as it <u>gains heat energy</u>.
4) The <u>heat energy</u> in the fluid can then be <u>converted</u> into a form of energy that's useful again — either in the <u>original device</u>, or for <u>other useful functions</u>. For example, some of the heat from a <u>car's engine</u> can be transferred to the air that's used to warm the <u>passenger compartment</u>.

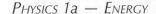

# Energy Transformation Diagrams

Energy transformation diagrams can be a great way of showing the efficiency of a device.

## The **thickness** of the **arrow** represents the **amount** of **energy**

The idea of Sankey diagrams is to make it easy to see at a glance how much of the total energy in is being usefully employed compared with how much is being wasted.

The thicker the arrow, the more energy it represents — so you see a big thick arrow going in, then several smaller arrows going off it to show the different energy transformations taking place.

You can have either a little sketch or a properly detailed diagram where the width of each arrow is proportional to the number of joules it represents.

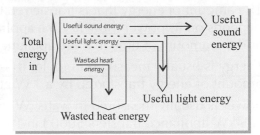

## Example — a sketch **diagram** for a **simple motor**:

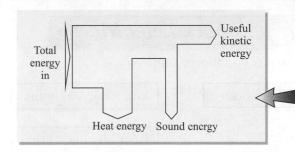

With sketches, they're likely to ask you to compare two different devices and say which is more efficient. You generally want to be looking for the one with the thickest useful energy arrow(s).

You don't know the actual amounts, but you can see that most of the energy is being wasted, and that it's mostly wasted as heat.

## Example — a detailed **diagram** for a **simple motor**:

In an exam, the most likely question you'll get about detailed Sankey diagrams is filling in one of the numbers or calculating the efficiency. The efficiency is straightforward enough if you can work out the numbers (see p.34).

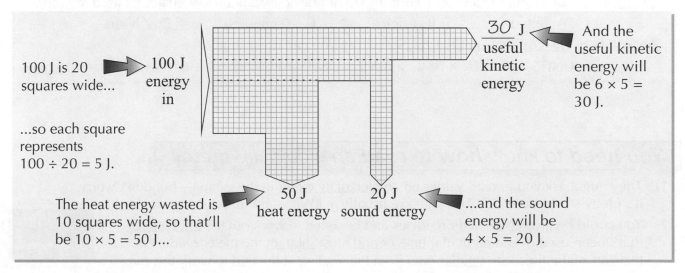

# The Cost of Electricity

Here's a page to help you deal with one of the tedious practicalities of life — <u>paying for electricity</u>.

## Kilowatt-hours (kWh) are "units" of energy

1) Electrical appliances <u>transfer</u> electrical energy into other forms (see p.33) — e.g. <u>sound</u> and <u>heat</u> energy in a <u>radio</u>.

2) The amount of <u>energy</u> that is transferred by an appliance depends on its <u>power</u> (<u>how fast</u> the appliance can transfer it) and the <u>amount of time</u> that the appliance is switched on.

**ENERGY = POWER × TIME**

3) Energy is usually measured in <u>joules</u> (J) — 1 J is the amount of energy transferred by a 1 W appliance in 1 s.

4) Power is usually measured in <u>watts</u> (W) or <u>kilowatts</u> (kW). A 5 kW appliance transfers 5000 J in 1 s.

> A <u>**KILOWATT-HOUR**</u> is the amount of electrical energy used by a <u>1 kW appliance</u> left on for <u>1 HOUR</u>.

5) When you're dealing with <u>large amounts</u> of electrical energy (e.g. the energy used by a home in one week), it's easier to think of the power and time in <u>kilowatts</u> and <u>hours</u> — rather than in <u>watts</u> and <u>seconds</u>.

6) So the standard units of electrical energy are <u>kilowatt-hours</u> (kWh) — <u>not joules</u>.

## The two easy formulas for calculating the cost of electricity

These must surely be the two most <u>trivial and obvious</u> formulas you'll ever see:

| No. of <u>UNITS</u> (kWh) used  =  <u>POWER</u> (in kW)  ×  <u>TIME</u> (in hours) | Units = kW × hours |

| <u>COST</u>  =  No. of <u>UNITS</u>  ×  <u>PRICE</u> per UNIT | Cost = Units × Price |

> <u>EXAMPLE</u>: An electricity supplier charges 14p per unit.
> Find the cost of leaving a 60 W light bulb on for:  a) 30 minutes   b) one year.
> <u>ANSWER</u>: a)  <u>No. of units = kW × hours</u> = 0.06 kW × ½ hr = 0.03 units.
> <u>Cost = units × price per unit</u>(14p) = 0.03 × 14p = <u>0.42p</u> for 30 mins.
> b)  <u>No. of units = kW × hours</u> = 0.06 kW × (24×365) hr = 525.6 units.
> <u>Cost = units × price per unit</u>(14p) = 525.6 × 14p = <u>£73.58</u> for one year.

> <u>EXAMPLE 2</u>:  Each unit of electricity costs 14p.  For how long can a 6 kW heater be used for 14p?
> A  6 hours           B  1 hour           C  10 minutes           D  7 hours
> <u>ANSWER 2</u>: <u>The cost of 1 unit is 14p</u>.  So for 14p you can use 1 unit.
> UNITS = POWER × TIME, so TIME = UNITS ÷ POWER = 1 ÷ 6 = 0.167 hours = <u>10 mins</u>

## You need to know how to read an electricity meter

1) They might ask you to read values off an <u>electricity meter</u> in the exam — but don't worry, it's pretty straightforward.  The units are usually in <u>kWh</u> — but make sure you <u>check</u>.

2) You could be given <u>two</u> meter readings and be asked to work out the <u>total energy</u> that's been used over a particular <u>time period</u>.  Just <u>subtract</u> the meter reading at the <u>start</u> of the time (the <u>smaller</u> one) from the reading at the <u>end</u> to work this out.

1 3 5 9 2 . 3 2 kWh
**Electricity Meter**

# Choosing Electrical Appliances

Knowing how to judge the <u>advantages</u> and <u>disadvantages</u> of different electrical appliances isn't just something you need for the exam — it's also a <u>genuinely useful life skill</u>, and this page is all about it.

## *Sometimes you have a* **choice** *of* **electrical equipment**

1) There are often a few <u>different appliances</u> that do the <u>same job</u>. In the exam, they might ask you to <u>weigh up</u> the <u>pros and cons</u> of different appliances and decide which one is <u>most suitable</u> for a particular <u>situation</u>.

2) You might need to work out whether one appliance uses <u>less energy</u> or is <u>more cost-effective</u> than another.

3) You might also need to think about the <u>practical</u> advantages and disadvantages of using different appliances. E.g. 'Can an appliance be used in areas with <u>limited electricity supplies</u>?'

4) You might get asked to compare two appliances that <u>you haven't seen before</u>. Just take your time and think about the <u>advantages</u> and <u>disadvantages</u> — you should be able to make a <u>sensible judgement</u>.

Here's an example of the sort of things you might have to compare:

## *E.g.* **clockwork radios** *and* **battery radios**

1) <u>Battery radios</u> and <u>clockwork radios</u> are both handy in areas where there is <u>no mains electricity</u> supply.

2) Clockwork radios work by storing <u>elastic potential energy</u> in a spring when someone winds them up. The elastic potential energy is <u>slowly released</u> and used to power the radio.

3) <u>Batteries</u> can be <u>expensive</u>, but powering a clockwork radio is <u>free</u>.

4) Battery power is also only useful if you can get hold of some <u>new batteries</u> when the old ones <u>run out</u>. You don't get that problem with clockwork radios — but it can get annoying to have to <u>keep winding them up</u> every few hours to recharge them.

5) Clockwork radios are also better for the <u>environment</u> — a lot of <u>energy</u> and <u>harmful chemicals</u> go into making batteries, and they're often <u>tricky</u> to dispose of safely.

## *You have a choice — so use it wisely*

Make sure you can <u>compare electrical devices</u> — remember to think about <u>suitability</u>, <u>initial cost</u>, <u>cost-effectiveness</u> and <u>practical</u> issues. The examiners will be looking for <u>sensible</u> and <u>reasoned</u> answers.

# Choosing Electrical Appliances

## You might be asked to use data to **compare two appliances**

**EXAMPLE**

A company is deciding whether to install a 720 W low-power heater, or a high-power 9 kW heater. The heater they choose will be on for 30 hours each week. Their electricity provider charges 7p per kWh of electricity. How much money per week would they save by choosing the low-power heater?

ANSWER: Weekly electricity used by the low-power heater
= 0.720 kW × 30 h = 21.6 kWh
Weekly electricity used by the high-power heater
= 9 kW × 30 h = 270 kWh
Total saving = (270 − 21.6) × 7 = £17.39 (to the nearest penny)

## Standard of living is affected by access to electricity

1) Most people in developed countries have access to mains electricity. However, many people living in the world's poorest countries don't — this has a big effect on their standard of living.

2) In the UK, our houses are full of devices that transform electrical energy into other useful types of energy. For example, not only is electric lighting useful and convenient, but it can also help improve safety at night.

3) Refrigerators keep food fresh for longer by slowing down the growth of bacteria. Refrigerators are also used to keep vaccines cold. Without refrigeration it's difficult to distribute important vaccines — this can have devastating effects on a country's population.

4) Electricity also plays an important role in improving public health in other ways. Hospitals in developed countries rely heavily on electricity, e.g. for X-ray machines. Without access to these modern machines, the diagnosis and treatment of patients would be poorer and could reduce life expectancy.

5) Communications are also affected by a lack of electricity. No electricity means no internet or phones — making it hard for people to keep in touch, or for people to send and receive news and information.

## Standard of living — your health, wealth and happiness

Electricity is something that we use everyday without realising the impact it has on our lives. Think about what you rely on every day and how your standard of living would change if it wasn't available.

# Warm-Up and Exam Questions

You must be getting used to the routine by now — the warm-up questions get you, well, warmed up, and the exam questions give you some idea of what you'll have to cope with on the day.

## Warm-Up Questions

1) What type of energy is stored in food?
2) Give an example of a device that uses elastic potential energy.
3) Modern appliances tend to be more energy-efficient than older ones. What does this mean?
4) Why is the efficiency of an appliance always less than 100%?
5) What is a 'unit' of electricity otherwise known as?
6) Give the formula for calculating the number of units of electricity used.

## Exam Questions

1   All electrical appliances conserve energy.

(a)   Complete the sentence below.

Energy can be transferred usefully, stored or dissipated,

but cannot be ........................................... or ........................................... .

*(1 mark)*

(b)   Describe the main energy transfers that take place in the following appliances.

(i)   A loud speaker.

*(1 mark)*

(ii)   A television.

*(1 mark)*

2   Paul is testing the efficiency of four different light bulbs.

(a)   He finds that the 'Brightlight Ecobulb' is 15% efficient.
Which of the Sankey diagrams below could represent this bulb?
Circle the correct answer.

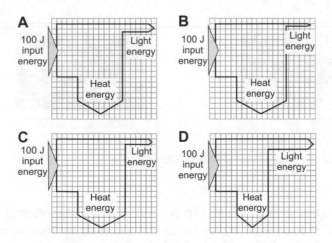

*(1 mark)*

(b)   Traditional light bulbs are commonly being replaced with LED lighting.
Give **two** advantages and **two** disadvantages of replacing traditional light bulbs
with LED lighting.

*(4 marks)*

## Exam Questions

3    A motor is supplied with 200 J of energy to lift a load.
The load gains 140 J of energy.

    (a)   What type of energy does the load gain when lifted by the motor?

*(1 mark)*

    (b)   Calculate the efficiency of the motor.
Clearly show how you work out your answer.

*(2 marks)*

4    A hair dryer is supplied with 1200 W of electrical power.
The hair dryer transforms this power into 120 W of sound energy and 100 W of kinetic energy.
The rest is transformed into heat energy.

    (a)   Calculate how much electrical power the hair dryer transforms into heat energy.

*(1 mark)*

    (b)   Calculate the efficiency of the hair dryer.
Write down the equation you use and clearly show how you work out your answer.

*(2 marks)*

    (c)   Suggest **one** way the hair dryer could be made more efficient.

*(1 mark)*

    (d)   It takes 4 minutes for a person to dry their hair.
Calculate how much electrical energy, in joules, is transformed in this time.

*(2 marks)*

5    John goes travelling for twelve weeks, but leaves some appliances (such as his freezer) switched on whilst he's away. He takes meter readings before his trip and on his return.
The meter readings are shown below.

 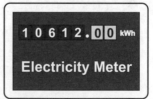

    (a)   Calculate the total energy used during this time.

*(1 mark)*

    (b)   His electricity supplier charges him 14p per kWh. When he returns home, he finds he has been billed £7.56 by his electricity supplier for the twelve weeks he was not at home. Is this bill correct? Show how you work out your answer.

*(2 marks)*

43

# Exam Questions

6 A car engine is supplied with 2000 kJ of chemical energy. It transfers 800 kJ of the energy into kinetic energy, 50 kJ into sound energy and 1150 J into heat energy.

(a) Complete the Sankey diagram to show the energy transfers for the car engine.

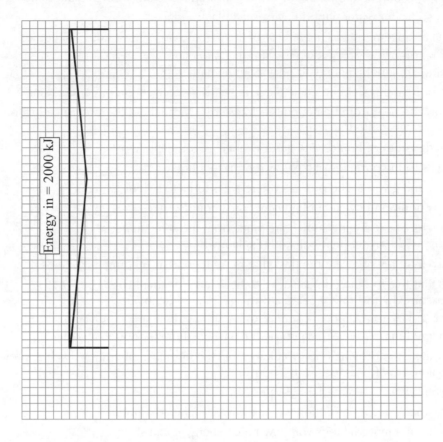

*(3 marks)*

(b) A heat exchanger is fitted to the engine.
Explain why a heat exchanger will help improve the engine's overall efficiency.

*(1 mark)*

7 *In this question you will be assessed on the quality of your English, the organisation of your ideas and your use of appropriate specialist vocabulary.*

The UN classify Angola as one of the world's least developed countries.
Many of Angola's population don't have access to mains electricity.

Describe how access to mains electricity could improve the standard of living in Angola.

*(6 marks)*

# Revision Summary for Physics 1a

It's all very well reading the pages and looking at the diagrams — but you won't have a hope of remembering it for your exam if you don't understand it. Have a go at these questions to see how much has gone in so far. If you struggle with any of them, have another read through the section and give the questions another go.

1)  Describe the three ways that heat energy can be transferred.
2)  True or false? An object that's cooler than its surroundings emits more radiation than it absorbs.
3)  Explain why solar hot water panels have a matt black surface.
4)  Describe the arrangement and movement of the particles in    a) solids    b) liquids    c) gases
5)  What is the name of the process where vibrating particles pass on their extra kinetic energy to neighbouring particles?
6)  Which type of heat transfer can't take place in solids — convection or conduction?
7)  Describe how the heat from heater coils is transferred throughout the water in a kettle. What is this process called?
8)  How do the densities of liquids and gases change as you heat them?
9)  What happens to the particles of a gas as it turns to a liquid?
10) What is the name given to the process where a gas turns to a liquid?
11) Why does evaporation have a cooling effect on a liquid?
12) The two designs of car engine shown are made from the same material. Which engine will transfer heat quicker? Explain why.

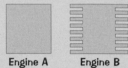
Engine A    Engine B

13) Describe two features of a vacuum flask that make it good at keeping hot liquids hot.
14) Do animals that live in cold climates tend to have large or small ears? Give one reason why this might be an advantage in a cold climate.
15)* If it costs £4000 to double glaze your house and the double glazing saves you £100 on energy bills every year, calculate the payback time for double glazing.
16) Name five ways of improving energy efficiency in the home. Explain how each improvement reduces the amount of heat lost from a house.
17) What can you tell from a material's U-value?
18) Would you expect copper or cotton wool to have a higher U-value?
19) What property of a material tells you how much energy it can store?
20)* An ornament has a mass of 0.5 kg. The ornament is made from a material that has a specific heat capacity of 1000 J/kg°C. How much energy does it take to heat the ornament from 20 °C to 200 °C?
21) Do heaters use materials that have a high or low heat capacity?
22) Name nine types of energy and give an example of each.
23) List the energy transformations that occur in a battery-powered toy car.
24) What is the useful type of energy delivered by a motor? In what form is energy wasted?
25)* What is the efficiency of a motor that converts 100 J of electrical energy into 70 J of useful kinetic energy?
26)* The following Sankey diagram shows how energy is converted in a catapult.

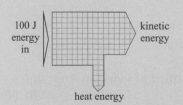
100 J energy in    kinetic energy

heat energy

a)    How much energy is converted into kinetic energy?
b)    How much energy is wasted?
c)    What is the efficiency of the catapult?

27)  What are the standard units of electrical energy?
28)* Calculate how many kWh of electrical energy are used by a 0.5 kW heater used for 15 minutes.
29)  Would a battery-powered radio or a clockwork radio be more suitable to use in rural Africa? Why?

# Energy Sources and Power Stations

There are <u>12</u> different types of <u>energy resource</u>.
They fit into <u>two broad types</u>: <u>renewable</u> and <u>non-renewable</u>.

## Non-renewable energy resources will run out one day

The <u>non-renewables</u> are the <u>three FOSSIL FUELS</u> and <u>NUCLEAR</u>:

1) <u>Coal</u>
2) <u>Oil</u>
3) <u>Natural gas</u>
4) <u>Nuclear fuels</u> (<u>uranium</u> and <u>plutonium</u>)

a) They will <u>all 'run out'</u> one day.
b) They all do <u>damage</u> to the environment.
c) But they provide <u>most of our energy</u>.

## Renewable energy resources will never run out

The <u>renewables</u> are:

1) <u>Wind</u>
2) <u>Waves</u>
3) <u>Tides</u>
4) <u>Hydroelectric</u>
5) <u>Solar</u>
6) <u>Geothermal</u>
7) <u>Food</u>
8) <u>Biofuels</u>

a) These will <u>never run out</u>.
b) Most of them do <u>damage the environment</u>, but in <u>less nasty</u> ways than non-renewables.
c) The trouble is they <u>don't provide much energy</u> and some of them are <u>unreliable</u> because they depend on the <u>weather</u>.

## Energy sources can be burned to drive turbines in power stations

<u>Most</u> of the electricity we use is <u>generated</u> from the four <u>NON-RENEWABLE</u> sources of energy (<u>coal</u>, <u>oil</u>, <u>gas</u> and <u>nuclear</u>) in <u>big power stations</u>, which are all <u>pretty much the same</u> apart from the <u>boiler</u>. <u>Learn</u> the <u>basic features</u> of the typical power station shown here.

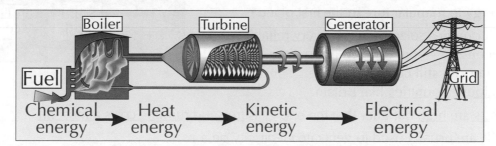

1) The <u>fossil fuel</u> is <u>burned</u> to convert its stored <u>chemical</u> energy into <u>heat</u> (thermal) energy.
2) The heat energy is used to <u>heat water</u> (or <u>air</u> in some fossil-fuel power stations) to produce steam.
3) The <u>steam</u> turns a <u>turbine</u>, converting <u>heat</u> energy into <u>kinetic</u> energy.
4) The turbine is connected to a <u>generator</u>, which transfers <u>kinetic</u> energy into <u>electrical</u> energy.

## It all boils down to steam...

Steam engines were invented as long ago as the <u>17th century</u>, and yet we're still using that idea to produce most of our electricity today, over <u>300 years later</u>. It's amazing when you think about it.

# Renewable Energy Sources

Renewable energy sources, like wind, waves and solar energy, will not run out. What's more, they do a lot less damage to the environment. They don't generate as much electricity as non-renewables though.

## Wind power — lots of little wind turbines

1) This involves putting lots of windmills (wind turbines) up in exposed places like on moors or round coasts.

2) Each wind turbine has its own generator inside it. The electricity is generated directly from the wind turning the blades, which turn the generator.

3) There's no pollution (except for a little bit when they're manufactured).

4) But they do spoil the view. You need about 1500 wind turbines to replace one coal-fired power station and 1500 of them cover a lot of ground — which would have a big effect on the scenery.

5) And they can be very noisy, which can be annoying for people living nearby.

6) There's also the problem of no power when the wind stops, and it's impossible to increase supply when there's extra demand.

7) The initial costs are quite high, but there are no fuel costs and minimal running costs.

8) There's no permanent damage to the landscape — if you remove the turbines, you remove the noise and the view returns to normal.

## Solar cells — expensive but no environmental damage

(well, there may be a bit caused by making the cells)

1) Solar cells generate electric currents directly from sunlight. Solar cells are often the best source of energy for calculators and watches which don't use much electricity.

2) Solar power is often used in remote places where there's not much choice (e.g. the Australian outback) and to power electric road signs and satellites.

3) There's no pollution. (Although they do use quite a lot of energy to manufacture in the first place.)

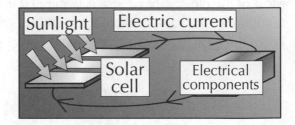

4) In sunny countries solar power is a very reliable source of energy — but only in the daytime. Solar power can still be cost-effective even in cloudy countries like Britain.

5) Initial costs are high but after that the energy is free and running costs almost nil.

6) Solar cells are usually used to generate electricity on a relatively small scale, e.g. powering individual homes.

7) It's often not practical or too expensive to connect them to the National Grid — the cost of connecting them to the National Grid can be enormous compared with the value of the electricity generated.

## People love the idea of wind power — just not in their back yard

Did you know you can now get rucksacks with built-in solar cells to charge up your mobile phone, MP3 player and digital camera while you're wandering around. Perfect for when you go on holiday.

# Renewable Energy Sources

Water can be used to turn <u>turbines</u> in the same way as wind. Wherever water is moving — in waves, rivers and tides, we can transfer its <u>kinetic energy</u> into <u>electrical energy</u>.

## *Hydroelectric power uses falling water*

1) <u>Hydroelectric power</u> usually requires the <u>flooding</u> of a <u>valley</u> by building a <u>big dam</u>.

2) <u>Rainwater</u> is caught and allowed out <u>through turbines</u>. There is <u>no pollution</u> (as such).

3) But there is a <u>big impact</u> on the <u>environment</u> due to the flooding of the valley (rotting vegetation releases methane and $CO_2$) and possible <u>loss of habitat</u> for some species (sometimes the loss of whole villages). The reservoirs can also look very <u>unsightly</u> when they <u>dry up</u>. Putting hydroelectric power stations in <u>remote valleys</u> tends to reduce their impact on humans.

4) A <u>big advantage</u> is it can provide an <u>immediate response</u> to an increased demand for electricity.

5) There's no problem with <u>reliability</u> except in times of <u>drought</u> — but remember this is Great Britain we're talking about.

6) <u>Initial costs are high</u>, but there's <u>no fuel</u> and <u>minimal running costs</u>.

7) It can be a useful way to generate electricity on a <u>small scale</u> in <u>remote areas</u>.

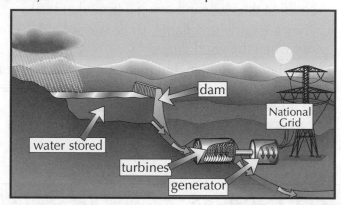

## *Pumped storage gives **extra supply** just when it's **needed***

1) Most large power stations have <u>huge boilers</u> which have to be kept running <u>all night</u> even though demand is <u>very low</u>. This means there's a <u>surplus</u> of electricity at night.

2) It's surprisingly <u>difficult</u> to find a way of <u>storing</u> this spare energy for <u>later use</u>.

3) <u>Pumped storage</u> is one of the <u>best solutions</u>.

4) In pumped storage, 'spare' <u>night-time electricity</u> is used to pump water up to a <u>higher reservoir</u>.

5) This can then be <u>released quickly</u> during periods of <u>peak demand</u> such as at <u>teatime</u> each evening, to supplement the <u>steady delivery</u> from the big power stations.

6) Remember, <u>pumped storage</u> uses the same <u>idea</u> as hydroelectric power, but it <u>isn't</u> a way of <u>generating</u> power — it's simply a way of <u>storing energy</u> which has <u>already</u> been generated.

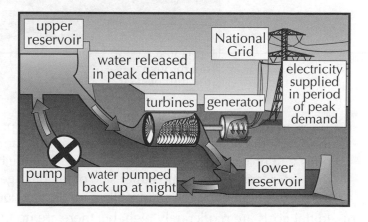

## *Pumped storage — saving energy for when you need it*

In Britain only a pretty <u>small percentage</u> of our electricity comes from <u>hydroelectric power</u> at the moment, but in some other parts of the world they rely much more heavily on it. For example, in the last few years, around <u>99%</u> of <u>Norway's</u> energy came from hydroelectric power.

# Renewable Energy Sources

It's easy to get confused between <u>wave power</u> and <u>tidal power</u> because they're both to do with the seaside — but don't.  They are <u>completely different</u>.

## Wave power — lots of little **wave-powered turbines**

1) You need lots of small <u>wave-powered turbines</u> located <u>around the coast</u>.

2) As waves come in to the shore they provide an <u>up and down motion</u> which can be used to drive a <u>generator</u>.

3) There is <u>no pollution</u>.  The main problems are <u>spoiling the view</u> and being a <u>hazard to boats</u>.

4) They are <u>fairly unreliable</u>, since waves tend to die out when the <u>wind drops</u>.

5) <u>Initial costs are high</u>, but there are <u>no fuel costs</u> and <u>minimal running costs</u>.  Wave power is never likely to provide energy on a <u>large scale</u>, but it can be <u>very useful</u> on <u>small islands</u>.

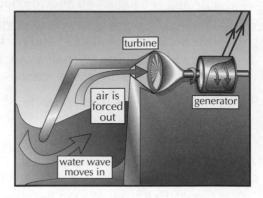

## Tidal barrages — using the **Sun and Moon's gravity**

1) <u>Tidal barrages</u> are <u>big dams</u> built across <u>river estuaries</u>, with <u>turbines</u> in them.

2) As the <u>tide comes in</u> it fills up the estuary to a height of <u>several metres</u> — it also drives the <u>turbines</u>. This water can then be allowed out <u>through the turbines</u> at a controlled speed.

3) The source of the energy is the <u>gravity</u> of the <u>Sun</u> and the <u>Moon</u>.

4) There is <u>no pollution</u>.  The main problems are <u>preventing free access by boats</u>, <u>spoiling the view</u> and <u>altering the habitat</u> of the wildlife, e.g. wading birds, sea creatures and animals who live in the sand.

5) Tides are <u>pretty reliable</u> in the sense that they happen <u>twice a day without fail</u>, and always near to the <u>predicted height</u>.  The only drawback is that the <u>height</u> of the tide is <u>variable</u> so lower (neap) tides will provide <u>significantly less energy</u> than the bigger 'spring' tides.  They also don't work when the water level is the <u>same</u> either side of the barrage — this happens four times a day because of the tides.  But tidal barrages are <u>excellent</u> for <u>storing energy</u> ready for periods of <u>peak demand</u>.

6) <u>Initial costs are moderately high</u>, but there are <u>no fuel costs</u> and <u>minimal running costs</u>. Even though it can only be used in <u>some</u> of the <u>most suitable estuaries</u> tidal power has the potential for generating a <u>significant amount</u> of energy.

## Learn about wave power and bid your cares goodbye

I do hope you appreciate the <u>big big differences</u> between <u>tidal power</u> and <u>wave power</u>.  They both involve seawater — but there the similarities end.  Lots of details then, just waiting to be absorbed.

# Renewable Energy Sources

There's yet <u>more energy</u> in piles of rubbish and underground — it makes you wonder why we even need to use oil. (If you are wondering about that, page 52 is all about comparing energy resources.)

## Geothermal energy — heat from underground

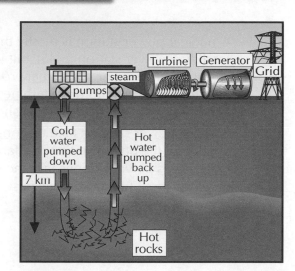

1) This is <u>only possible</u> in <u>volcanic areas</u> where <u>hot rocks</u> lie quite near to the <u>surface</u>. The source of much of the heat is the <u>slow decay</u> of various <u>radioactive elements</u>, including <u>uranium</u>, deep inside the Earth.

2) <u>Steam</u> and <u>hot water</u> rise to the surface and are used to drive a <u>generator</u>.

3) This is actually <u>brilliant free energy</u> with no real environmental problems.

4) In some places, geothermal heat is used to <u>heat buildings directly</u>, without being converted to electrical energy.

5) The <u>main drawback</u> with geothermal energy is there <u>aren't</u> very many <u>suitable locations</u> for power plants.

6) Also, the <u>cost</u> of building a power plant is often <u>high</u> compared to the <u>amount</u> of energy we can get out of it.

## Biofuels are made from plants and waste

1) Biofuels are <u>renewable energy resources</u>. They're used to generate electricity in <u>exactly</u> the same way as fossil fuels (see p.45) — they're <u>burnt</u> to heat up <u>water</u>.

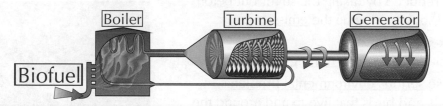

2) They can be also used in some <u>cars</u> — just like fossil fuels.

3) Biofuels can be <u>solids</u> (e.g. straw, nutshells and woodchips), <u>liquids</u> (e.g. ethanol) or <u>gases</u> (e.g. methane 'biogas' from sludge digesters).

4) We can get <u>biofuels</u> from organisms that are <u>still alive</u> or from dead organic matter — like fossil fuels, but from <u>organisms</u> that have been living much more <u>recently</u>.

5) E.g. <u>crops</u> like sugar cane can be fermented to produce <u>ethanol</u>, or plant oils can be modified to produce <u>biodiesel</u>.

*Sludge digesters are used in sewage processing.*

## Sugar cane to ethanol — a terrible waste in my opinion

Biofuels sound quite futuristic, but believe it or not, biofuel mixed with petrol or diesel was actually used in some cars before WW2. Biofuel never really became successful though because of <u>cheap</u> oil. One big advantage of biofuels is they don't release as much <u>greenhouse gas</u> compared with common transport fuels like petrol and diesel. They aren't completely non-polluting though, as you'll see on p.51.

# Energy Sources and the Environment

Nuclear reactors generate electricity in a similar way to fossil fuel power stations.
But one big difference is that they **don't** burn a fuel to generate **heat energy**.

## *Nuclear reactors are just fancy boilers*

1) A nuclear power station is mostly the same as a fossil fuel power station (p.45), but with nuclear fission of uranium or plutonium producing the heat to make steam to drive turbines, etc. The difference is in the boiler, as shown here:

2) Nuclear power stations take the longest time of all the power stations to start up. Natural gas power stations take the shortest time of all the fossil fuel power stations.

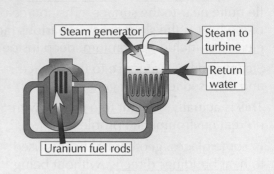

Steam generator    Steam to turbine

Return water

Uranium fuel rods

## *Non-renewables are linked to environmental problems*

1) All three fossil fuels (coal, oil and gas) release $CO_2$ into the atmosphere when they're burned. For the same amount of energy produced, coal releases the most $CO_2$, followed by oil then gas. All this $CO_2$ adds to the greenhouse effect, and contributes to global warming.

2) Burning coal and oil releases sulfur dioxide, which causes acid rain. Acid rain can be harmful to trees and soils and can have far-reaching effects in ecosystems.

3) Acid rain can be reduced by taking the sulfur out before the fuel is burned, or cleaning up the emissions.

4) Coal mining makes a mess of the landscape, especially "open-cast mining".

5) Oil spillages cause serious environmental problems, affecting mammals and birds that live in and around the sea. We try to avoid them, but they'll always happen.

6) Nuclear power is clean but the nuclear waste is very dangerous and difficult to dispose of.

7) Nuclear fuel (i.e. uranium) is relatively cheap but the overall cost of nuclear power is high due to the cost of the power plant and final decommissioning.

8) Nuclear power always carries the risk of a major catastrophe like the Chernobyl disaster in 1986.

## *Energy production — full of pros and cons*

Acid rain was first discovered back in the 1800s but it wasn't until the 1960s and 70s that the effects were seen at their worst. Acid rain collected in lakes and rivers, totally wiping out some species of wildlife and destroying ecosystems. The sulfur dioxide travelled in the atmosphere for hundreds of miles, meaning that pollution created in the UK lead to devastating effects in places like Scandinavia.

# Energy Sources and the Environment

Whilst some energy resources can seem like the <u>solution</u> to all our energy problems, they've all got <u>issues</u> — and <u>biofuels</u> are no exception. Read this page carefully.

## *Biofuels have their disadvantages too*

1) Biofuels (see p.49) are a relatively <u>quick</u> and 'natural' source of energy and are supposedly <u>carbon neutral</u>.

2) There is still debate into the impact of biofuels on the environment, once the <u>full energy</u> that goes into the <u>production</u> is considered.

3) In some regions, large areas of <u>forest</u> have been <u>cleared</u> to make room to grow <u>biofuels</u>, resulting in lots of species losing their <u>natural habitats</u>. The decay and burning of this vegetation also increases <u>$CO_2$</u> and <u>methane</u> emissions.

4) Biofuels have <u>potential</u>, but their use is limited by the amount of available <u>farmland</u> that can be dedicated to their production.

*Huge areas of land are needed to produce biofuels on a large scale.*

> The <u>plants</u> that grew to <u>produce the waste</u> (or to <u>feed the animals</u> that produced the dung) <u>absorbed carbon dioxide</u> from the atmosphere as they were growing. When the waste is burnt, this $CO_2$ is <u>re-released</u> into the <u>atmosphere</u>. So it has a <u>neutral effect</u> on <u>atmospheric $CO_2$ levels</u> (although this only really works if you keep growing plants at the same rate you're burning things). Biofuel production also creates <u>methane</u> emissions — a lot of this comes from the <u>animals</u>.

## *Carbon capture can reduce the impact of carbon dioxide*

1) <u>Carbon capture and storage</u> (CCS) is used to <u>reduce</u> the amount of $CO_2$ building up in the atmosphere and <u>reduce</u> the strength of the <u>greenhouse effect</u>.

2) CCS works by <u>collecting</u> the $CO_2$ from power stations <u>before</u> it is released into the atmosphere.

3) The captured $CO_2$ can then be <u>pumped</u> into empty <u>gas fields</u> and <u>oil fields</u> like those under the North Sea. It can be safely <u>stored</u> without it adding to the greenhouse effect.

4) CCS is a <u>new technology</u> that's <u>developing quickly</u>. New ways of storing $CO_2$ are being explored, including <u>storing</u> $CO_2$ dissolved in <u>seawater</u> at the bottom of the ocean and <u>capturing</u> $CO_2$ with <u>algae</u>, which can then be used to <u>produce oil</u> that can be used as a <u>biofuel</u>.

# Comparison of Energy Resources

## Setting up a power station

Because coal and oil are running out fast, many old <u>coal- and oil-fired power stations</u> are being <u>taken out of use</u>. Often they're being <u>replaced</u> by <u>gas-fired power stations</u> because they're <u>quick</u> to <u>set up</u>, there's still quite a lot of <u>gas left</u> and gas <u>doesn't pollute as badly</u> as coal and oil.  But gas is <u>not</u> the <u>only option</u>.

When looking at the options for a <u>new power station</u>, there are <u>several factors</u> to consider:
How much it <u>costs</u> to set up and run, <u>how long</u> it takes to <u>build</u>, <u>how much power</u> it can generate, etc.
Then there are also the trickier factors like <u>damage to the environment</u> and <u>impact on local communities</u>. And because these are often <u>very contentious</u> issues, getting <u>permission</u> to build certain types of power station can be a <u>long-running</u> process, and hence <u>increase</u> the overall <u>set-up time</u>.
The time and <u>cost</u> of <u>decommissioning</u> (shutting down) a power plant can also be a crucial factor.

## Set-up costs

<u>Renewable</u> resources often need <u>bigger power stations</u> than non-renewables for the <u>same output</u>.  And as you'd expect, the <u>bigger</u> the power station, the <u>more expensive</u> it is.

<u>Nuclear reactors</u> and <u>hydroelectric dams</u> also need <u>huge</u> amounts of <u>engineering</u> to make them <u>safe</u>, which bumps up the cost.

## Set-up/decommissioning time

These are both affected by the <u>size</u> of the power station, the <u>complexity</u> of the engineering and also the <u>planning issues</u> (e.g. <u>discussions</u> over whether a nuclear power station should be built on a stretch of <u>beautiful coastline</u> can last <u>years</u>).  <u>Gas</u> is one of the <u>quickest</u> to set up.  <u>Nuclear</u> power stations take by far the <u>longest</u> (and cost the most) to <u>decommission</u>.

## Reliability issues

All the <u>non-renewables</u> are <u>reliable energy providers</u> (until they run out).

Many of the <u>renewable</u> sources <u>depend on the weather</u>, which means they're pretty <u>unreliable</u> here in the UK.  The exceptions are <u>tidal</u> power and <u>geothermal</u> (which <u>don't</u> depend on weather).

## Running/fuel costs

<u>Renewables</u> usually have the <u>lowest running costs</u>, because there's <u>no</u> actual <u>fuel</u> involved.

## Location issues

This is fairly <u>common sense</u> — a <u>power station</u> has to be <u>near</u> to the <u>stuff it runs on</u>.

<u>Solar</u> — <u>anywhere</u>, though the sunnier the better

<u>Gas</u> — <u>anywhere</u> there's piped gas (most of the UK)

<u>Hydroelectric</u> — <u>hilly</u>, rainy places with <u>floodable valleys</u>, e.g. the Lake District, Scottish Highlands

<u>Wind</u> — <u>exposed</u>, <u>windy</u> places like moors and coasts or out at sea

<u>Oil</u> — near the <u>coast</u> (oil transported by sea)

<u>Waves</u> — on the <u>coast</u>

<u>Coal</u> — near <u>coal mines</u>, e.g. Yorkshire, Wales

<u>Nuclear</u> — <u>away from people</u> (in case of disaster), <u>near water</u> (for cooling)

<u>Tidal</u> — big <u>river estuaries</u> where a dam can be built

<u>Geothermal</u> — fairly limited, only in places where <u>hot rocks</u> are <u>near the Earth's surface</u>

## Environmental issues

If there's a <u>fuel</u> involved, there'll be <u>waste pollution</u> and you'll be <u>using up resources</u>.

If it <u>relies on the weather</u>, it's often got to be in an <u>exposed place</u> where it sticks out like a <u>sore thumb</u>.

<u>Atmospheric Pollution</u>
Coal, Oil, Gas,
(+ others, though less so)

<u>Visual Pollution</u>
Coal, Oil, Gas, Nuclear, Tidal, Waves, Wind, Hydroelectric,

<u>Other Problems</u>
Nuclear (dangerous waste, explosions, contamination), Hydroelectric (dams bursting)

<u>Using Up Resources</u>
Coal, Oil, Gas, Nuclear

<u>Noise Pollution</u>
Coal, Oil, Gas, Nuclear, Wind

<u>Disruption of Habitats</u>
Hydroelectric, Tidal, Biofuels.

<u>Disruption of Leisure Activities</u> (e.g. boats)
Waves, Tidal

# Electricity and the National Grid

The <u>National Grid</u> is the <u>network</u> of pylons and cables that covers <u>the whole of Britain</u>, getting electricity to homes everywhere. Whoever you pay for your electricity, it's the National Grid that gets it to you.

## Electricity is distributed via the National Grid...

1) The <u>National Grid</u> takes electrical energy from <u>power stations</u> to where it's needed in <u>homes</u> and <u>industry</u>.

2) It enables power to be <u>generated</u> anywhere on the grid, and then be <u>supplied</u> anywhere else on the grid.

3) To transmit the <u>huge</u> amount of <u>power</u> needed, you need either a <u>high voltage</u> or a <u>high current</u>.

4) The <u>problem</u> with a <u>high current</u> is that you lose <u>loads of energy</u> through <u>heat</u> in the cables.

*You might come across the term 'potential difference' — this is just another way of saying 'voltage'.*

5) It's much <u>cheaper</u> to <u>boost the voltage</u> up <u>really high</u> (to 400 000 V) and keep the current <u>very low</u>.

## ...With a little help from pylons and transformers

1) To get the voltage to 400 000 V to transmit power requires <u>transformers</u> as well as <u>big pylons</u> with <u>huge insulators</u> — but it's <u>still cheaper</u>.

2) The transformers have to <u>step</u> the voltage <u>up</u> at one end, for <u>efficient transmission</u>, and then bring it back down to <u>safe, usable levels</u> at the other end.

3) The <u>voltage</u> is <u>increased</u> ('<u>stepped up</u>') using a <u>step-up transformer</u>.

4) It's then <u>reduced</u> again ('<u>stepped down</u>') at the consumer end using a <u>step-down transformer</u>.

---

### Step up the voltage, then step it back down again

You don't need to know the <u>details</u> about exactly what transformers are and how they work — just that they increase and decrease the <u>voltage</u> to <u>minimise power losses</u> in the National Grid.

# Electricity and the National Grid

## There are **different ways** to **transmit electricity**

1) Electrical energy can be moved around by cables <u>buried in the ground</u>, as well as in <u>overhead</u> power lines.

2) Each of these different options has its <u>pros and cons</u>:

|  | Setup cost | Maintenance | Faults | How it looks | Affected by weather | Reliability | How easy to set up | Disturbance to land |
|---|---|---|---|---|---|---|---|---|
| Overhead Cables | lower | lots needed | easy to access | ugly | yes | less reliable | easy | minimal |
| Underground Cables | higher | minimal | hard to access | hidden | no | more reliable | hard | lots |

## *Supply* and *demand*

1) The National Grid needs to <u>generate</u> and <u>direct</u> all the energy that the country needs — our energy demands keep on <u>increasing</u> too.

2) In order to meet these demands in the future, the <u>energy supplied</u> to the National Grid will need to <u>increase</u>, or the <u>energy demands</u> of consumers will need to <u>decrease</u>.

3) In the future, <u>supply</u> can be <u>increased</u> by opening <u>more</u> power plants or increasing their power output (or by doing <u>both</u>).

4) <u>Demand</u> can be <u>reduced</u> by consumers using more <u>energy-efficient</u> appliances, and being more <u>careful</u> not to waste energy in the home (e.g. turning off the lights or running washing machines at cooler temperatures).

## *Energy demands are ever increasing*

The National Grid has been working nationwide since 1935 and has gone through many changes and updates since then to meet increasing energy demands. Get a good idea of what we can do to ensure that supply and demand <u>stay in balance</u> — including using <u>energy-efficient appliances</u>. Make sure you know the pros and cons of <u>underground</u> and <u>over-ground</u> electricity transmission too.

# Warm-Up and Exam Questions

Hopefully the last few pages have stuck, but there's only one way to check — and that's with some questions. Warm up questions to get you started, and exam questions to really get your teeth into.

## Warm-Up Questions

1) Name three different renewable energy resources.
2) Explain how pumped storage systems work.
3) Give two ways in which using coal as an energy source causes problems.
4) Describe the major problems with using nuclear fuel to generate electricity.
5) Explain what is meant by biofuels.

## Exam Questions

1    Geothermal energy can be described as a renewable energy source.

(a)   Describe what is meant by geothermal energy.

*(1 mark)*

(b)   Describe what 'renewable energy' means.

*(1 mark)*

(c)   Give **two** disadvantages of using geothermal energy to generate electricity.

*(2 marks)*

2    An old coal-fired power station has an output of 2 MW (2 million watts).
The electricity generating company plans to replace it with wind turbines
which have a maximum output of 4000 W each.

(a)   Calculate the minimum number of wind turbines required to replace the
old power station.

*(1 mark)*

(b)   Suggest why more wind turbines than this might be needed in reality.

*(1 mark)*

(c)   Give **two** reasons why some people might oppose the wind farm development.

*(2 marks)*

(d)   The wind turbines will need to be connected to the National Grid.
Explain why the National Grid uses step-up transformers.

*(2 marks)*

3    The inhabitants of a remote island do not have the resources or expertise to build a nuclear
power plant. They have no access to fossil fuels.

(a)   The islanders have considered using wind, solar and hydroelectric
power to generate electricity. Suggest **two** other renewable energy
resources they could use.

*(2 marks)*

(b)   The islanders decide that both solar and hydroelectric power could reliably
generate enough electricity for all their needs. Suggest **two** other factors they
should consider when deciding which method of electricity generation to use.

*(2 marks)*

# Wave Basics

Waves transfer <u>energy</u> from one place to another without transferring any <u>matter</u> (stuff).

## Waves have amplitude, wavelength and frequency

1) The <u>amplitude</u> is the displacement from the <u>rest position</u> to the <u>crest</u> (NOT from a trough to a crest).

2) The <u>wavelength</u> is the length of a <u>full cycle</u> of the wave, e.g. from <u>crest to crest</u>.

3) <u>Frequency</u> is the <u>number of complete waves</u> passing a certain point <u>per second</u> OR the <u>number of waves</u> produced by a source <u>each second</u>. Frequency is measured in hertz (Hz). 1 Hz is <u>1 wave per second</u>.

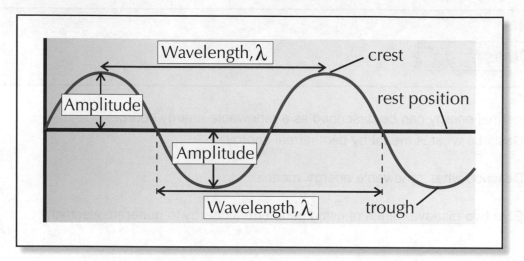

## Transverse waves have sideways vibrations

<u>Most waves</u> are <u>transverse</u>:

1) <u>Light</u> and <u>all other EM waves</u>.

2) <u>Ripples</u> on water.

3) <u>Waves</u> on <u>strings</u>.

4) A <u>slinky spring</u> wiggled up and down.

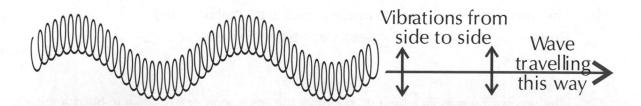

Vibrations from side to side

Wave travelling this way

### In <u>TRANSVERSE</u> waves the vibrations are <u>PERPENDICULAR</u> (at <u>90°</u>) to the <u>DIRECTION OF ENERGY TRANSFER</u> of the wave.

## Wiggling from side to side — must be transverse

First things first — get that diagram at the top of the page <u>memorised</u>. Make sure you are <u>completely clear</u> on the definitions of <u>wave amplitude</u> and <u>wavelength</u> — they are both <u>fundamental</u> to physics and <u>very easy</u> to get <u>wrong</u>. There's no time like the present, so get learning.

# Wave Basics

If a wave isn't transverse, it will be <u>longitudinal</u>. All waves, transverse or longitudinal, have a <u>velocity</u> equal to their <u>wavelength</u> multiplied by their <u>frequency</u>.

## *Longitudinal waves have vibrations along the same line*

Examples of <u>longitudinal waves</u> are:
1) <u>Sound waves</u> and <u>ultrasound</u>.
2) <u>Shock waves</u>, e.g. seismic waves.
3) A <u>slinky spring</u> when you <u>push</u> the end.

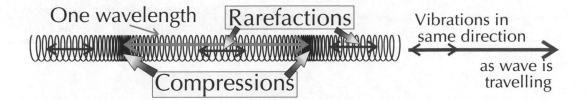

One wavelength   Rarefactions   Vibrations in same direction

Compressions

as wave is travelling

In <u>LONGITUDINAL</u> waves the vibrations are <u>PARALLEL</u> to the <u>DIRECTION OF ENERGY TRANSFER</u> of the wave.

## *Wave speed = frequency × wavelength*

The equation below applies to <u>all waves</u>.

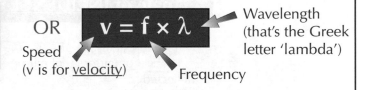

| Speed = Frequency × Wavelength |
| (m/s)      (Hz)         (m) |

OR   $v = f \times \lambda$

Speed (v is for <u>velocity</u>)

Frequency

Wavelength (that's the Greek letter 'lambda')

<u>EXAMPLE:</u> A radio wave has a frequency of $92.2 \times 10^6$ Hz. Find its wavelength. (The speed of all EM waves is $3 \times 10^8$ m/s.)

<u>ANSWER:</u> You're trying to find $\lambda$ using f and v, so you've got to rearrange the equation. So $\lambda = v \div f = 3 \times 10^8 \div 9.22 \times 10^7 = \underline{3.25 \text{ m}}$.

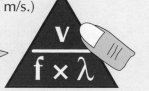

$$\frac{v}{f \times \lambda}$$

The <u>speed</u> of a wave is <u>usually independent</u> of the <u>frequency</u> or <u>amplitude</u> of the wave.

## *Compressions and rarefactions — must be longitudinal*

Get that $v = f \times \lambda$ equation <u>imprinted</u> on your brain. When you've done <u>that</u>, try this question: A sound wave travelling in a solid has a frequency of $\underline{1.9 \times 10^4}$ Hz and a wavelength of <u>12.5</u> cm. Find its speed.*

# Wave Properties

Now you've mastered the <u>wave basics</u> (go back and read pages 56 and 57 if you're not so sure), it's time to talk about some wave properties. First up, <u>reflection</u>...

## *All waves can be reflected, refracted and diffracted*

1) When waves arrive at an obstacle (or meet a new material), their <u>direction</u> of travel can be <u>changed</u>.

2) This can happen by <u>reflection</u> (see below) or by <u>refraction</u> or <u>diffraction</u> (see page 60).

## *Reflection of light lets us see things*

1) <u>Reflection of light</u> is what allows us to <u>see</u> objects. Light bounces off them into our eyes.

2) When light travelling in the <u>same direction</u> reflects from an <u>uneven surface</u> such as a <u>piece of paper</u>, the light reflects off <u>at different angles</u>.

3) When light travelling in the <u>same direction</u> reflects from an <u>even surface</u> (<u>smooth and shiny</u> like a <u>mirror</u>) then it's all reflected at the <u>same angle</u> and you get a <u>clear reflection</u>.

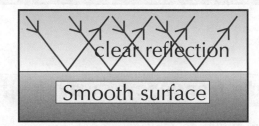

4) The <u>LAW OF REFLECTION</u> applies to <u>every reflected ray</u>:

### Angle of <u>INCIDENCE</u> = Angle of <u>REFLECTION</u>

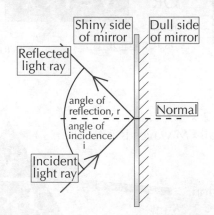

*The <u>normal</u> is an imaginary line that's perpendicular (at right angles) to the surface at the point of incidence (where the light hits the surface).*

Note that these two angles are <u>ALWAYS</u> defined between the ray itself and the <u>NORMAL</u>, dotted above. <u>Don't ever</u> label them as the angle between the ray and the <u>surface</u>.

## *Reflect on this page a while*

Reflection, refraction and diffraction are <u>wave phenomena</u> that can happen to <u>any wave</u> — <u>transverse</u> or <u>longitudinal</u>. So shock waves can be reflected, sound waves can be refracted and light waves can be diffracted. Panic not — page 60 has lots more on wave phenomena.

# Wave Properties

This page is all about drawing <u>ray diagrams</u>. It's a vital skill — questions on ray diagrams appear in the exams year after year. The best way to learn is plenty of <u>practice</u>.

## *Draw a **ray diagram** for an **image** in a **plane mirror***

You need to be able to <u>reproduce</u> this entire diagram of <u>how an image is formed</u> in a <u>PLANE MIRROR</u>. Learn these <u>important points</u>:

1) The <u>image</u> is the <u>same size</u> as the <u>object</u>.

2) It is <u>AS FAR BEHIND</u> the mirror as the object is <u>in front</u>.

3) The image is <u>virtual</u> and <u>upright</u>. The image is virtual because the object appears to be <u>behind</u> the mirror.

4) The image is <u>laterally inverted</u> — the left and right sides are <u>swapped</u>, i.e. the object's <u>left</u> side becomes its <u>right</u> side in the <u>image</u>.

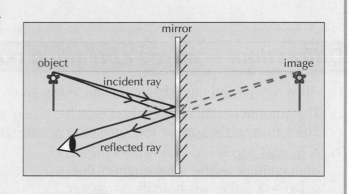

1) First off, draw the <u>virtual image</u>. <u>Don't</u> try to draw the rays first. Follow the rules in the above box — the image is the <u>same size</u>, and it's <u>as far behind</u> the mirror as the object is in <u>front</u>.

2) Next, draw a <u>reflected ray</u> going from the top of the virtual image to the top of the eye. Draw a <u>bold line</u> for the part of the ray between the mirror and eye, and a <u>dotted line</u> for the part of the ray between the mirror and virtual image.

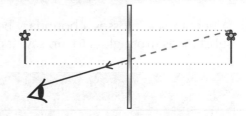

3) Now draw the <u>incident ray</u> going from the top of the object to the mirror. The incident and reflected rays follow the <u>law of reflection</u> — but you <u>don't</u> actually have to measure any angles. Just draw the ray from the <u>object</u> to the <u>point</u> where the reflected ray <u>meets the mirror</u>.

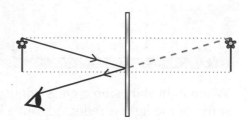

4) Now you have an <u>incident ray</u> and <u>reflected ray</u> for the <u>top</u> of the image. Do <u>steps 2 and 3 again</u> for the <u>bottom</u> of the <u>eye</u> — a reflected ray going from the image to the bottom of the eye, then an incident ray from the object to the mirror.

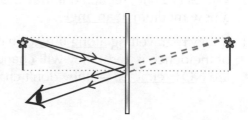

# Refraction and Diffraction

If you thought <u>reflection</u> was good, you'll just love <u>diffraction</u> and <u>refraction</u>. If you didn't find reflection interesting then I'm afraid it's tough luck — you need to know about <u>all three</u> of them.

## *Diffraction* and *refraction* are a bit more **complicated**

1) Reflection's quite <u>straightforward</u>, but there are other ways that waves can be made to change direction.

2) They can be <u>refracted</u> — which means they go through a new material but <u>change direction</u>.

3) Or they can be <u>diffracted</u> — the waves 'bend round' obstacles, causing the waves to spread out.

## *Diffraction* — waves *spreading out*

1) All waves <u>spread out</u> ('<u>diffract</u>') at the edges when they pass through a <u>gap</u> or <u>pass an obstacle</u>.

2) The amount of diffraction depends on the size of the gap relative to the wavelength of the wave. The <u>narrower the gap</u>, or the <u>longer the wavelength</u>, the <u>more</u> the wave spreads out.

3) A <u>narrow gap</u> is one that is the same order of magnitude as the <u>wavelength</u> of the wave — i.e. they're about the <u>same size</u>.

4) So whether a gap counts as narrow or not depends on the wave in question.

5) <u>Light</u> has a very <u>small wavelength</u> (about 0.0005 mm), so it can be diffracted but it needs a <u>really small gap</u>.

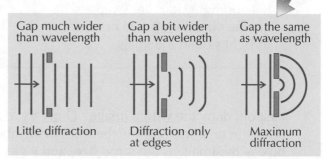

Gap much wider than wavelength — Little diffraction

Gap a bit wider than wavelength — Diffraction only at edges

Gap the same as wavelength — Maximum diffraction

## *Refraction* — *changing the speed* of a wave *can change its direction*

1) When a wave crosses a boundary between two substances (from glass to air, say) it <u>changes direction</u>:

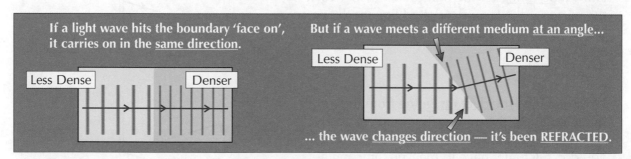

If a light wave hits the boundary 'face on', it carries on in the <u>same direction</u>.

Less Dense — Denser

But if a wave meets a different medium <u>at an angle</u>...

Less Dense — Denser

... the wave <u>changes direction</u> — it's been <u>REFRACTED</u>.

2) When light shines on a glass <u>window pane</u>, some of the light is reflected, but a lot of it passes through the glass and gets <u>refracted</u> as it does so.

3) Waves are <u>only</u> refracted if they meet a new medium <u>at an angle</u>.

4) If they're travelling <u>along the normal</u> (i.e. the angle of incidence is zero) they will <u>change speed</u>, but are <u>NOT refracted</u> — they don't change direction.

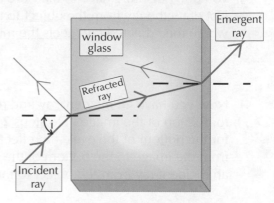

Emergent ray

window glass

Refracted ray

Incident ray

# Warm-Up and Exam Questions

Learning facts and practising exam questions is the only recipe for sure-fire success.
That's what the questions on this page are all about. All you have to do — is do them.

## Warm-Up Questions

1) What type of wave are EM waves — transverse or longitudinal?
2) Give the formula for calculating the speed of a wave.
3) Describe what happens when a wave passes through a narrow gap.
4) True or false: a wave entering a new medium along the path of the normal will not be refracted.
5) Describe the direction of vibrations in a longitudinal wave.

## Exam Questions

1    Look at this displacement-time graph for a water wave.

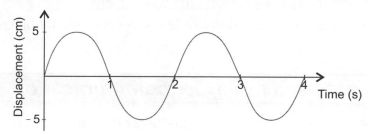

(a)  State whether water waves are transverse or longitudinal.

*(1 mark)*

(b)  Give the amplitude of this wave.

*(1 mark)*

(c)  Calculate the frequency of the wave.

*(1 mark)*

(d)  If the frequency of the wave doubles but its speed stays the same,
describe what will happen to its wavelength.

*(1 mark)*

2    The diagram below shows a student looking at a
pencil from behind a screen using a plane mirror.

(a)  Name the wave property that allows the student to see the pencil.

*(1 mark)*

(b)  Draw rays of light to complete the ray diagram below, showing
the virtual image of the pencil seen by the student.

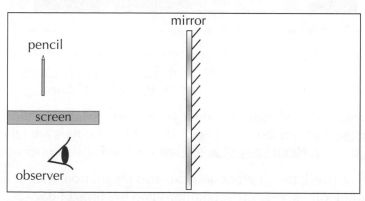

*(3 marks)*

# EM Waves and Communication

Electromagnetic (EM) <u>waves</u> have a lot in common with one another, but their <u>differences</u> make them useful to us in different ways.

## There's a continuous *spectrum* of *EM waves*

EM waves with <u>different wavelengths</u> (or frequencies) have different properties. We group them into <u>seven basic types</u>, but the different regions actually merge to form a <u>continuous spectrum</u>. They're shown below with increasing frequency and energy (decreasing wavelength) from left to right.

| RADIO WAVES | MICRO WAVES | INFRA RED | VISIBLE LIGHT | ULTRA VIOLET | X-RAYS | GAMMA RAYS |
|---|---|---|---|---|---|---|
| $1\ m - 10^4\ m$ | $10^{-2}\ m$ (1 cm) | $10^{-5}\ m$ (0.01 mm) | $10^{-7}\ m$ | $10^{-8}\ m$ | $10^{-10}\ m$ | $10^{-12}\ m$ |

*wavelength* →

1) EM waves vary in <u>wavelength</u> from around $\underline{10^{-15}\ m}$ to more than $\underline{10^4\ m}$.

2) All the different types of EM wave travel at the <u>same speed</u> ($3 \times 10^8$ m/s) in a <u>vacuum</u> (e.g. space).

3) EM waves with <u>higher frequencies</u> have <u>shorter wavelengths</u>.

4) Because of their <u>different properties</u>, different EM waves are used for <u>different purposes</u>.

## *Radio waves* are used mainly for *communication*

1) <u>Radio waves</u> are EM radiation with wavelengths longer than about 10 cm.

2) <u>Long-wave radio</u> (wavelengths of <u>1 – 10 km</u>) can be transmitted from London, say, and received halfway round the world. That's because long wavelengths <u>diffract</u> (bend, see p.60) around the curved surface of the Earth.

3) <u>Long-wave radio</u> wavelengths can also <u>diffract</u> around <u>hills</u>, into <u>tunnels</u> and all sorts.

4) This <u>diffraction effect</u> makes it possible for radio signals to be <u>received</u> even if the receiver <u>isn't</u> in <u>line of the sight</u> of the <u>transmitter</u>.

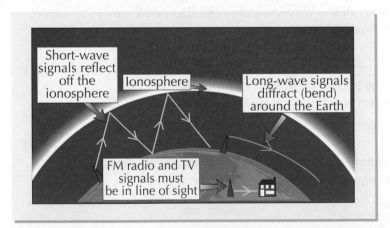

5) The radio waves used for <u>TV and FM radio</u> transmissions have very short wavelengths (10 cm – 10 m). To get reception, you must be in <u>direct sight of the transmitter</u> — the signal doesn't bend around hills or travel far <u>through</u> buildings.

6) <u>Short-wave radio</u> signals (wavelengths of about <u>10 m – 100 m</u>) can, like long-wave, be received at <u>long distances</u> from the transmitter. That's because they are <u>reflected</u> (see p.58) from the <u>ionosphere</u> — an <u>electrically charged layer</u> in the Earth's upper atmosphere.

7) <u>Medium-wave</u> signals (well, the shorter ones) can also reflect from the ionosphere, depending on atmospheric conditions and the time of day.

# EM Waves and Their Uses

Radio waves aren't the only waves used for communication — other EM waves come in <u>pretty handy</u> too. The most important thing is to think about how the <u>properties</u> of a wave relate to its <u>uses</u>.

## *Microwaves are used for satellite communication and mobile phones*

1) Communication to and from <u>satellites</u> (including satellite TV signals and satellite phones) uses microwaves. But you need to use microwaves which can <u>pass easily</u> through the Earth's <u>watery atmosphere</u>. Radio waves <u>can't</u> do this.

2) For satellite TV, the signal from a <u>transmitter</u> is transmitted into space...

3) ... where it's picked up by the satellite's receiver dish <u>orbiting</u> thousands of kilometres above the Earth. The satellite <u>transmits</u> the signal back to Earth in a different direction...

4) ... where it's received by a <u>satellite dish</u> on the ground.

5) Mobile phone calls also travel as <u>microwaves</u> between your phone and the nearest <u>transmitter</u>. Some wavelengths of microwaves are <u>absorbed</u> by <u>water</u> molecules and <u>heat</u> them up.

6) If the water in question happens to be in <u>your cells</u>, you might start to <u>cook</u> — so some people think using your mobile a lot (especially next to your <u>head</u>), or living near a <u>mast</u>, could damage your <u>health</u>. There isn't any conclusive evidence either way yet.

7) And microwaves are used by <u>remote-sensing</u> satellites — to 'see' through the clouds and monitor oil spills, track the movement of icebergs, see how much rainforest has been chopped down and so on.

## *Mobile phone use — safe radiation or harmful microwaves?*

One study on the effects of mobile phones on health looked at <u>over 400 000 people</u> and found <u>no connection</u> between mobile phone use and occurrence of brain tumours. But, mobile phone use has <u>increased dramatically</u> in the last 15 years and there may be <u>long term effects</u> that we don't know about.

# EM Waves and Their Uses

Here's another page on the uses of EM waves — this time it's all about <u>infrared</u> and <u>visible light</u>.

## *Infrared waves* are used for *remote controls* and *optical fibres*

1) <u>Infrared</u> waves are used in lots of <u>wireless remote controllers</u>.

2) Remote controls work by <u>emitting</u> different <u>patterns</u> of infrared waves to send <u>different commands</u> to an appliance, e.g. a TV.

3) <u>Optical fibres</u> (e.g. those used in phone lines) can carry <u>data</u> over long distances very quickly.

4) They use both <u>infrared</u> waves and <u>visible light</u>.

5) The signal is carried as <u>pulses</u> of light or infrared radiation and is <u>reflected</u> off the sides of a very narrow <u>core</u> from one end of the fibre to the other.

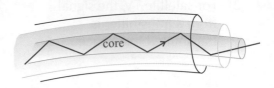

## *Visible light* is useful for *photography*

It sounds pretty obvious, but <u>photography</u> would be <u>tricky</u> without visible light.

1) Cameras use a <u>lens</u> to focus <u>visible light</u> onto a light-sensitive <u>film</u> or electronic <u>sensor</u>.

2) The lens <u>aperture</u> controls <u>how much</u> light enters the camera (like the pupil in an eye).

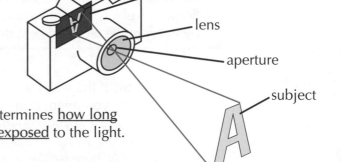

light-sensitive film or sensor

lens

aperture

subject

3) The <u>shutter speed</u> determines <u>how long</u> the film or sensor is <u>exposed</u> to the light.

4) By varying the <u>aperture</u> and <u>shutter speed</u> (and also the <u>sensitivity</u> of the film or the sensor), a photographer can capture as much or as little light as they want in their photograph.

## *Infrared radiation — turning on your telly since the 1980s*

<u>Different</u> types of <u>electromagnetic wave</u> each have different uses in <u>technology</u> as we've seen over the last few pages. Make sure you learn all the uses of <u>infrared radiation</u> and <u>visible light</u> from this page.

# Warm-Up and Exam Questions

There was lots of information about electromagnetic waves on those last few pages. See what you can remember by first answering the warm-up questions, then by moving onto the exam questions.

## Warm-Up Questions

1) Which type of EM wave has the highest energy?
2) Which type of EM wave has the longest wavelength?
3) Explain why microwaves are used in satellite communications.
4) Which type of EM wave has the lowest frequency?
5) What type of EM wave is used in traditional photography?

## Exam Questions

1    An electromagnetic wave has a wavelength of $1 \times 10^{-5}$ m.

    (a)   State what type of EM wave this is.

*(1 mark)*

    (b)   Give **one** possible use of the EM wave stated in part (a).

*(1 mark)*

    (c)   Mobile phones use microwave signals. Explain why people might be concerned that mobile phone use could be hazardous to health.

*(2 marks)*

2    Radio waves are used for communication.

    (a)   Complete the diagram below to show the paths that the following types of radio waves can take around the Earth from the transmitter to receiver. Label each path.

       (i)    Long-wave radio waves.

       (ii)   Short-wave radio waves.

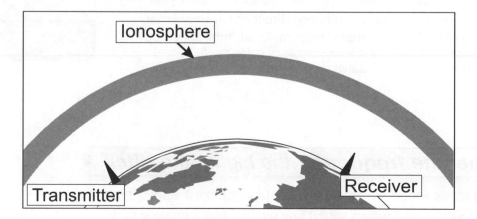

*(2 marks)*

    (b)   Name the property of waves that allows long-wave radio waves to be sent great distances around the earth.

*(1 mark)*

    (c)   Explain why receivers for FM radio waves need to be in direct line of sight of the transmitter.

*(2 marks)*

# Sound Waves

We hear sounds when <u>vibrations</u> reach our <u>eardrums</u>. You'll need to know how sound waves work.

## Sound travels as a wave

1) <u>Sound waves</u> are caused by <u>vibrating objects</u>. These mechanical vibrations are passed through the surrounding medium as a series of compressions. They're a type of <u>longitudinal wave</u> (see page 57).

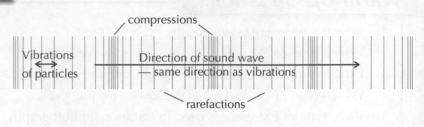

2) Sometimes the sound will eventually travel through someone's <u>inner ear</u> and reach their <u>eardrum</u>, at which point the person might <u>hear it</u>.

3) Sound generally travels <u>faster in solids</u> than in liquids, and faster in liquids than in gases.

4) Sound can't travel in <u>space</u>, because it's mostly a <u>vacuum</u> (there are no particles).

## Sound waves can reflect and refract

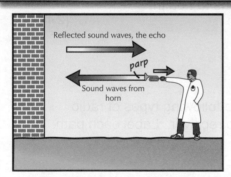

1) Sound waves will be <u>reflected</u> by <u>hard flat surfaces</u>.

2) This is very noticeable in an <u>empty room</u>. A big empty room sounds <u>completely different</u> once you've put <u>carpet</u>, <u>curtains</u> and a bit of <u>furniture</u> in it. That's because these things <u>absorb</u> the sound quickly and stop it <u>echoing</u> around the room. <u>Echoes</u> are just <u>reflected</u> sound waves.

3) You hear a <u>delay</u> between the <u>original</u> sound and the <u>echo</u> because the echoed sound

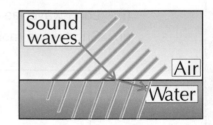

waves have to <u>travel further</u>, and so take <u>longer</u> to reach your ears.

4) <u>Sound waves</u> will also refract (change direction) as they enter <u>different media</u>. As they enter <u>denser</u> material, they <u>speed up</u>. (However, since sound waves are always <u>spreading out so much</u>, the change in direction is <u>hard to spot</u> under normal circumstances.)

## The higher the frequency, the higher the pitch

1) <u>High frequency</u> sound waves sound <u>high pitched</u> like a <u>squeaking mouse</u>.

2) <u>Low frequency</u> sound waves sound <u>low pitched</u> like a <u>mooing cow</u>.

3) <u>Frequency</u> is the number of <u>complete vibrations</u> each second — so a wave that has a frequency of 100 Hz vibrates 100 times each second.

4) Common <u>units</u> are <u>kHz</u> (1000 Hz) and <u>MHz</u> (1 000 000 Hz).

5) <u>High frequency</u> (or high pitch) also means <u>shorter wavelength</u> (see p.57).

6) The <u>loudness</u> of a sound depends on the <u>amplitude</u> (p.56) of the sound wave. The <u>bigger</u> the amplitude, the <u>louder</u> the sound.

# The Origin of the Universe

OK. Let's not kid ourselves — this is a pretty <u>daunting</u> topic. How the universe started is obviously open to debate, but physicists have got some <u>neat ideas</u> based on their observations of the <u>stars</u>.

## The **universe** seems to be **expanding**

As big as the universe already is, it looks like it's getting even bigger.
All its <u>galaxies</u> seem to be moving away from each other. There's good evidence for this...

## Light from other galaxies is red-shifted

1) Different chemical elements <u>absorb</u> different <u>frequencies</u> (see p.62) of light.

2) Each element produces a <u>specific pattern</u> of <u>dark lines</u> at the frequencies that it <u>absorbs</u> in the visible spectrum.

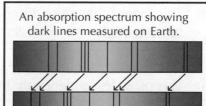

An absorption spectrum showing dark lines measured on Earth.

3) When we look at <u>light from distant galaxies</u> we can see the <u>same patterns</u> but at <u>slightly lower frequencies</u> than they should be — they're shifted towards the <u>red end</u> of the spectrum. This is called <u>red-shift</u>.

The same absorption spectrum measured from light from a distant galaxy. The dark lines in this spectrum are red-shifted.

4) It's the same effect as the vrrroomm from a racing car — the engine sounds <u>lower-pitched</u> when the car's gone past you and is <u>moving away</u> from you. This is called the Doppler effect.

## The **Doppler effect**

1) When something that emits waves moves <u>towards</u> you or <u>away</u> from you, the <u>wavelengths</u> and <u>frequencies</u> of the waves seem <u>different</u> — compared to when the source of the waves is <u>stationary</u>.

2) The <u>frequency</u> of a source moving <u>towards</u> you will seem <u>higher</u> and its <u>wavelength</u> will seem <u>shorter</u>.

3) The <u>frequency</u> of a source moving <u>away</u> from you will seem <u>lower</u> and its <u>wavelength</u> will seem longer.

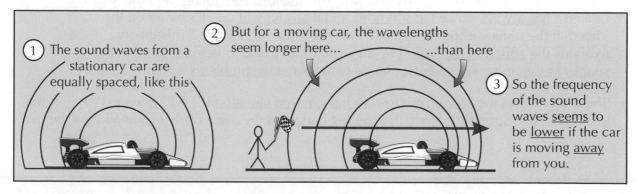

① The sound waves from a stationary car are equally spaced, like this

② But for a moving car, the wavelengths seem longer here... ...than here

③ So the frequency of the sound waves <u>seems</u> to be <u>lower</u> if the car is moving <u>away</u> from you.

4) The Doppler effect happens to both <u>longitudinal</u> waves (e.g. sound) and <u>transverse</u> waves (e.g. light and microwaves).

# The Origin of the Universe

Once upon a time there was a really <u>Big Bang</u> — that's the <u>most convincing theory</u> we've got at the moment. But it's not an idea plucked from nowhere — there's good evidence to support it.

## The **further away** a galaxy is, the **greater** the **red-shift**

1) <u>Measurements</u> of the red-shift suggest that <u>all the galaxies</u> are <u>moving away from us</u> very quickly — and it's the <u>same result</u> whichever direction you look in.

2) <u>More distant</u> galaxies have <u>greater</u> red-shifts than nearer ones.

3) This means that more distant galaxies are <u>moving away</u> from us <u>faster</u> than nearer ones.

4) This provides evidence that the whole universe is <u>expanding</u>.

## It all **started off** with a very **Big Bang** (probably)

Right now, distant galaxies are moving <u>away</u> from us — the <u>further</u> away a galaxy is from the us, the <u>faster</u> they're moving away. But something must have <u>got them going</u>. That 'something' was probably a <u>big explosion</u> — so they called it the <u>Big Bang</u>...

1) According to this theory, all the matter and energy in the universe must have been compressed into a <u>very small space</u>. Then it <u>exploded</u> from that single 'point' and started expanding.

2) The <u>expansion</u> is still going on. We can use the current <u>rate of expansion</u> of the universe to estimate its <u>age</u>. Our best guess is that the Big Bang happened about <u>14 billion years ago</u>.

3) The Big Bang isn't the only game in town. The '<u>Steady State</u>' theory says that the universe <u>has always</u> existed <u>as it is now</u>, and it <u>always will</u> do. It's based on the idea that the universe appears pretty much <u>the same everywhere</u>. This theory explains the <u>apparent expansion</u> by suggesting that matter is being <u>created</u> in the spaces as the universe expands. But there are some <u>big problems</u> with this theory.

4) The discovery of the <u>cosmic microwave background radiation</u> (CMBR) (see next page) some years later was <u>strong evidence</u> that the Big Bang was the more likely explanation of the two.

## The Big Bang — it's the best theory we've got

Whichever way astronomers and astrophysicists look into space, they see galaxies getting <u>further</u> and <u>further apart</u>. The natural conclusion from this observation is that if things are getting further apart, they must have at one point been really <u>close together</u>. And what triggered that single point to suddenly expand into the universe that we know today? It's <u>anybody's guess</u>.

# The Origin of the Universe

The Big Bang is the currently accepted theory because of the <u>cosmic microwave background radiation</u>.

## There's **uniform microwave radiation** from all **directions**

1) Scientists have detected <u>low frequency electromagnetic radiation</u> coming from <u>all parts</u> of the universe.

2) This radiation is largely in the <u>microwave</u> part of the EM spectrum (see p.62). It's known as the <u>cosmic microwave background radiation</u> (CMBR).

3) The <u>Big Bang theory</u> is the <u>only</u> theory that can explain the CMBR.

4) Just after the Big Bang while the universe was still <u>extremely hot</u>, everything in the universe emitted very <u>high frequency radiation</u>. As the universe <u>expanded</u> it has <u>cooled</u>, and this radiation has dropped in frequency and is now seen as <u>microwave radiation</u>.

## The **Big Bang theory** has its **limitations**

1) Today <u>nearly all</u> astronomers agree there <u>was</u> a Big Bang. However, there are <u>some</u> who still believe in the Steady State theory. Some of these say the <u>evidence</u> just points that way. Others maybe <u>don't want to change their mind</u> — that would mean admitting they were <u>wrong</u> in the first place.

2) The Big Bang theory <u>isn't perfect</u>. As it stands, it's <u>not</u> the whole explanation of the universe — there are observations that the theory can't yet explain. E.g. for complicated reasons that you don't need to know, the Big Bang theory predicts that the universe's expansion should be <u>slowing down</u> — but as far as we can tell it's actually <u>speeding up</u>.

3) The Big Bang explains the universe's expansion well, but it isn't an explanation for what actually <u>caused</u> the explosion in the first place, or what the <u>conditions</u> were like before the explosion (or if there was a 'before').

4) It seems most likely the Big Bang theory will be <u>adapted</u> in some way to account for its weaknesses rather than just <u>dumped</u> — it explains so much so well that scientists will need a lot of persuading to drop it altogether.

## Time and space — it's funny old stuff isn't it...

<u>Proving</u> a scientific theory is impossible. If enough evidence points a certain way, then a theory can look pretty <u>convincing</u>. But that doesn't <u>prove</u> it's a <u>fact</u> — <u>new evidence</u> may change people's minds.

# Warm-Up and Exam Questions

You know the drill — some warm-up questions to get you thinking about what you've just read, and some exam questions to see how far you can apply your knowledge.  Get cracking.

## Warm-Up Questions

1) True or false: sound travels as a transverse wave.
2) How does the frequency of a sound wave affect the pitch of the sound?
3) What is an echo?
4) Describe the Steady State theory of the universe.

## Exam Questions

1    The diagram below shows an ambulance
     speeding away from an observer with its siren on.

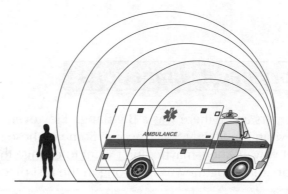

(a)   (i)    Describe what happens to the observed wavelength of sound waves as the
             ambulance travels towards and then away from the observer.

*(2 marks)*

(ii)   Give the name of this effect.

*(1 mark)*

(iii)  Describe how the pitch of the sound reaching the observer
       will change as the ambulance moves away from him.

*(1 mark)*

A similar effect has been discovered in observations of the light from distant galaxies.

(b)   Describe the movement of distant galaxies as viewed from Earth.

*(1 mark)*

2    (a)   Briefly describe the currently accepted theory for the origin of the universe.

*(2 marks)*

(b)   Red-shift is a key piece of evidence for the currently accepted
      theory on the origin of the universe.

(i)    Explain how the relationship between a galaxy's distance and its
       observed red-shift suggests that the universe is expanding.

*(3 marks)*

(ii)   Give **one** other piece of evidence that supports the
       currently accepted theory for the origin of the universe.

*(1 mark)*

# Revision Summary for Physics 1b

It's business time — another chance for you to see which bits went in and which bits you need to flick back and have another read over. Do as many of the questions as you can and then try the tricky ones after you've had another chance to read the pages you struggled on. You know it makes sense.

1) What is meant by a non-renewable energy resource?
   Name four different non-renewable energy resources.

2) Explain how electricity is generated in a gas-fired power station.
   Describe the useful energy transfers that occur.

3) Describe how the following renewable resources are used to generate electricity.
   State one advantage and one disadvantage for each resource.

   a) wind      b) solar energy      c) the tide      d) waves      e) geothermal energy

4) Why are hydroelectric power stations often located in remote valleys?

5) What is the purpose of pumped storage?

6) Why is wave power only a realistic major energy source on small islands?

7) What is the source of energy for tidal barrages?

8) Apart from generating electricity, how else can geothermal heat be used?

9) How are biofuels produced? Give two examples of biofuels.

10) Name two places that carbon dioxide can be stored after carbon capture.

11) Name six factors that should be considered when a new power station is being planned.

12) Which three energy sources are linked most strongly with habitat disruption?

13) Explain why a very high electrical voltage is used to transmit electricity in the National Grid.

14) Draw a diagram to illustrate frequency, wavelength and amplitude of a wave.

15)*Find the speed of a wave with frequency 50 kHz and wavelength 0.3 cm.

16) a) Sketch a diagram of a ray of light being reflected in a mirror.
    b) Label the normal and the angles of incidence and reflection.

17) Why does light bend as it moves between air and water?

18) Draw a diagram showing a wave diffracting through a gap.

19) What size should the gap be in order to maximise diffraction?
    a) much larger than the wavelength    b) the same size as the wavelength
    c) a bit bigger than the wavelength

20) Sketch the EM spectrum with all its details. Put the lowest frequency waves on the left.

21) What type of wave do television remote controls usually use?

22) Which two types of EM wave are commonly used to send signals along optical fibres?

23) Why can't sound waves travel in space?

24) Are high frequency sound waves high pitched or low pitched?

25) If a wave source is moving towards you, will the observed frequency of its waves be higher or lower than their actual frequency?

26) What do red-shift observations tell us about the universe?

27) Describe the 'Big Bang' theory for the origin of the universe. What evidence is there for this theory?

# Velocity and Distance-Time Graphs

Speed and velocity aren't the same thing, you know. There's more to velocity than meets the eye.

## Speed and velocity are both how fast you're going

Speed and velocity are both measured in m/s (or km/h or mph). They both simply say how fast you're going, but there's a subtle difference between them which you need to know:

> Speed is just how fast you're going (e.g. 30 mph or 20 m/s) with no regard to the direction.
> Velocity however must also have the direction specified, e.g. 30 mph north or 20 m/s, 060°.

Seems kinda fussy I know, but they expect you to remember that distinction, so there you go.

## Distance-time graphs

These are a very nifty way of describing something travelling through time and space:

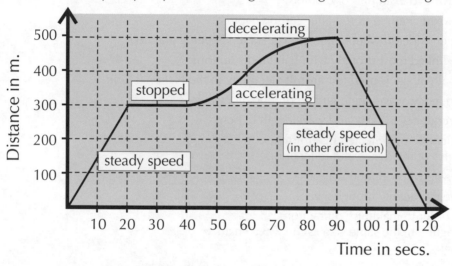

As you probably know, speed = distance ÷ time. So the gradient of a distance-time graph tells you how fast your object is travelling. This is because the gradient is the change in the distance (vertical axis) divided by the change in time (horizontal axis). See — it's easy when you know how.

### Very important notes:

1) <u>Gradient = speed</u>.
2) <u>Flat</u> sections are where it's <u>stationary</u> — it's <u>stopped</u>.
3) <u>Straight</u> uphill or downhill sections mean it is travelling at a <u>steady speed</u>.
4) The <u>steeper</u> the graph, the <u>faster</u> it's going.
5) <u>Downhill</u> sections mean it's <u>going back</u> toward its starting point.
6) <u>Curves</u> represent <u>acceleration</u> or <u>deceleration</u>.
7) A <u>steepening</u> curve means it's <u>speeding up</u> (increasing gradient).
8) A <u>levelling off</u> curve means it's <u>slowing down</u> (decreasing gradient).

## Calculating speed from a distance-time graph — it's just the gradient

For example the speed of the return section of the graph is:

$$\text{Speed} = \text{gradient} = \frac{\text{vertical}}{\text{horizontal}} = \frac{500}{30} = 16.7 \text{ m/s}$$

Don't forget that you have to use the scales of the axes to work out the gradient. Don't measure in cm!

# Acceleration and Velocity-Time Graphs

If something is <u>speeding up</u>, we say that it is <u>accelerating</u>.

## *Acceleration is how quickly velocity is changing*

Acceleration is <u>definitely not</u> the same as <u>velocity</u> or <u>speed</u>.

> 1) Acceleration is <u>how quickly</u> the velocity is <u>changing</u>.
> 2) This change in velocity can be a <u>CHANGE IN SPEED</u> or a <u>CHANGE IN DIRECTION</u> or <u>both</u>.

(You only have to worry about the change in speed bit for calculations.)

## *Acceleration — the formula:*

$$\text{acceleration} = \frac{\text{change in velocity}}{\text{time taken}}$$

*Acceleration is the change in velocity (m/s) per second (s), = m/s².*

Well, it's <u>just another formula</u>.
And it's got a <u>formula triangle</u> like all the others.

Mind you, there are <u>two tricky things</u> with this one:

First there's the 'v – u', which means working out the '<u>change in velocity</u>', as shown in the example below, rather than just putting a <u>simple value</u> for velocity or speed in.

*Here 'v' is the <u>final velocity</u> and 'u' is the <u>initial velocity</u>.*

Secondly there's the <u>unit</u> of acceleration, which is <u>m/s²</u>.
<u>Not m/s</u>, which is <u>velocity</u>, but <u>m/s²</u>. Got it? No? Let's try once more: <u>Not m/s</u>, but <u>m/s²</u>.

## *Example*

> A skulking cat accelerates from 2 m/s to 6 m/s in 5.6 s. Find its acceleration.
>
> <u>ANSWER:</u> Using the formula triangle:
> a = (v – u) / t = (6 – 2) / 5.6 = 4 ÷ 5.6 = <u>0.71 m/s²</u>

# Acceleration and Velocity-Time Graphs

Here's the distance-time graph's big brother — the <u>velocity-time</u> graph.

## *Velocity-time* graphs

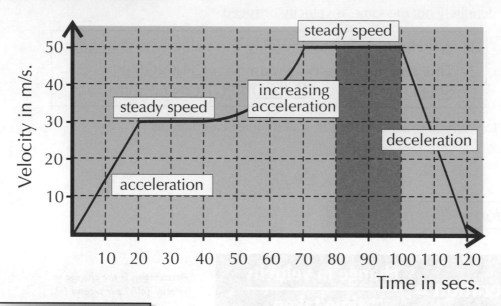

### *Very important notes:*

1) <u>GRADIENT = ACCELERATION</u>.
2) <u>Flat sections</u> represent <u>steady speed</u>.
3) The <u>steeper</u> the graph, the <u>greater</u> the <u>acceleration</u> or <u>deceleration</u>.
4) <u>Uphill</u> sections (/) are <u>acceleration</u>.
5) <u>Downhill</u> sections (\) are <u>deceleration</u>.
6) The <u>area</u> under any section of the graph (or all of it) is equal to the <u>distance travelled</u> in that <u>time interval</u>.
7) A <u>curve</u> means <u>changing acceleration</u>.

## *Calculating **acceleration**, **velocity** and **distance** from a **V-T** graph*

1) The <u>acceleration</u> represented by the <u>first section</u> of the graph is:

$$\underline{\text{Acceleration}} = \text{gradient} = \frac{\text{vertical change}}{\text{horizontal change}} = \frac{30}{20} = \underline{1.5 \text{ m/s}^2}$$

2) The <u>velocity</u> at any point is simply found by <u>reading the value</u> off the <u>velocity axis</u>.
3) The <u>distance travelled</u> in any time interval is equal to the <u>area</u> under the graph. For example, the distance travelled between t = 80 s and t = 100 s is equal to the <u>shaded area</u>, which is equal to $20 \times 50 = \underline{1000 \text{ m}}$.

---

## *Don't get distance-time graphs and velocity-time graphs confused*

Make sure you know all there is to know about velocity-time graphs — i.e. learn those numbered points. You work out acceleration from the graph simply by applying the acceleration formula — change in velocity is the change on the vertical axis and time taken is the change on the horizontal axis.

# Weight, Mass and Gravity

Now for something a bit more attractive — the force of gravity.

## Gravitational force is the force of attraction between all masses

Gravity attracts all masses, but you only notice it when one of the masses is really really big, e.g. a planet. Anything near a planet or star is attracted to it very strongly.

This has two important effects:

1) On the surface of a planet, it makes all things accelerate (see p.73) towards the ground (all with the same acceleration, g, which is about 10 m/s$^2$ on Earth).

2) It gives everything a weight.

## Weight and mass are not the same

1) Mass is just the amount of 'stuff' in an object. For any given object this will have the same value anywhere in the universe.

2) Weight is caused by the pull of the gravitational force. In most questions the weight of an object is just the force of gravity pulling it towards the centre of the Earth.

3) An object has the same mass whether it's on Earth or on the Moon — but its weight will be different. A 1 kg mass will weigh less on the Moon (about 1.6 N) than it does on Earth (about 10 N), simply because the gravitational force pulling on it is less.

4) Weight is a force measured in newtons. It's measured using a spring balance or newton meter. Mass is not a force. It's measured in kilograms with a mass balance (an old-fashioned pair of balancing scales).

## The very important formula relating mass, weight and gravity

### weight = mass × gravitational field strength

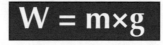

*The acceleration due to gravity and the gravitational field strength are always the same value, no matter what planet or moon you're on.*

1) Remember, weight and mass are not the same. Mass is in kg, weight is in newtons.

2) The letter "g" represents the strength of the gravity and its value is different for different planets. On Earth g ≈ 10 N/kg. On the Moon, where the gravity is weaker, g is only about 1.6 N/kg.

3) This formula is hideously easy to use:

> EXAMPLE: What is the weight, in newtons, of a 5 kg mass, both on Earth and on the Moon?
>
> ANSWER: "W = m × g". On Earth: W = 5 × 10 = 50 N   (The weight of the 5 kg mass is 50 N.)
> On the Moon: W = 5 × 1.6 = 8 N   (The weight of the 5 kg mass is 8 N.)

See what I mean. Hideously easy — as long as you've learnt what all the letters mean.

# Warm-Up and Exam Questions

Here's another set of questions to test your knowledge.
Make sure you can answer them all before you go steaming on.

## Warm-Up Questions

1) What does the gradient of a distance-time graph show?
2) What are the units of acceleration? and of mass? and of weight?
3) A car goes from 0 to 30 m/s in 6 seconds. Calculate its acceleration.
4) Name the force that keeps the Earth orbiting around the Sun.

## Exam Questions

1    A racing car is driven round a circular track of length 2400 m at a constant speed of 45 m/s.

   (a)  Explain why the car's velocity is not constant.

   *(1 mark)*

   (b)  On one lap, the speed of the car increases from 45 m/s to 59 m/s over a period of
        5 seconds.  Calculate its acceleration.

   *(2 marks)*

2    The graph below shows the distance of a shuttle-bus from its start point plotted against time.

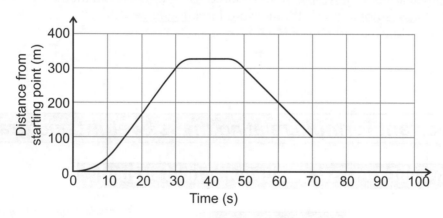

   Use the graph to answer the following questions:
   (a)  Between 15 and 30 seconds:
        (i)   how far does the bus travel?

   *(1 mark)*

        (ii)  how fast is the bus going?

   *(2 marks)*

   (b)  For how long does the bus stop?

   *(1 mark)*

   (c)  Describe the bus's speed and direction between 50 and 70 seconds.

   *(1 mark)*

   (d)  Between 70 and 100 seconds, the bus slows, coming to a standstill at 100 s to finish
        up where it started.  Show this on the graph.

   *(1 mark)*

# Exam Questions

3   The diagram below shows the velocity of a cyclist plotted against time.

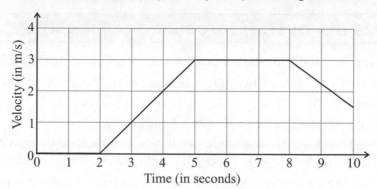

(a)   Describe the motion of the cyclist between 5 and 8 seconds.

*(1 mark)*

(b)   Describe what is happening to the cyclist's speed between 8 and 10 seconds.

*(1 mark)*

(c)   Calculate how far the cyclist travelled between 2 and 5 seconds.

*(1 mark)*

4   A spring increases in length when masses are suspended from it, as shown.  When a metal ball with a mass of 0.1 kg is suspended from the spring, the spring stretches by 3 cm.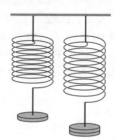

If the experiment was repeated on Mars, the spring would only be stretched by 1.1 cm.

(a)   Suggest and explain why the spring would stretch less on Mars than on Earth.

*(3 marks)*

(b)   Calculate the value of $g$ on Mars, assuming that $g$ on Earth is 10 m/s$^2$.

*(3 marks)*

5   A stone falls from the edge of a cliff.  After falling for 1 second the stone has a downwards velocity of 10 m/s.

(a)   Calculate the stone's acceleration during the first second it falls.

*(1 mark)*

(b)   Assuming no air resistance, calculate the stone's velocity after three seconds of falling.

*(2 marks)*

(c)   The stone has a mass of 0.12 kg.  Calculate its weight.

*(2 marks)*

(d)   Describe the effect of doubling the stone's mass on its acceleration due to gravity.

*(1 mark)*

6   Which of the following masses exert a gravitational attraction on other masses — the Sun, the Earth, a human being, a feather, an atom?  Explain your answer.

*(1 mark)*

# Resultant Forces

Gravity isn't the only force in town — there are other forces such as <u>driving forces</u> or <u>air resistance</u>. What you need to be able to work out is how all these forces <u>add up together</u>.

## *Resultant force is the overall force on a point or object*

The notion of <u>resultant force</u> is a really important one for you to get your head round:

1) In most <u>real</u> situations there are at least <u>two forces</u> acting on an object along any direction.

2) The <u>overall</u> effect of these forces will decide the <u>motion</u> of the object
— whether it will <u>accelerate</u>, <u>decelerate</u> or stay at a <u>steady speed</u>.

3) If you have a <u>number of forces</u> acting at a single point, you can replace them with a <u>single force</u> (so long as the single force has the <u>same effect on the motion</u> as the original forces acting all together).

4) If the forces all act along the same line (they're all parallel and act in the same or the opposite direction), the <u>overall effect</u> is found by just <u>adding or subtracting</u> them.

5) The overall force you get is called the <u>resultant force</u>.

### Example: **stationary teapot** — all forces **balance**

1) The force of <u>GRAVITY</u> (or weight) is acting <u>downwards</u>.
2) This causes a <u>REACTION FORCE</u> (see p.80) from the surface <u>pushing up</u> on the object.
3) This is the <u>only way</u> it can be in <u>BALANCE</u>.
4) <u>Without</u> a reaction force, it would <u>accelerate downwards</u> due to the pull of gravity.
5) The <u>resultant</u> force on the teapot is zero: 10 N – 10 N = 0 N.

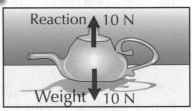

*Remember that forces are always measured in newtons (N).*

## *A resultant force means a change in velocity*

1) If there is a resultant force acting on an object, then the object will <u>change its state of rest or motion</u>.

2) In other words it causes a <u>change in the object's velocity</u>.

## *You should be able to find the resultant force acting in a straight line*

<u>EXAMPLE:</u> Benny is driving in his car. He applies a driving force of <u>1000 N</u>, but has to overcome air resistance of <u>600 N</u>.
What is the <u>resultant force</u>? Will the car's velocity <u>change</u>?

*Driving Force:*
*1000 N*

*Air Resistance:*
*600 N*

*Resultant Force:*
*400 N*

<u>ANSWER:</u> Say that the forces pointing to the <u>left</u> are pointing in the <u>positive direction</u>.
The resultant force = 1000 N – 600 N = <u>400 N to the left</u>.
If there is a resultant force then there is always an acceleration, so Benny's velocity <u>will</u> change.

# Forces and Acceleration

Around about the time of the Great Plague in the 1660s, a chap called <u>Isaac Newton</u> worked out his <u>Laws of Motion</u>. At first they might seem kind of obscure or irrelevant, but if you can't understand this page then you'll never understand <u>forces and motion</u>.

## An object needs a **force** to start **moving**

> If the resultant force on a <u>stationary</u> object is <u>zero</u>, the object will <u>remain stationary</u>.

Things <u>don't just start moving</u> on their own, there has to be a <u>resultant force</u> (see p.78) to get them started.

## No resultant force means no change in velocity

> If there is <u>no resultant force</u> on a <u>moving</u> object it'll just carry on moving at the <u>same velocity</u>.

1) When a train or car or bus or anything else is <u>moving</u> at a <u>constant velocity</u> then the <u>forces</u> on it must all be <u>balanced</u>.

2) Never let yourself entertain the <u>ridiculous idea</u> that things need a constant overall force to <u>keep</u> them moving — NO NO NO NO NO NO!

3) To keep going at a <u>steady speed</u>, there must be <u>zero resultant force</u> — and don't you forget it.

## A resultant force means acceleration

> If there is a <u>non-zero resultant force</u>, then the object will <u>accelerate</u> in the direction of the force.

1) A non-zero <u>resultant</u> force will always produce <u>acceleration</u> (or deceleration).

2) This "acceleration" can take <u>five</u> different forms: <u>Starting</u>, <u>stopping</u>, <u>speeding up</u>, <u>slowing down</u> and <u>changing direction</u>.

3) On a force diagram, the <u>arrows</u> will be <u>unequal</u>:

<u>Don't ever say</u>: "If something's moving there must be an overall resultant force acting on it". Not so. If there's an <u>overall</u> force it will always <u>accelerate</u>.

You get <u>steady</u> speed when there is <u>zero</u> resultant force.
I wonder how many times I need to say that same thing before you remember it?

# Forces and Acceleration

More on forces and acceleration here. The big equation to learn is <u>F = ma</u> — it's a really important one and you <u>will</u> be tested on it. Remember that the F is always the <u>resultant force</u> — that's important too.

## A **non-zero** resultant force produces an **acceleration**

Any <u>resultant force</u> will produce <u>acceleration</u>, and this is the <u>formula</u> for it:

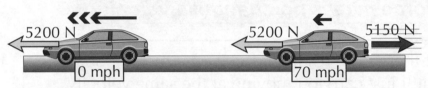

$$F = ma \qquad \text{or} \qquad a = F/m$$

m = mass in kilograms (kg)    a = acceleration in metres per second squared (m/s²)
F is the <u>resultant force</u> in newtons (N)

> <u>EXAMPLE</u>: A car of mass of 1750 kg has an engine which provides a driving force of 5200 N. At 70 mph the drag force acting on the car is 5150 N.
>
> Find its acceleration: a) when first setting off from rest    b) at 70 mph.

<u>ANSWER</u>: 1) First draw a force diagram for both cases (no need to show the vertical forces):

5200 N    0 mph          5200 N    5150 N    70 mph

2) Work out the resultant force and acceleration of the car in each case.

Resultant force = 5200 N          Resultant force = 5200 − 5150 = 50 N

a = F/m = 5200 ÷ 1750 = <u>3.0 m/s²</u>    a = F/m = 50 ÷ 1750 = <u>0.03 m/s²</u>

## Reaction forces are equal and opposite

> When <u>two objects interact</u>, the forces they exert on each other are <u>equal and opposite</u>.

1) That means if you <u>push</u> something, say a shopping trolley, the trolley will <u>push back</u> against you, <u>just as hard</u>.

2) And as soon as you <u>stop</u> pushing, <u>so does the trolley</u>. Kinda clever really.

3) So far so good. The slightly tricky thing to get your head round is this — if the forces are always equal, <u>how does anything ever go anywhere</u>? The important thing to remember is that the two forces are acting on <u>different objects</u>.

### Example — a pair of ice skaters

When skater A pushes on skater B (the '<u>action</u>' force), she feels an equal and opposite force from skater B's hand (the '<u>reaction</u>' force).

Both skaters feel the <u>same sized force</u>, in <u>opposite directions</u>, and so accelerate away from each other.

Skater A will be <u>accelerated</u> more than skater B, though, because she has a smaller mass — remember <u>a = F/m</u>.

Skater A    Skater B    mass = 55 kg    mass = 65 kg

It's the same sort of thing when you go <u>swimming</u>. You <u>push</u> back against the <u>water</u> with your arms and legs, and the water pushes you forwards with an <u>equal-sized force</u> in the <u>opposite direction</u>.

# Frictional Force and Terminal Velocity

Friction is found nearly everywhere and it acts to <u>slow down</u> and <u>stop</u> moving objects. Sometimes friction is a pain, but at other times it's very helpful.

## *Friction is always there to **slow things down***

1) If an object has <u>no force</u> propelling it along it will always <u>slow down and stop</u> because of <u>friction</u> (unless you're in space where there's nothing to rub against).
2) Friction always acts in the <u>opposite</u> direction to movement.
3) To travel at a <u>steady</u> speed, the driving force needs to <u>balance</u> the frictional forces.
4) You get friction between <u>two surfaces</u> in contact, or when an object passes <u>through a fluid</u> (<u>drag</u>).

## *Resistance or "**drag**" from **fluids** (air or liquid)*

Most of the resistive forces are caused by <u>air resistance</u> or "<u>drag</u>". The most important factor <u>by far</u> in <u>reducing drag</u> in fluids is keeping the shape of the object <u>streamlined</u>.

The <u>opposite</u> extreme is a <u>parachute</u> which is about as <u>high drag</u> as you can get — which is, of course, <u>the whole idea</u>.

## *Drag **increases** as the **speed increases***

<u>Frictional forces</u> from fluids always <u>increase with speed</u>.

A car has <u>much more</u> friction to <u>work against</u> when travelling at <u>70 mph</u> compared to <u>30 mph</u>. So at 70 mph the engine has to work <u>much harder</u> just to maintain a <u>steady speed</u>.

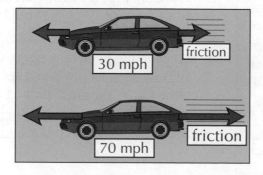

---

### *Friction's annoying when it's slowing down your boat, car or lorry...*

... but it can be useful too. As well as stopping parachutists ending up as nasty messes on the floor, friction's good for <u>other stuff</u> — e.g. without it, you wouldn't be able to walk or run or skip or write.

# Frictional Force and Terminal Velocity

Frictional forces <u>increase</u> with speed — but only up to a certain point.  Read on...

## *Objects falling through fluids reach a terminal velocity*

1) When falling objects first <u>set off</u>, the force of gravity is <u>much more</u> than the <u>frictional force</u> slowing them down, so they accelerate.

2) As the <u>speed increases</u> the friction <u>builds up</u>.

3) This gradually <u>reduces</u> the <u>acceleration</u> until eventually the <u>frictional force</u> is <u>equal</u> to the <u>accelerating force</u> and then it won't accelerate any more.

4) It will have reached its maximum speed or <u>terminal velocity</u> and will fall at a steady speed.

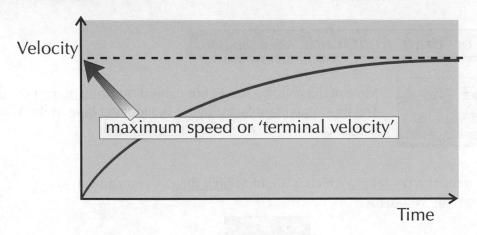

## *Terminal velocity of falling objects depends on shape and area*

1) The <u>accelerating force</u> acting on <u>all</u> falling objects is <u>gravity</u> and it would make them all fall at the <u>same</u> rate, if it wasn't for <u>air resistance</u>.

2) This means that on the Moon, where there's <u>no air</u>, hammers and feathers dropped simultaneously will hit the ground <u>together</u>.

3) However, on Earth, <u>air resistance</u> causes things to fall at <u>different</u> speeds, and the <u>terminal velocity</u> of any object is determined by its <u>drag</u> in <u>comparison</u> to its <u>weight</u>.

4) The frictional force depends on its <u>shape and area</u>.

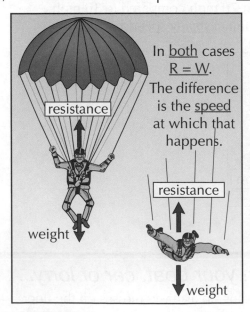

In <u>both</u> cases R = W. The difference is the <u>speed</u> at which that happens.

5) The most important example is the human <u>skydiver</u>.

6) Without his parachute open he has quite a <u>small</u> area and a force of "<u>W = mg</u>" pulling him down.

7) He reaches a <u>terminal velocity</u> of about <u>120 mph</u>.

8) But with the parachute <u>open</u>, there's much more <u>air resistance</u> (at any given speed) and still only the same force "<u>W = mg</u>" pulling him down.

9) This means his <u>terminal velocity</u> comes right down to about <u>15 mph</u>, which is a <u>safe speed</u> to hit the ground at.

# Warm-Up and Exam Questions

You're about halfway through this section and it's time for some more questions.

## Warm-Up Questions

1) A rowing boat is being pulled to shore by two people with a force of 30 N each. A force of 10 N is resisting the movement in the opposite direction. What is the resultant force on the boat?

2) What is the resultant force on a body moving at constant velocity?

3) What happens to the acceleration of a body if the resultant force on it is doubled?

4) In which direction does friction act on a body — with or against the body's motion?

## Exam Questions

1   Two parachutists, A and B, are members of the same club.

   (a)   The diagram shows the forces acting on parachutist A.

      (i)   What is the resultant force acting on parachutist A?

                                           *(1 mark)*

900 N

900 N

      (ii)   Describe the velocity of parachutist A.

                                           *(1 mark)*

   (b)   Parachutist B is in free fall.
The total mass of parachutist B and her equipment is 70 kg.

      (i)   What will the force of air resistance on parachutist B be when she reaches terminal velocity? Explain your answer.

                                           *(3 marks)*

      (ii)   Which parachutist, A or B, would have a higher terminal velocity? Explain your answer.

                                           *(3 marks)*

   (c)   Explain why a parachutist slows down when they open their parachute.

                                           *(1 mark)*

2   Stefan weighs 600 newtons. He is accelerating upwards in a lift at 2.5 m/s².

   (a)   The forces acting on Stefan are his weight and the upwards force exerted on him by the floor of the lift. Which force is greater? Explain your answer.

                                           *(2 marks)*

   (b)   Calculate the size of the resultant force acting on Stefan.

                                           *(3 marks)*

3   Damien's cricket bat has a mass of 1.2 kg. He uses it to hit a ball with a mass of 160 g forwards with a force of 500 N.

   (a)   State the force that the ball exerts on the bat.
Explain your answer.

                                           *(2 marks)*

   (b)   Which is greater — the acceleration of the bat or the ball? Explain your answer.

                                           *(2 marks)*

# Stopping Distances

If you <u>need to stop</u> in a <u>given distance</u>, then the <u>faster</u> you're going, the <u>bigger the braking force</u> you'll need. But there are lots of <u>other factors</u> that also affect <u>how far</u> you travel before you stop...

## Many factors affect your total stopping distance

1) If you <u>need to stop</u> in a <u>given distance</u>, then the <u>faster</u> a vehicle's going, the <u>bigger braking force</u> it'll need.

2) Likewise, for any given braking force, the <u>faster</u> you're going, the <u>greater your stopping distance</u>. But in real life it's not quite that simple — if your maximum braking force isn't enough, you'll go further before you stop.

3) The total <u>stopping distance</u> of a vehicle is the distance covered in the time between the driver <u>first spotting</u> a hazard and the vehicle coming to a <u>complete stop</u>.

4) The <u>stopping distance</u> is <u>the sum</u> of the <u>thinking distance</u> and the <u>braking distance</u>.

### 1) Thinking distance

*"The distance the vehicle travels during the driver's reaction time".*

*The reaction time is the time between the driver spotting a hazard and taking action.*

It's affected by <u>two main factors</u>:

a) How fast you're going — Whatever your reaction time, the <u>faster</u> you're going, the <u>further</u> you'll go.

b) How dopey you are — This is affected by <u>tiredness</u>, <u>drugs</u>, <u>alcohol</u> and a <u>careless</u> blasé attitude.

<u>Bad visibility</u> and <u>distractions</u> can also be a major factor in accidents — lashing rain, messing about with the radio, bright oncoming lights, etc. might mean that a driver <u>doesn't notice</u> a hazard until they're quite close to it. It <u>doesn't</u> affect your thinking distance, but you <u>start thinking</u> about stopping <u>nearer</u> to the hazard, and so you're <u>more likely</u> to crash.

### 2) Braking distance

*"The distance the car travels under the breaking force".*

It's affected by <u>four main factors</u>:

a) How fast you're going — The <u>faster</u> you're going, the <u>further</u> it takes to stop.

b) How good your brakes are — All brakes must be checked and maintained <u>regularly</u>. Worn or faulty brakes will let you down <u>catastrophically</u> just when you need them the <u>most</u>, i.e. in an <u>emergency</u>.

c) How good the tyres are — Tyres should have a minimum <u>tread depth</u> of <u>1.6 mm</u> in order to be able to get rid of the <u>water</u> in wet conditions. Leaves, diesel spills and muck on the road can <u>greatly increase</u> the braking distance, and cause the car to <u>skid</u> too.

d) How good the grip is — This depends on <u>three things</u>:
1) <u>road surface</u>, 2) <u>weather</u> conditions, 3) <u>tyres</u>.

<u>Wet</u> or <u>icy roads</u> are always much more <u>slippy</u> than dry roads, but often you only discover this when you try to <u>brake</u> hard. You don't have as much grip, so you travel further before stopping.

The figures below for typical stopping distances are from the Highway Code. It's frightening to see just how far it takes to stop when you're going at 70 mph.

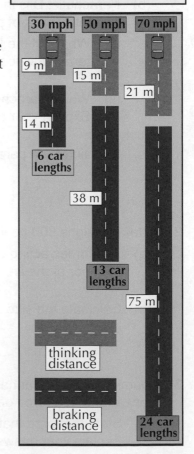

30 mph | 50 mph | 70 mph
9 m
15 m
21 m
14 m
6 car lengths
38 m
13 car lengths
75 m
thinking distance
braking distance
24 car lengths

# Work Done

Work (like a lot of things) means something slightly different in Physics than it does in everyday life.

## Doing **work** involves **transferring energy**

> When a force moves an object through a distance,
> ENERGY IS TRANSFERRED and WORK IS DONE.

That statement sounds far more complicated than it needs to.  Try this:

1) Whenever something moves, something else is providing some sort of 'effort' to move it.

2) The thing putting the effort in needs a supply of energy (like fuel or food or electricity etc.).

3) It then does 'work' by moving the object — and one way or another it transfers the energy it receives (as fuel) into other forms.

4) Whether this energy is transferred 'usefully' (e.g. by lifting a load) or is 'wasted' (e.g. lost as heat through friction), you can still say that 'work is done'.  Just like Batman and Bruce Wayne, 'work done' and 'energy transferred' are indeed 'one and the same'.  (And they're both given in joules.)

## It's just **another trivial formula**:

$$\text{work done} = \text{force} \times \text{distance}$$

Whether the force is friction or weight or tension in a rope, it's always the same.  To find how much energy has been transferred (in joules), you just multiply the force in N by the distance moved in m.

## Example

> Some kids drag an old tractor tyre 5 m over rough ground.
> They pull with a total force of 340 N.  Find the energy transferred.
>
> ANSWER:  W = F×d  = 340 × 5 = 1700 J.

---

## Remember "energy transferred" and "work done" are the same thing

By lifting something up you do work by transferring chemical energy to gravitational potential energy (p.86).

# Potential and Kinetic Energy

Gravitational potential energy is the energy an object has because of its height. Kinetic energy is the energy something has when it is moving. But it isn't just the definitions of them you need to know...

## *Gravitational potential energy is energy due to height*

### gravitational potential energy = mass × g × height

1) Gravitational potential energy (measured in joules) is the energy that an object has by virtue of (because of) its vertical position in a gravitational field.

2) When an object is raised vertically, work is done against the force of gravity (it takes effort to lift it up) and the object gains gravitational potential energy.

3) On Earth the gravitational field strength (g) is approximately 10 N/kg.

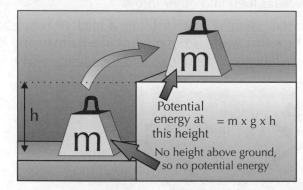

Potential energy at this height $= m \times g \times h$

No height above ground, so no potential energy

EXAMPLE: An object of mass 47 kg is slowly raised through 6.3 m. Find the gain in potential energy.

ANSWER: Just plug the numbers into the formula:
$E_p = mgh = 47 \times 10 \times 6.3 = \underline{2961\ J}$ (Joules because it's energy.)

## *Kinetic energy is energy of movement*

Anything that's moving has kinetic energy.
There's a slightly tricky formula for it, so you have to concentrate a little bit harder for this one.

### kinetic energy = ½ × mass × speed$^2$

$$\frac{E_k}{\tfrac{1}{2} \times m \times v^2}$$

EXAMPLE: A car of mass 2450 kg is travelling at 38 m/s. Calculate its kinetic energy.

ANSWER: It's pretty easy. You just plug the numbers into the formula — but watch the 'v²'!
$E_k = \tfrac{1}{2}mv^2 = \tfrac{1}{2} \times 2450 \times 38^2 = \underline{1\ 768\ 900\ J}$ (Joules because it's energy.)

Remember, the kinetic energy of something depends both on mass and speed.
The more it weighs and the faster it's going, the bigger its kinetic energy will be.

small mass, not fast low kinetic energy

big fast lorries Ltd

big mass, very fast high kinetic energy

# Kinetic Energy

Moving objects have kinetic energy — to <u>stop</u> them, that energy needs to be <u>transferred</u> into other types.

## *Kinetic energy transferred is work done*

*Conservation of energy states that energy can never be created or destroyed — only converted into different forms.*

### *When a car is moving it has kinetic energy*

1) A <u>moving car</u> can have a lot of <u>kinetic energy</u>. To slow a car down this kinetic energy needs to be <u>converted into other types of energy</u> (using the law of conservation of energy).

2) To stop a car, the <u>kinetic energy</u> ($\frac{1}{2}mv^2$) has to be <u>converted to heat energy</u> as <u>friction</u> between the <u>wheels</u> and the <u>brake pads</u>, causing the <u>temperature</u> of the brakes to <u>increase</u>:

> **Kinetic Energy Transferred = Work Done by Brakes**
> $$\frac{1}{2} \times m \times v^2 = F \times d$$

m = <u>mass</u> of car and passengers (in kg)
v = <u>speed</u> of car (in m/s)
F = maximum <u>braking force</u> (in N)
d = <u>braking distance</u> (in m)

### *Falling objects convert Eₚ into Eₖ...*

When something falls, its <u>potential energy</u> (see p. 86) is <u>converted</u> into <u>kinetic energy</u>. So the <u>further</u> it falls, the <u>faster</u> it goes.

> **Kinetic energy <u>gained</u> = Potential Energy <u>lost</u>**

### *...and some of this Eₖ is transferred into heat and sound*

1) When <u>meteors</u> and <u>space shuttles</u> enter the atmosphere, they have a <u>very high kinetic energy</u>.

2) <u>Friction</u> due to collisions with particles in the atmosphere transfers some of their kinetic energy to <u>heat energy</u> and <u>work is done</u>.

3) The temperatures can become so <u>extreme</u> that <u>most</u> meteors <u>burn up</u> completely and never hit the Earth.

4) Only the biggest meteors make it through to the Earth's surface — these are called <u>meteorites</u>.

5) Space shuttles have heat shields made from <u>special materials</u> which lose heat <u>quickly</u>, allowing the shuttle to re-enter the atmosphere <u>without burning up</u>.

## *Ek and Ep are closely linked for falling objects*

The braking distance of a vehicle increases as speed increases. <u>Doubling</u> the speed <u>increases</u> the braking distance by a factor of <u>four</u>, and <u>tripling</u> the speed increases it by <u>nine times</u>. It's all do with $v^2$.

# Forces and Elasticity

Forces aren't just important for cars and falling objects — you can <u>stretch things</u> with them as well.

## *Elastic objects store energy as elastic potential energy*

1) When you apply a force to an object you may cause it to <u>stretch</u> and <u>change in shape</u>.

2) Any object that can <u>go back</u> to its <u>original shape</u> after the force has been removed is an <u>elastic object</u>.

3) <u>Work is done</u> to an elastic object to <u>change</u> its shape.
   This energy is not lost but is <u>stored</u> by the object as <u>elastic potential energy</u>.

4) The elastic potential energy is then <u>converted to kinetic energy</u> when the <u>force is removed</u> and the object returns to its original shape, e.g. when a spring or an elastic band bounces back.

## *Extension of an elastic object is directly proportional to force...*

If a spring is supported at the top and then a weight attached to the bottom, it <u>stretches</u>.

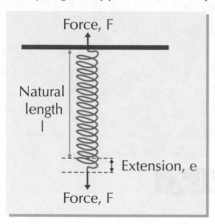

Force, F

Natural length
l

Extension, e

Force, F

1) The <u>extension, e</u>, of a stretched spring (or other elastic object) is <u>directly proportional</u> to the load or <u>force</u> applied, <u>F</u>. The extension is measured in metres, and the force is measured in newtons.

2) This is the equation you need to learn:

$$F = k \times e$$

3) k is the <u>spring constant</u>. Its value depends on the <u>material</u> that you are stretching and it's measured in newtons per metre (N/m).

## *...but this stops working when the force is great enough*

There's a <u>limit</u> to the amount of force you can apply to an object for the extension to keep on increasing <u>proportionally</u>.

1) The graph shows <u>force against extension</u> for an elastic object.

2) For small forces, force and extension are <u>proportional</u>. So the first part of the graph shows a straight-line relationship between force and extension.

3) There is a <u>maximum</u> force that the elastic object can take and still extend proportionally. This is known as the <u>limit of proportionality</u> and is shown on the graph at the point marked P.

4) If you increase the force <u>past</u> the limit of proportionality, the material will be <u>permanently stretched</u>. When the force is <u>removed</u>, the material will be <u>longer</u> than at the start.

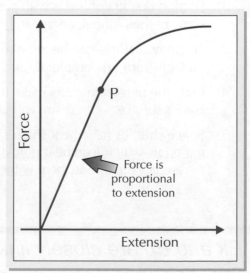

Force

P

Force is proportional to extension

Extension

# Warm-Up and Exam Questions

There were lots of definitions and equations to get to grips with on the last five pages.
Try these questions to see what you can remember.

## Warm-Up Questions

1) What is meant by 'thinking distance' as part of the total stopping distance of a car?
2) What must be added to thinking distance to find the total stopping distance of a car?
3) Why can 'work done' be measured in the same units as energy?
4) What is gravitational potential energy?
5) Why don't many meteors hit the Earth?
6) What type of energy does an elastic object store when work is done to it?
7) What happens to a spring if you stretch it past its limit of proportionality?

## Exam Questions

1   The graph below shows how thinking distance and stopping distance vary with speed.

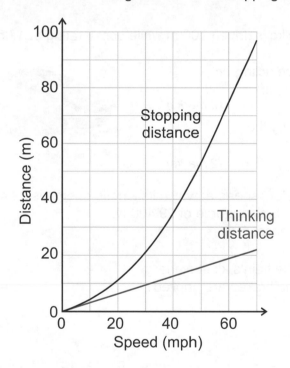

(a) Use the graph to determine the following distances for a car travelling at 40 mph.
   (i)   Thinking distance
   (ii)  Total stopping distance
   (iii) Braking distance

*(3 marks)*

(b) Which is greater at 50 miles per hour, thinking distance or braking distance?

*(1 mark)*

(c) Is stopping distance proportional to speed?
    Explain how this can be seen from the graph.

*(2 marks)*

   *If you need some help with part c) — see page 13.*

# Exam Questions

2    A teacher is setting up an experiment.

(a)  He lifts a 2.5 kg mass from the floor onto a table that is 1.3 m tall.
Calculate the gain in gravitational potential energy of the mass.
(Use g = 10 N/kg.)

*(2 marks)*

(b)  The mass is accidentally knocked off the table and falls to the floor.
Calculate the speed of the mass as it hits the floor.

*(3 marks)*

(c)  The teacher shows his students an experiment to show how
a spring extends when masses are hung from it.  When a force
of 4 N is applied to the spring, the spring extends by 3.5 cm.

Calculate the spring constant of the spring.
Clearly show how you work out your answer.

*(3 marks)*

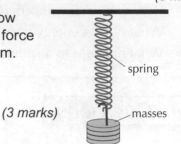

spring

masses

3    A train with a mass of 40 000 kg is driven 700 m while accelerating at 1.05 m/s$^2$.

(a)  Calculate the driving force acting on
the train.  Ignore any friction.

*(2 marks)*

(b)  Calculate the work done by the
driving force.

*(2 marks)*

(c)  The train reaches a constant speed at which its kinetic energy is 29 400 000 J.
It then decelerates with a braking force of 29 400 N.
Calculate its braking distance.

*(2 marks)*

(d)  What form of energy is the train's kinetic energy
transformed into when the brakes are applied?

*(1 mark)*

4    A car with a mass of 2750 kg is travelling at 12 m/s.
(a)  Calculate its kinetic energy.

*(2 marks)*

(b)  A van with a mass of 3120 kg is travelling at the same speed.
Which has more kinetic energy?

*(1 mark)*

(c)  The car accelerates and reaches a constant speed at which its kinetic energy
is 550 000 J.  The car then brakes and comes to rest in 25 m.
Calculate its braking force.

*(2 marks)*

# Power

Power is a concept that pops up in both <u>forces</u> and <u>electricity</u>. This is because, at its most fundamental level, power is just about the rate of <u>energy transferred</u> — and energy is transferred wherever you look.

## *Power is the "rate of doing work" — i.e. how much per second*

Power is <u>not</u> the same thing as <u>force</u>, nor <u>energy</u>. A <u>powerful</u> machine is not necessarily one which can exert a strong <u>force</u> (though it usually ends up that way).
A <u>powerful</u> machine is one which transfers <u>a lot of energy in a short space of time</u>.
This is the <u>very easy formula</u> for power:

$$\text{Power} = \frac{\text{Work done (or energy transferred)}}{\text{Time taken}} \qquad P = \frac{E}{t}$$

$$\frac{E}{P \times t}$$

## *Power is measured in watts (or J/s)*

The proper unit of power is the <u>watt</u>. <u>One watt = 1 joule of energy transferred per second</u>.
<u>Power</u> means "how much energy <u>per second</u>", so <u>watts</u> are the same as "<u>joules per second</u>" (J/s).
Don't ever say "watts per second" — it's <u>nonsense</u>.

> <u>EXAMPLE:</u> A motor transfers 4.8 kJ of useful energy in 2 minutes. Find its power output.
>
> <u>ANSWER:</u> P = E / t = 4800/120 = 40 W (or 40 J/s)
>
> (Note that the kJ had to be turned into J, and the minutes into seconds.)

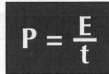

4.8 kJ of useful energy in 2 minutes

## *Calculating your power output*

There are a few different ways to measure the power output of a <u>person</u>:

### *a) The timed run upstairs:*

In this case the "<u>energy transferred</u>" is the <u>potential energy you gain</u> (= mgh).
Hence <u>Power = mgh/t</u>

62 kg    12 m    Time taken = 14 s

Power output
= En. transferred/time
= mgh/t
= (62×10×12)÷14
= <u>531 W</u>

### *b) The timed acceleration:*

This time the <u>energy transferred</u> is the <u>kinetic energy you gain</u> (= ½mv²).
Hence <u>Power = ½mv²/t</u>

62 kg    0 ➡ 8 m/s    time taken = 4 s

Power output
= En. transferred/time
= ½mv²/t
= (½×62×8²)÷4
= <u>496 W</u>

To get <u>accurate results</u> from these experiments, you have to do them several times and find an <u>average</u>.

---

## *Watt is the unit of power?*

Power is the amount of energy transferred per second, and it's measured in <u>watts</u>. The watt is named after James Watt, a Scottish inventor and engineer who did a lot of work on steam engines in the 1700s. Nice. Make sure you <u>learn the formula</u> and power questions should be easy.

# Momentum and Collisions

A <u>large</u> rugby player running very <u>fast</u> is going to be a lot harder to stop than a scrawny one out for a Sunday afternoon stroll — that's <u>momentum</u> for you.

## *Momentum = mass × velocity*

1) Momentum (p) is a <u>property</u> of <u>moving objects</u>.

2) The <u>greater</u> the <u>mass</u> of an object and the <u>greater</u> its <u>velocity</u> (see p. 72) the <u>more momentum</u> the object has.

3) Momentum is a <u>vector</u> quantity — it has size <u>and</u> direction (like <u>velocity</u>, but not speed).

$$\text{Momentum (kg m/s)} = \text{Mass (kg)} \times \text{Velocity (m/s)}$$

## *Momentum before = momentum after*

In a <u>closed system</u>, the total momentum <u>before</u> an event (e.g. a collision) is the same as <u>after</u> the event. This is called <u>Conservation of Momentum</u>.

*A closed system is just a fancy way of saying that no external forces act.*

### Example 1: Collisions

Two skaters approach each other, collide and move off together as shown. At what velocity do they move after the collision?

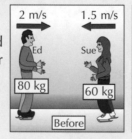

1) Choose which direction is <u>positive</u>.
   I'll say "<u>positive</u>" means "<u>to the right</u>".

2) <u>Total momentum before</u> collision
   = momentum of Ed + momentum of Sue
   = {80 × 2} + {60 × (–1.5)}
   = <u>70 kg m/s</u>

3) <u>Total momentum after</u> collision
   = momentum of Ed and Sue together
   = <u>140 × v</u>

4) So 140v = 70, i.e. <u>v = 0.5 m/s to the right</u>

### Example 2: Explosions

A gun fires a bullet as shown. At what speed does the gun move backwards?

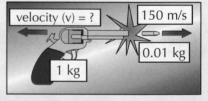

1) Choose which direction is <u>positive</u>.
   Again, I reckon "<u>positive</u>" means "<u>to the right</u>".

2) <u>Total momentum before</u> firing = <u>0 kg m/s</u>

3) <u>Total momentum after</u> firing
   = momentum of bullet + momentum of gun
   = (0.01 × 150) + (1 × v)
   = <u>1.5 + v</u>

   *This is the gun's recoil.*

   The momentum of a system <u>before</u> an explosion is <u>zero</u>, so, due to <u>conservation of momentum</u>, the total momentum after an explosion is <u>zero too</u>.

4) So 1.5 + v = 0, i.e. v = –1.5 m/s
   So the gun moves <u>backwards</u> at <u>1.5 m/s</u>.

## *Momentum's a pretty fundamental bit of Physics — learn it well*

Momentum is always <u>conserved</u> in collisions and explosions when there are no external forces acting.

# Car Design and Safety

Nowadays, cars usually come with lots of different <u>safety features</u> all designed to <u>slow</u> you down over a <u>longer time</u> in a crash. This page is all about how they <u>work</u>.

## *Forces* cause *changes* in *momentum*

1) When a <u>force</u> acts on an object, it causes a <u>change</u> in momentum.

2) A <u>larger</u> force means a <u>faster</u> change of momentum (and so a greater <u>acceleration</u>).

3) Likewise, if someone's momentum changes <u>very quickly</u> (like in a <u>car crash</u>), the <u>forces</u> on the body will be very <u>large</u>, and more likely to cause <u>injury</u>.

4) This is why cars are designed with safety features that slow people down over a <u>longer time</u> when they have a crash — the longer it takes for a change in <u>momentum</u>, the <u>smaller</u> the <u>force</u>.

## Cars are *designed* to *convert kinetic energy safely* in a crash

1) If a car crashes it will <u>slow down very quickly</u> — this means that a lot of <u>kinetic energy</u> is converted into other forms of energy in a <u>short amount of time</u>, which can be dangerous for the <u>people</u> inside.

2) In a crash, there'll be a <u>big change in momentum</u> over a <u>very short time</u>, so the people inside the car experience <u>huge forces</u> that could be fatal.

3) Cars are <u>designed</u> to convert the <u>kinetic energy</u> of the car and its passengers in a way that is <u>safest</u> for the car's occupants. They often do this by <u>increasing the time</u> over which momentum changes happen, which <u>lessens</u> the forces on the passengers.

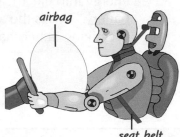

*airbag*

*seat belt*

### *Examples*

CRUMPLE ZONES at the front and back of the car crumple up <u>on impact</u>.

- The car's kinetic energy is converted into other forms of energy by the car body as it <u>changes shape</u>.
- Crumple zones <u>increase the impact time</u>, decreasing the force produced by the change in momentum.

SEAT BELTS stretch slightly, <u>increasing the time</u> taken for the wearer to stop. This <u>reduces the forces</u> acting in the chest. Some of the kinetic energy of the wearer is <u>absorbed</u> by the seat belt <u>stretching</u>.

SIDE IMPACT BARS are strong metal tubes fitted into car door panels. They help direct the kinetic energy of the crash <u>away from the passengers</u> to other areas of the car, such as the crumple zones.

AIR BAGS also slow you down more <u>gradually</u> and prevent you from <u>hitting hard surfaces</u> inside the car.

# Car Design and Safety

Here's a bit more about the design of cars.
First up, a new type of <u>braking system</u> that <u>stores</u> energy rather than wasting it. How handy.

## Brakes do **work** against the **kinetic energy** of the car

1) When you <u>apply the brakes</u> to slow down a car, <u>work is done</u> (see p.85).

2) The brakes reduce the <u>kinetic energy</u> of the car by transferring it into <u>heat</u> (and sound) energy (see p.87).

3) In <u>traditional</u> braking systems that would be the <u>end of the story</u>, but new <u>regenerative braking systems</u> used in some <u>electric</u> or <u>hybrid</u> cars <u>make use</u> of the energy, instead of converting it all into heat during braking.

### Regenerative braking systems:

1) <u>Regenerative brakes</u> use the <u>system</u> that <u>drives</u> the vehicle to do the <u>majority of the braking</u>.

2) Rather than converting the kinetic energy of the vehicle into heat energy, the brakes put the vehicle's <u>motor into reverse</u>. With the motor running <u>backwards</u>, the wheels are <u>slowed</u>.

3) At the same time, the motor acts as an <u>electric generator</u>, converting kinetic energy into <u>electrical energy</u> that is stored as <u>chemical energy</u> in the vehicle's <u>battery</u>. This is the advantage of regenerative brakes — they <u>store</u> the energy of braking rather than <u>wasting</u> it. It's a nifty chain of energy transfer.

## Cars have different power ratings

1) The <u>size</u> and <u>design</u> of car engines determine how <u>powerful</u> they are.

2) The <u>more powerful</u> an engine is, the more <u>energy</u> it transfers from its <u>fuel</u> every second, and so the <u>faster</u> its top speed can be.

3) E.g. the <u>power output</u> of a typical small car will be around 50 kW and a sports car will be about 100 kW (some are <u>much</u> higher).

*Sports car power = 100 kW*

*Small car power = 50 kW*

4) Cars are also designed to be <u>aerodynamic</u>. This means that they are shaped in such a way that <u>air flows</u> very easily and smoothly past them, so minimising their <u>air resistance</u>.

5) Cars reach their <u>top speed</u> when the resistive force <u>equals</u> the driving force provided by the engine (see p.82).

6) So, with <u>less air resistance</u> to overcome, the car can reach a <u>higher speed</u> before this happens. Aerodynamic cars therefore have <u>higher top speeds</u>.

### The more powerful an engine, the faster it transfers energy from fuel
The more powerful the engine of a car, generally the <u>faster</u> its top speed will be. Make sure you can say why cars are designed to be <u>aerodynamic</u> — it isn't just so they look better.

# Warm-Up and Exam Questions

It's very nearly the end of this section. But don't shed a tear — try these questions instead.

## Warm-Up Questions

1) What is meant by power in terms of work done?
2) Give the equation for momentum.
3) What is meant by the conservation of momentum?
4) Name two safety features that increase the time taken for the car driver to stop in a collision.
5) Give two factors that will affect the top speed of a car.

## Exam Questions

1  The images below show two different cars, car A and car B.

Car A                          Car B

(a) Car A has side impact bars.
Describe how side impact bars work during a crash to help protect passengers.

*(2 marks)*

(b) Both cars have seat belts.
Explain why seat belts are made of a slightly stretchy material.

*(3 marks)*

(c) Car A is more aerodynamic than car B.
Explain why aerodynamic cars tend to have higher top speeds.

*(3 marks)*

2  Two ice hockey players are skating towards the puck. Player A has a mass of 100 kg and is travelling right at 6 m/s. Player B has a mass 80 kg and is travelling left at 9 m/s.

(a) Calculate the momentum of:

(i) Player A

*(2 marks)*

(ii) Player B

*(2 marks)*

(b) The two players collide and become joined together.

(i) Calculate the speed of the two joined players just after the collision.

*(3 marks)*

(ii) State the direction they move.

*(1 mark)*

# Exam Questions

3    The picture shown below is a hybrid bus used for public transport in a city centre.

(a)   The engine of the bus has a power rating of 90 kW.
     Calculate the energy transferred by the engine in 5 seconds.

*(2 marks)*

(b)   The bus has a regenerative braking system which is used to store energy in the
     battery of the bus.
     (i)    Explain how a regenerative braking system works.

*(3 marks)*

     (ii)   Give **one** advantage of regenerative braking systems over
            traditional braking systems.

*(1 mark)*

4    A runner of mass 60 kg is taking part in some training exercises.
    It takes him 50 s to run from the bottom to the top of a hill which
    is 35 m high.

    Calculate his power during the run.  (Assume g = 10 N/kg).
    Clearly show how you work out your answer.

*(4 marks)*

5    A fast-moving neutron collides with a uranium-235 atom and bounces off.
    The diagram shows the particles before and after the collision.

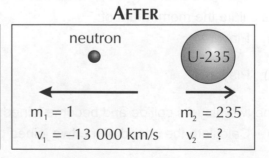

|  | BEFORE |  |  | AFTER |  |
|---|---|---|---|---|---|
| neutron | | U-235 | neutron | | U-235 |
| $m_1 = 1$ | | $m_2 = 235$ | $m_1 = 1$ | | $m_2 = 235$ |
| $v_1 = 14\,000$ km/s | | $v_2 = 0$ km/s | $v_1 = -13\,000$ km/s | | $v_2 = ?$ |

    Find the velocity of the U-235 atom after the collision.

*(3 marks)*

# Static Electricity

Static electricity is all about charges which are <u>not</u> free to move, e.g. in insulating materials. This causes them to build up in one place and it often ends with a <u>spark</u> or a <u>shock</u> when they do finally move.

## Build-up of *static* is caused by *friction*

1) When certain <u>insulating</u> materials are <u>rubbed</u> together, negatively charged electrons will be <u>scraped off one</u> and <u>dumped</u> on the other.

2) This'll leave a <u>positive</u> static charge on one and a <u>negative</u> static charge on the other.

3) <u>Which way</u> the electrons are transferred <u>depends</u> on the <u>two materials</u> involved.

4) Electrically charged objects <u>attract</u> small objects placed near them.
   (Try this: rub a balloon on a woolly pully — then put it near tiddly bits of paper and watch them jump.)

5) The classic examples are <u>polythene</u> and <u>acetate</u> rods being rubbed with a <u>cloth duster</u>, as shown in the diagrams.

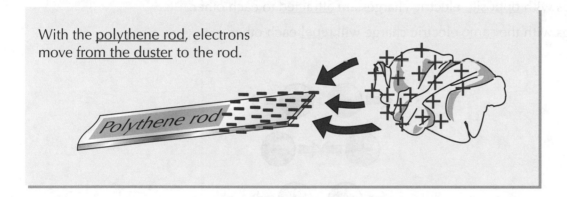

With the <u>polythene rod</u>, electrons move <u>from the duster</u> to the rod.

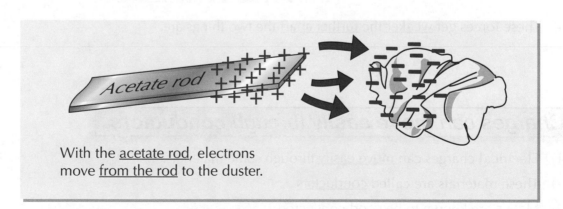

With the <u>acetate rod</u>, electrons move <u>from the rod</u> to the duster.

---

## Static electricity is caused by electrons being transferred

Static electricity's great fun. You must have tried it — rubbing a balloon against your jumper and trying to get it to stick to the ceiling. It really works... well, sometimes. Bad hair days are caused by static too — it builds up on your hair, so your strands of hair repel each other. Which is nice...

# Static Electricity

## Only electrons move — never the positive charges

1) <u>Watch out for this in exams</u>. Both +ve and –ve electrostatic charges are only ever produced by the movement of <u>electrons</u>.

2) The positive charges <u>definitely do not move</u>!

3) A positive static charge is always caused by electrons <u>moving</u> away elsewhere.

4) The material that <u>loses</u> the electrons loses some negative charge, and is <u>left with an equal positive charge</u> (see previous page). Don't forget!

## Like charges repel, opposite charges attract

1) This is <u>easy</u> and, I'd have thought, <u>kind of obvious</u>. When two electrically charged objects are brought close together they <u>exert a force</u> on one another.

2) Two things with <u>opposite</u> electric charges are <u>attracted</u> to each other.

3) Two things with the <u>same</u> electric charge will <u>repel</u> each other.

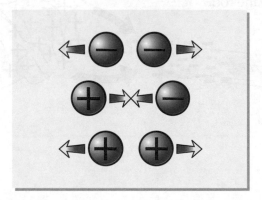

4) These forces get <u>weaker</u> the <u>further apart</u> the two things are.

## Charges can move easily through conductors

1) Electrical charges can <u>move easily</u> through some materials.

2) These materials are called <u>conductors</u>.

3) <u>Metals</u> are known to be <u>good</u> conductors.

## Don't forget that opposites attract

The bog standard electrical charge carrier is the electron. Those little devils get just about everywhere in metals, taking charge pretty much wherever you want it. But in insulators they're stuck and can't move easily — it's only when they're manually scraped off that they ever get to go anywhere.

# Warm-Up and Exam Questions

By this point you'll probably have worked out that static electricity isn't the most exciting of topics. Don't worry — there are just these few questions before you get on to much more interesting stuff.

## Warm-Up Questions

1) Is a polythene rod an insulator or a conductor?
2) What are the two types of electric charge?
3) Do similar charges attract or repel one another?
4) Are metals good or bad insulators?

## Exam Questions

1   Jane hangs an uncharged balloon from a thread. She brings
    a negatively charged polythene rod towards the balloon.
    The diagram below shows how the positive and negative
    charges in the balloon rearrange themselves when she does this.

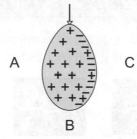

   (a)   In which of the positions labelled A, B and C on the diagram
         did Jane hold the polythene rod? Explain your answer.

                                                                            *(2 marks)*

   (b)   Jane brings the rod closer to the balloon.
         Explain why the balloon swings towards it.

                                                                            *(2 marks)*


2   A positive static charge builds up on a cloth when it is used to wipe a surface.

   (a)   Describe the movement of charged particles that gives the cloth its charge.

                                                                            *(1 mark)*

   (b)   The cloth has a relative charge of +23.
         Circle the correct answer below to show the charge on the surface.

         | +23 |      | +46 |      | -46 |      | -23 |

                                                                            *(1 mark)*

   (c)   The cloth is an insulator so charges can't easily flow through it.
         Give **one** example of a material that charges can flow easily through.

                                                                            *(1 mark)*

# Current and Potential Difference

Isn't electricity great. Mind you it's pretty bad news if the words don't mean anything to you...

1) Current is the flow of electric charge round the circuit. Current will only flow through a component if there is a potential difference across that component. Unit: ampere, A.
2) Potential difference is the driving force that pushes the current round. Unit: volt, V.
3) Resistance is anything in the circuit which slows the flow down. Unit: ohm, Ω.

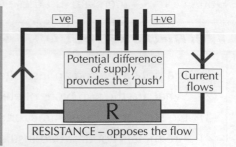
RESISTANCE – opposes the flow

**The greater the resistance across a component, the smaller the current that flows (for a given potential difference across the component).**

## Total charge through a circuit depends on current and time

1) Current is the rate of flow of charge. When current (I) flows past a point in a circuit for a length of time (t) then the charge (Q) that has passed is given by this formula:

$$\text{Current} = \frac{\text{Charge}}{\text{Time}} \qquad I = \frac{Q}{t}$$

2) Current is measured in amperes (A), charge is measured in coulombs (C), time is measured in seconds (s).
3) More charge passes around the circuit when a bigger current flows.

EXAMPLE: A battery charger passes a current of 2.5 A through a cell over a period of 4 hours. How much charge does the charger transfer to the cell altogether?

ANSWER: $Q = I \times t = 2.5 \times (4 \times 60 \times 60) = 36\,000$ C (36 kC).

## Potential difference (P.D.) is the work done per unit charge

1) The potential difference (or voltage) is the work done (the energy transferred, measured in joules, J) per coulomb of charge that passes between two points in an electrical circuit.
2) It's given by this formula:

$$\text{P.D.} = \frac{\text{Work done}}{\text{Charge}}$$

3) So, the potential difference across an electrical component is the amount of energy that is transferred by that electrical component (e.g. to light and heat energy by a bulb) per unit of charge.
4) Voltage and potential difference mean the same thing. You can use either in your exam and scoop up the marks (so long as you use it correctly).

# Circuits — The Basics

Formulas are mighty pretty and all, but you might have to design some <u>electrical circuits</u> as well one day. For that you're going to need <u>circuit symbols</u>...

## Circuit symbols *you should* **know** *— learn them well*

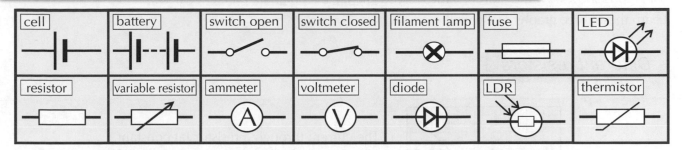

| cell | battery | switch open | switch closed | filament lamp | fuse | LED |
| resistor | variable resistor | ammeter | voltmeter | diode | LDR | thermistor |

## The standard *test circuit*

This is the circuit you use if you want to know the <u>resistance of a component</u>. You find the resistance by measuring the <u>current through</u> and the <u>potential difference across</u> the component. It is absolutely the most <u>bog standard</u> circuit you could know. <u>So know it</u>.

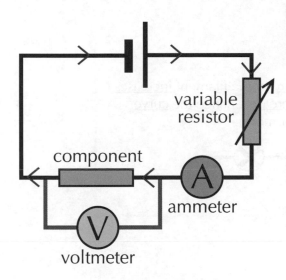

### The *ammeter*

1) Measures the <u>current</u> (in <u>amps</u>) flowing through the component.

2) Must be placed <u>in series</u> (see p.106).

3) Can be put <u>anywhere</u> in series in the <u>main circuit</u>, but <u>never</u> in parallel like the voltmeter.

### The *voltmeter*

1) Measures the <u>potential difference</u> (in <u>volts</u>) across the component.

2) Must be placed <u>in parallel</u> (see p.108) around the <u>component</u> under test — <u>NOT</u> around the variable resistor or the battery!

## *Five important points*

1) This <u>very basic</u> circuit is used for testing <u>components</u>, and for getting <u>V-I graphs</u> from them (see next page).

2) The <u>component</u>, the <u>ammeter</u> and the <u>variable resistor</u> are all in <u>series</u>, which means they can be put in <u>any order</u> in the main circuit. The <u>voltmeter</u>, on the other hand, can only be placed <u>in parallel</u> around the <u>component under test</u>, as shown. Anywhere else is a definite <u>no-no</u>.

3) As you <u>vary</u> the <u>variable resistor</u> it alters the <u>current</u> flowing through the circuit.

4) This allows you to take several <u>pairs of readings</u> from the <u>ammeter</u> and <u>voltmeter</u>.

5) You can then <u>plot</u> these values for <u>current</u> and <u>voltage</u> on a <u>V-I graph</u> and find the <u>resistance</u>.

# Resistance and V = I × R

With your current and your potential difference measured, you can now make some graphs...

## Three hideously important potential difference-current graphs

V-I graphs show how the current varies as you change the potential difference (P.D.).
Learn these three graphs really well:

### Different resistors

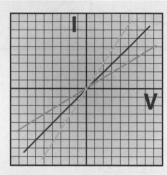

The current through a resistor (at constant temperature) is directly proportional to P.D.
Different resistors have different resistances, hence the different slopes.

### Filament lamp

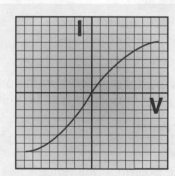

As the temperature of the filament increases, the resistance increases, hence the curve (see next page for more).

### Diode

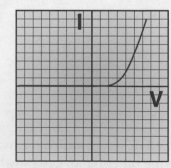

Current will only flow through a diode in one direction, as shown. The diode has very high resistance in the opposite direction.

## You have to be able to interpret V-I graphs for your exam

Learn the shape of each of the three graphs above — and make sure you can explain why they're shaped that way too. There's more on the next page about the shape of the filament lamp graph.

# Resistance and V = I × R

Prepare yourself to meet the <u>most important</u> equation in electrics, bar none.
But first up, a bit more about resistance...

## Resistance *increases* with *temperature*

1) When an electrical charge flows through a resistor, some of the electrical
energy is <u>transferred to heat energy</u> and the resistor gets <u>hot</u>.

2) This heat energy causes the <u>ions</u> in the conductor to <u>vibrate more</u>.

3) This makes it <u>more difficult</u> for the charge-carrying electrons to get through the
resistor — the <u>current can't flow</u> as easily and the <u>resistance increases</u>.

4) For most resistors there is a <u>limit</u> to the amount of current that can flow.

5) More current means an <u>increase</u> in <u>temperature</u>, which means an
<u>increase</u> in <u>resistance</u>, which means the <u>current decreases</u> again.

6) This is why the graph for the filament lamp <u>levels off</u> at high currents (see previous page).

## Resistance, *potential difference* and *current*: V = I × R

# Potential Difference = Current × Resistance

For the <u>straight-line graphs</u> on the previous page, the resistance of the
component is <u>steady</u> and is equal to the <u>inverse</u> of the <u>gradient</u> of the line, or
"<u>1/gradient</u>". In other words, the <u>steeper</u> the graph the <u>lower</u> the resistance.

If the graph <u>curves</u>, it means the resistance is <u>changing</u>. In that case R can be found for any point
by taking the <u>pair of values</u> (V, I) from the graph and sticking them in the formula <u>R = V/I</u>. Easy.

### Example

> Voltmeter V reads 6 V and resistor R is 4 Ω.
> What is the current through ammeter A?
>
> <u>ANSWER</u>:  Use the formula triangle for V = I × R.
> We need to find I, so the version we need is I = V/R.
> The answer is then: I = 6 ÷ 4 = <u>1.5 A</u>.

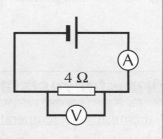

---

*Learn the all important formula: V = I × R*

Make sure you can explain why the <u>resistance</u> of a resistor <u>increases</u> as its <u>temperature increases</u>. And
you need to know that formula inside out, back to front, upside down — it's really useful and important.

# Circuit Devices

You might consider yourself a bit of an <u>expert</u> in circuit components — you're enlightened about bulbs, you're switched on to switches... Just make sure you know these ones as well — they're a <u>bit trickier</u>.

## *Current only flows in **one direction** through a **diode***

1) A diode is a special device made from <u>semiconductor</u> material such as <u>silicon</u>.

2) It is used to <u>regulate</u> the <u>potential difference</u> in circuits.

3) It lets current flow freely through it in <u>one direction</u>, but <u>not</u> in the other (i.e. there's a very high resistance in the <u>reverse</u> direction).

4) This turns out to be really useful in various <u>electronic circuits</u>.

## *Light-emitting diodes are **very useful***

1) A <u>light-emitting diode</u> (LED) emits light when a current flows through it in the <u>forward direction</u>.

2) LEDs are being used more and more as lighting, as they use a much <u>smaller current</u> than other forms of lighting.

3) LEDs indicate the presence of current in a circuit. They're often used in appliances (e.g. TVs) to show that they are <u>switched on</u>.

4) They're also used for the numbers on <u>digital clocks</u>, in <u>traffic lights</u> and in <u>remote controls</u>.

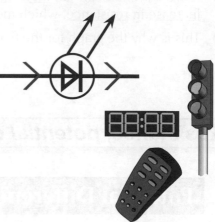

## *A **Light-Dependent Resistor** or "LDR"*

1) An LDR is a resistor that is <u>dependent</u> on the <u>intensity</u> of <u>light</u>. Simple really.

2) In <u>bright light</u>, the resistance <u>falls</u>.

3) In <u>darkness</u>, the resistance is <u>highest</u>.

4) They have lots of applications including <u>automatic night lights</u>, outdoor lighting and <u>burglar detectors</u>.

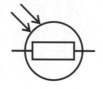

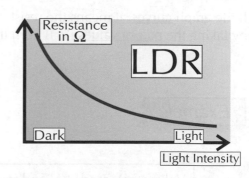

Resistance in Ω

LDR

Dark | Light

Light Intensity

## *Thermistor resistance decreases as temperature increases*

1) A <u>thermistor</u> is a <u>temperature dependent</u> resistor.

2) In <u>hot</u> conditions, the resistance <u>drops</u>.

3) In <u>cool</u> conditions, the resistance goes <u>up</u>.

4) Thermistors make useful <u>temperature detectors</u>, e.g. <u>car engine</u> temperature sensors and electronic <u>thermostats</u>.

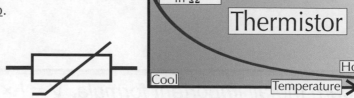

Resistance in Ω

Thermistor

Cool | Hot

Temperature

# Warm-Up and Exam Questions

Phew — circuits aren't the easiest thing in the world, are they?  Make sure you've understood the last few pages by trying these questions.  If you get stuck, just go back and re-read the relevant page.

## Warm-Up Questions

1) What are the units of resistance?
2) Write down the formula that links potential difference, work done and charge.
3) Draw the symbol for a light-emitting diode (LED).
4) Give one use of a light-dependant resistor (LDR).
5) What happens to the resistance of a thermistor as temperature increases?

## Exam Questions

1    Shown below is a circuit diagram for a standard test circuit.

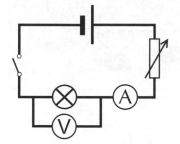

(a) When the switch is closed, the ammeter reads 0.3 A and the voltmeter reads 1.5 V.

   (i) Calculate the resistance of the filament lamp.

   *(2 marks)*

   (ii) The switch is closed for 35 seconds.  Calculate the total charge that flows through the filament lamp.

   *(2 marks)*

(b) The variable resistor is used to increase the resistance in the circuit. Describe how this will affect the current flowing through the circuit.

   *(1 mark)*

(c) The resistance of a filament lamp changes with temperature.

   (i) On the graph to the right, sketch the potential difference-current graph for a filament lamp.

   *(1 mark)*

   (ii) Explain why the resistance of the filament lamp increases as the temperature of the filament increases.

   *(3 marks)*

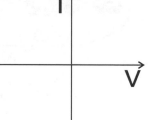

2    The graph below shows current against potential difference (P.D.) for a diode.

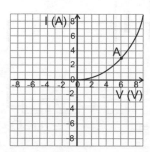

(a) Explain why the graph shows zero current for negative P.D.s.
   *(1 mark)*

(b) Calculate the resistance of the diode at the point marked A.
   *(2 marks)*

(c) Light emitting diodes (LEDs) are often used for lighting. Give **one** advantage of using LEDs instead of filament lamps.
   *(1 mark)*

# Series Circuits

You need to be able to tell the difference between series and parallel circuits <u>just by looking at them</u>. You also need to know the <u>rules</u> about what happens with both types. Read on.

## *Series* circuits — *all or nothing*

1) In <u>series circuits</u>, the different components are connected <u>in a line</u>, <u>end to end</u>, between the +ve and –ve of the power supply (except for <u>voltmeters</u>, which are always connected <u>in parallel</u>, but they don't count as part of the circuit).

2) If you remove or disconnect <u>one</u> component, the circuit is <u>broken</u> and they all <u>stop</u>.

3) This is generally <u>not very handy</u>, and in practice <u>very few things</u> are connected in series.

## *1) Potential difference is* **shared***:*

In series circuits the <u>total P.D.</u> of the <u>supply</u> is <u>shared</u> between the various <u>components</u>. So the <u>voltages</u> round a series circuit <u>always add up</u> to equal the <u>source voltage</u>:

$$V = V_1 + V_2 + ...$$

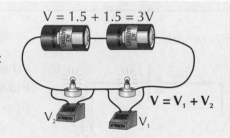

## *2) Current is the* **same** *everywhere:*

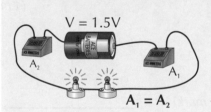

1) In series circuits the <u>same current</u> flows through <u>all parts</u> of the circuit, i.e:

$$A_1 = A_2$$

2) The <u>size</u> of the current is determined by the <u>total P.D.</u> of the cells and the <u>total resistance</u> of the circuit: i.e. $I = V/R$

## *3) Resistance* **adds up***:*

1) In series circuits the <u>total resistance</u> is just the <u>sum</u> of all the resistances:

$$R = R_1 + R_2 + R_3$$

2) The <u>bigger</u> the <u>resistance</u> of a component, the bigger its <u>share</u> of the <u>total P.D.</u>

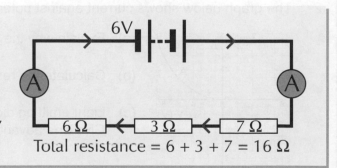

# Series Circuits

It's <u>not enough</u> to know how circuits work in theory, it's important that you can calculate the currents, potential differences and resistances in a <u>range of examples</u>. There's a nice example on this page to help you see how all the theory from the last page can be <u>put into practice</u>.

## Cell voltages *add up*:

1) There is a bigger potential difference when more cells are in series, provided the cells are all <u>connected</u> the <u>same way</u>.

2) For example when two batteries of voltage 1.5 V are <u>connected in series</u> they supply 3 V <u>between them</u>.

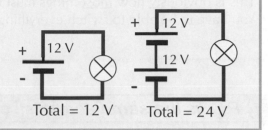

Total = 12 V    Total = 24 V

## Example on *series circuits*

<u>Potential differences</u> add to equal the <u>source P.D.</u>:
1.5 + 2 + 2.5 = 6 V

<u>Total resistance</u> is the sum of the resistances in the circuit: 3 + 4 + 5 = 12 Ω

<u>Current</u> flowing through all parts of the circuit
= V/R = 6/12 = 0.5 A

(If an extra cell was added of P.D. 3 V then the P.D. across each resistor would increase and the current would increase too.)

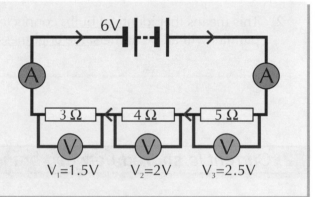

## Christmas *fairy lights* are sometimes wired in *series*

1) <u>Christmas fairy lights</u> are about the <u>only</u> real-life example of things connected in <u>series</u>, and it can be a real <u>pain</u> when the <u>whole lot go out</u> just because <u>one</u> of the bulbs breaks.

2) The only <u>advantage</u> is that the bulbs can be <u>very small</u> because the total 230 V is <u>shared out</u> between them, so each bulb only has a <u>small</u> potential difference across it.

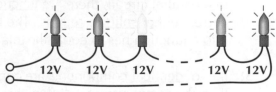

*Mains voltage is 230 V.*

## Series circuits aren't used very much in the real world

A lot of fairy lights are actually done on a <u>parallel circuit</u> (see next page) these days — they have an adapter that lowers the voltage, so the lights can still be diddy but it doesn't matter if one of them blows.

# Parallel Circuits

Parallel circuits are much more <u>sensible</u> than series circuits.  First up, the reason why...

## Parallel circuits — *independence* and *isolation*

1) In <u>parallel circuits</u>, each component is <u>separately</u> connected to the +ve and –ve of the <u>supply</u>.

2) If you remove or disconnect <u>one</u> of them, it will <u>hardly affect</u> the others at all.

3) This is <u>obviously</u> how <u>most</u> things must be connected, for example in <u>cars</u> and in <u>household electrics</u>.
   You have to be able to switch everything on and off <u>separately</u>.

### 1) P.D. is the *same* across *all* components:

1) In parallel circuits <u>all</u> components get the <u>full source P.D.</u>,
   so the voltage is the <u>same</u> across all components:

$$V_1 = V_2 = V_3$$

2) This means that <u>identical bulbs</u> connected in
   parallel will all be at the <u>same brightness</u>.

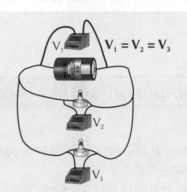

$$V_1 = V_2 = V_3$$

### 2) Current is *shared* between branches:

1) In parallel circuits the <u>total current</u> flowing
   around the circuit is equal to the <u>total</u> of all the
   currents through the <u>separate components</u>.

$$A = A_1 + A_2 + \ldots$$

2) In a parallel circuit, there are <u>junctions</u> where the
   current either <u>splits</u> or <u>rejoins</u>.  The total current going
   <u>into</u> a junction has to equal the total current <u>leaving</u>.

3) If two <u>identical components</u> are connected in parallel
   then the <u>same current</u> will flow through each component.

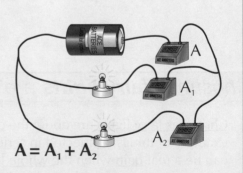

$$A = A_1 + A_2$$

---

## *All the electrics in your house will be wired in parallel circuits*

Parallel circuits might look a bit scarier than series ones, but they're much <u>more useful</u> — and you
don't have to learn as many equations for them.  Remember: each branch has the <u>same voltage</u>
across it, and the <u>total current</u> is equal to the <u>sum</u> of the currents through each of the branches.

# Parallel Circuits

This page covers some useful examples of <u>parallel circuits</u>.

## *Voltmeters* and *ammeters* are *exceptions* to the rule:

1) Ammeters and voltmeters are <u>exceptions</u> to the series and parallel rules.

2) Ammeters are <u>always</u> connected in <u>series</u> even in a parallel circuit.

3) Voltmeters are <u>always</u> connected in <u>parallel with a component</u> even in a series circuit.

## *Example on parallel circuits*

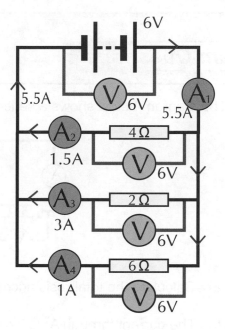

1) The <u>P.D.</u> across each resistor in the circuit is the same as the <u>supply P.D.</u> Each voltmeter will read 6 V.

2) The <u>current</u> through each <u>resistor</u> will be <u>different</u> because they have different values of <u>resistance</u>.

3) The current through the <u>battery</u> is the same as the <u>sum</u> of the other currents in the branches.
i.e. $A_1 = A_2 + A_3 + A_4 \Rightarrow A_1 = 1.5 + 3 + 1 = 5.5$ A

## *Everything* **electrical** *in a* **car** *is connected in* **parallel**

<u>Parallel connection</u> is <u>essential</u> in a car to give these <u>two features</u>:

1) Everything can be <u>turned on and off separately</u>.

2) Everything always gets the <u>full voltage</u> from the battery.

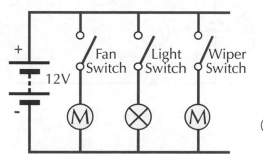

(M) *is the symbol for a motor.*

The only <u>slight effect</u> is that when you turn <u>lots of things on</u> the lights may go <u>dim</u> because the battery can't provide <u>full voltage</u> under <u>heavy load</u>. This is normally a <u>very slight</u> effect.

You can spot the same thing at home when you turn a kettle on, if you watch very carefully.

# Warm-Up and Exam Questions

Those last few pages had lots more stuff on circuits and electricity.
Try these out to see what you can remember...

## Warm-Up Questions

1) Give one disadvantage of series circuits.
2) How do you work out the total resistance in a series circuit?
3) In an electrical circuit, would you put an ammeter in series or parallel?
4) In a parallel circuit, is the p.d. across all the components the same or different?
5) Are circuits in cars connected in series or parallel?

## Exam Questions

1    The diagram below shows a series circuit.

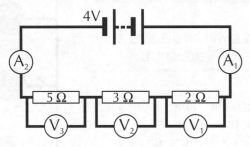

(a)   Calculate the total resistance in the circuit.

*(2 marks)*

(b)   The current through $A_1$ is 0.4 A.  What is the current through $A_2$?
Explain your answer.

*(2 marks)*

(c)   $V_1$ reads 0.8 V and $V_2$ reads 1.2 V.
Calculate the reading on $V_3$.

*(2 marks)*

2    A parallel circuit is connected as shown.

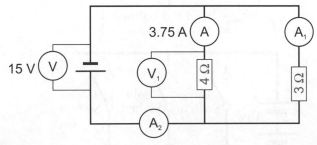

Calculate the readings on:
(a)   Voltmeter $V_1$.

*(1 mark)*

(b)   Ammeter $A_1$.

*(2 marks)*

(c)   Ammeter $A_2$.

*(2 marks)*

# Revision Summary for Physics 2a

Well done — you've made it to the end of another section. There are loads of bits and bobs about forces, motion and electricity which you have to learn. The best way to find out what you know is to get stuck in to these revision questions...

1) What's the difference between speed and velocity?

2)* Write down the formula for acceleration. What's the acceleration of a object that starts off from rest and reaches a speed of 14 m/s in 0.4 seconds?

3) Explain how to find speed, distance and acceleration from a velocity-time graph.

4) Explain the difference between mass and weight.

5) Explain what is meant by a "resultant force".

6) If an object has zero resultant force on it, can it be moving? Can it be accelerating?

7)* Write down the formula relating resultant force and acceleration.
A resultant force of 30 N pushes a trolley of mass 4 kg. What will be its acceleration?

8)* A skydiver has a mass of 75 kg. At 80 mph, the drag force on the skydiver is 650 N.
Find the acceleration of the skydiver at 80 mph (take g = 10 N/kg).

9)* A man pushes a tree with a force of 120 N. What is the size of the reaction force that the man feels pushing back at him?

10) What is "terminal velocity"?

11) What are the two different parts of the overall stopping distance of a car?

12)*Write down the formula for work done. A dog drags a big branch 12 m over the next-door neighbour's front lawn, pulling with a force of 535 N. How much work was done?

13)*A 4 kg cheese is taken 30 m up a hill before being rolled back down again. If g = 10 N/kg, how much gravitational potential energy does the cheese have at the top of the hill?

14)*What's the formula for kinetic energy? Find the kinetic energy of a 78 kg object moving at 23 m/s.

15)*Calculate the kinetic energy of the same 78 kg object just as it hits the floor after falling through 20 m.

16)*A car of mass 1000 kg is travelling at a velocity of 2 m/s when a sheep runs out 5 m in front.
If the driver immediately applies the maximum braking force of 395 N, can he avoid hitting it?

17) Write down the equation that relates the force on a spring and its extension.

18)*Calculate the power output of a 78 kg runner when she runs 20 m up a staircase in 16.5 seconds.

19) If the total momentum of a system before a collision is zero, what is the total momentum of the system after the collision?

20) Explain how seat belts, crumple zones, side impact bars and air bags are useful in a crash.

21) What is the advantage of using regenerative braking systems?

22) What causes the build-up of static electricity? Which particles move when static builds up?

23) True or false: the greater the resistance of a component, the smaller the current that flows through it?

24)*240 C of charge is carried though a wire in a circuit in one minute.
How much current has flowed through the wire?

25) Draw a diagram of the circuit that you would use to find the resistance of a motor.

26) Sketch typical potential difference-current graphs for:
a) a resistor,  b) a filament lamp,  c) a diode. Explain the shape of each graph.

27) Explain how resistance of a component changes with its temperature in terms of ions and electrons.

28)*What potential difference is required to push 2 A of current through a 0.6 Ω resistor?

29) Describe how the resistance of an LDR varies with light intensity. Give an application of an LDR.

30)*A 4 Ω bulb and a 6 Ω bulb are connected in series with a 12 V battery.
a) How much current flows through the 4 Ω bulb?
b) What is the P.D over the 6 Ω bulb?
c) What would the P.D. over the 6 Ω bulb be if the two bulbs were connected in parallel?

# Mains Electricity

Electric current is the <u>movement of charge carriers</u>. To transfer energy, it <u>doesn't matter which way</u> the charge carriers are going. That's why an <u>alternating current</u> works. Read on to find out more...

## *Mains supply is AC, battery supply is DC*

1) The UK mains supply is approximately <u>230 volts</u>.

2) It is an <u>AC supply</u> (alternating current), which means the current is <u>constantly</u> changing direction.

3) The frequency of the AC mains supply is <u>50 cycles per second</u> or <u>50 Hz</u> (hertz).

4) By contrast, cells and batteries supply <u>direct current</u> (DC).
This just means that the current always keeps flowing in the <u>same direction</u>.

## *Electricity supplies can be shown on an oscilloscope screen*

1) A <u>cathode ray oscilloscope</u> (CRO) is basically a <u>voltmeter</u>.

2) If you plug an <u>AC supply</u> into an oscilloscope, you get a '<u>trace</u>' on the screen that shows how the voltage of the supply changes with <u>time</u>. The trace goes up and down in a <u>regular pattern</u> — some of the time it's positive and some of the time it's negative.

3) If you plug in a <u>DC supply</u>, the trace you get is just a <u>straight line</u>.

4) The <u>vertical height</u> of the AC trace at any point shows the <u>input voltage</u> at that point.
By measuring the height of the trace you can find the potential difference of the AC supply.

5) For DC it's a <u>lot simpler</u> — the voltage is just the distance from the <u>straight line trace</u> to the centre line.

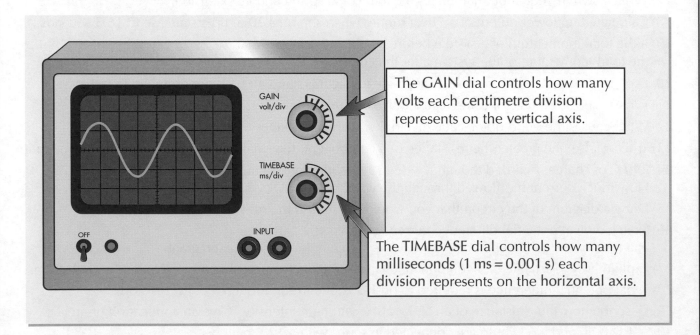

The GAIN dial controls how many volts each centimetre division represents on the vertical axis.

The TIMEBASE dial controls how many milliseconds (1 ms = 0.001 s) each division represents on the horizontal axis.

# Mains Electricity

## Learn how to **read** an **oscilloscope trace**

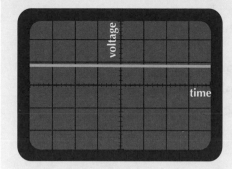

A <u>DC source</u> is always at the <u>same voltage</u>, so you get a <u>straight line</u>.

An <u>AC source</u> gives a <u>regularly repeating wave</u>. From that, you can work out the <u>period</u> and the <u>frequency</u> of the supply.

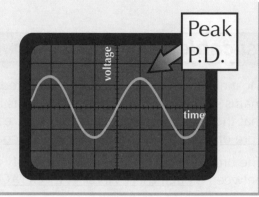

Peak P.D.

You work out the frequency using:

$$\text{Frequency (Hz)} = \frac{1}{\text{Time period (s)}}$$

## Example

The trace to the right comes from an oscilloscope with the timebase set to 5 ms/div. Find:

a) the time period, and b) the frequency of the AC supply.

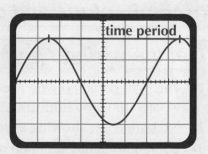

Time period = the time to complete one cycle.
1 ms = 0.001 s.

<u>ANSWER</u>:

a) To find the time period, measure the horizontal distance between two peaks. The time period of the signal is 6 divisions. Multiply by the timebase:
Time period = 5 ms × 6 = <u>0.03 s</u>

b) Using the frequency formula:
Frequency = 1/0.03 = <u>33 Hz</u>

## *Be prepared to use traces like these to do calculations*

Because mains power is AC, its current can be increased or decreased using a device called a transformer (see pages 176 -178). The lower the current in power transmission lines, the less energy is wasted as heat.

# Electricity in the Home

It's important to know how to correctly <u>wire a plug</u> — plugs that aren't wired correctly are <u>dangerous</u>.

## *Hazards in the home* — *eliminate them before they eliminate you*

A likely <u>exam question</u> will show you a picture with various <u>electrical hazards</u>, and then ask you to <u>list all the hazards</u>. This should be mostly <u>common sense</u>, but it'll help if you already know some of the likely hazards, so learn these 9 examples:

1) <u>Long cables</u>.
2) <u>Frayed cables</u>.
3) <u>Cables</u> in contact with something <u>hot</u> or <u>wet</u>.
4) <u>Water near sockets</u>.
5) <u>Shoving</u> things into sockets.

6) <u>Damaged plugs</u>.
7) <u>Too many</u> plugs into one socket.
8) Lighting sockets <u>without bulbs in</u>.
9) Appliances without their <u>covers</u> on.

## *Most cables have three separate wires*

1) Most electrical appliances are connected to the mains supply by <u>three-core</u> cables. This means that they have <u>three wires</u> inside them, each with a <u>core of copper</u> and a <u>coloured plastic coating</u>.

2) The brown <u>LIVE WIRE</u> in a mains supply alternates between a <u>HIGH +VE AND –VE VOLTAGE</u>.

3) The blue <u>NEUTRAL WIRE</u> is always at <u>0V</u>. Electricity normally flows in and out through the live and neutral wires only.

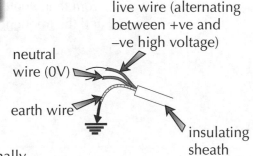

live wire (alternating between +ve and –ve high voltage)

neutral wire (0V)

earth wire

insulating sheath

4) The green and yellow <u>EARTH WIRE</u> is for protecting the wiring, and for safety — it works together with a fuse to prevent fire and shocks. It is attached to the metal casing of the plug and <u>carries the electricity to earth</u> (and away from you) should something go wrong and the live or neutral wires touch the metal case.

## *Three-pin plugs and cables* — *learn the safety features*

### *Get the wiring right*

1) The <u>right coloured wire</u> is connected to each pin, and <u>firmly screwed</u> in.
2) <u>No bare wires</u> showing inside the plug.
3) <u>Cable grip</u> tightly fastened over the cable <u>outer layer</u>.
4) Different appliances need <u>different</u> amounts of electrical energy. <u>Thicker</u> cables have <u>less resistance</u>, so they carry <u>more current</u>.

Rubber or plastic case

Earth Wire Green/Yellow

Fuse

Neutral Wire Blue

Live Wire Brown

Cable grip

Brass Pins

### *Plug features*

1) The <u>metal parts</u> are made of copper or brass because these are <u>very good conductors</u>.
2) The case, cable grip and cable insulation are made of <u>rubber</u> or <u>plastic</u> because they're really good <u>insulators</u>, and <u>flexible</u> too.
3) This all keeps the electricity flowing <u>where it should</u>.

# Fuses and Earthing

Questions about fuses are an exam favourite because they <u>cover lots of stuff</u> — electrical current, resistance, energy transfers and electrical safety. Learn this page and make sure you've got it sussed.

## *Earthing* and *fuses* prevent *electrical overloads*

The earth wire and fuse (or circuit breaker) are included in electrical appliances for safety and work together like this:

1) If a <u>fault</u> develops in which the <u>live wire</u> somehow touches the <u>metal case</u>, then because the case is <u>earthed</u>, <u>too great a current</u> flows in through the <u>live wire</u>, through the <u>case</u> and out down the <u>earth wire</u>.

2) This <u>surge</u> in current <u>melts the fuse</u> (or trips the circuit breaker in the live wire) when the amount of current is greater than the fuse rating. This <u>cuts off</u> the <u>live supply</u> and <u>breaks the circuit</u>.

3) This <u>isolates</u> the <u>whole appliance</u>, making it <u>impossible</u> to get an electric <u>shock</u> from the case. It also prevents the risk of <u>fire</u> caused by the heating effect of a large current.

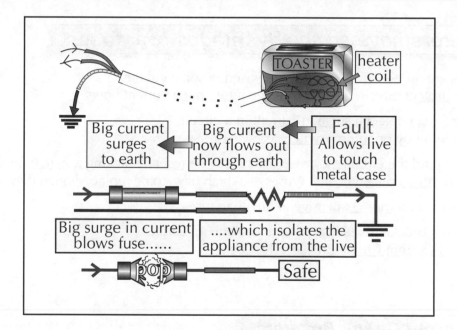

4) As well as people, fuses and earthing are there to <u>protect the circuits and wiring</u> in your appliances from getting <u>fried</u> if there is a <u>current surge</u>.

5) <u>Fuses</u> should be <u>rated</u> as near as possible but <u>just higher</u> than the <u>normal operating current</u>.

6) The <u>larger the current</u>, the <u>thicker the cable</u> you need to carry it. That's why the <u>fuse rating</u> needed for cables usually <u>increases</u> with <u>cable thickness</u>.

## *Fuses — you'll find them in exams and kettles*

<u>Safety precautions</u> on modern appliances mean it's pretty difficult to get electrocuted by them. But that's only so long as they are in <u>good condition</u> and you're not doing <u>something really stupid</u>. Watch out for frayed wires, don't overload plugs, and for goodness sake don't use a knife to get toast out of a toaster when it is switched on. Turn over to the next page to find out more about safety precautions that you might find in your home.

# Fuses and Earthing

Earthing is another way in which we can prevent appliances giving us an electric shock.

## *Insulating materials make appliances "double insulated"*

1) All appliances with metal cases are usually "earthed" to reduce the danger of electric shock.

2) "Earthing" just means the case must be attached to an earth wire.

3) An earthed conductor can never become live.

4) If the appliance has a plastic casing and no metal parts showing then it's said to be double insulated.

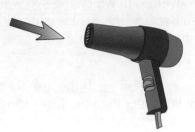

5) Anything with double insulation like that doesn't need an earth wire — just a live and neutral.

6) Cables that only carry the live and neutral wires are known as two-core cables.

## *Circuit breakers have some advantages over fuses*

1) Circuit breakers are an electrical safety device used in some circuits. Like fuses, they protect the circuit from damage if too much current flows.

2) When circuit breakers detect a surge in current in a circuit, they break the circuit by opening a switch.

3) A circuit breaker (and the circuit they're in) can easily be reset by flicking a switch on the device. This makes them more convenient than fuses — which have to be replaced once they've melted.

4) They are, however, a lot more expensive to buy than fuses.

5) One type of circuit breaker used instead of a fuse and an earth wire is a Residual Current Circuit Breakers (RCCBs):

### *Residual Current Circuit Breakers*

1) Normally exactly the same current flows through the live and neutral wires. If somebody touches the live wire, a small but deadly current will flow through them to the earth. This means the neutral wire carries less current than the live wire. The RCCB detects this difference in current and quickly cuts off the power by opening a switch.

2) They also operate much faster than fuses — they break the circuit as soon as there is a current surge — no time is wasted waiting for the current to melt a fuse. This makes them safer.

3) RCCBs even work for small current changes that might not be large enough to melt a fuse. Since even small current changes could be fatal, this means RCCBs are more effective at protecting against electrocution.

# Energy and Power in Circuits

Electricity is just another form of <u>energy</u> — which means that it is always <u>conserved</u>.

## *Energy is transferred from cells and other sources*

Anything which <u>supplies electricity</u> is also supplying <u>energy</u>.

So cells, batteries, generators, etc. all <u>transfer energy</u> to components in the circuit:

| <u>Motion</u>: motors | <u>Light</u>: light bulbs | <u>Heat</u>: Hair dryers/kettles | <u>Sound</u>: speakers |

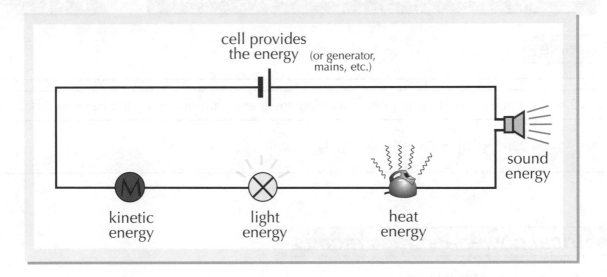

## *All resistors produce heat when a current flows through them*

1) Whenever a <u>current</u> flows through anything with <u>electrical resistance</u> (which is pretty much everything) then <u>electrical energy</u> is converted into <u>heat energy</u>.

2) The <u>more current</u> that flows, the more heat is produced.

3) A <u>bigger voltage</u> means more heating because it pushes more current through.

4) <u>Filament bulbs</u> work by passing a current through a very <u>thin wire</u>, heating it up so much that it glows. Rather obviously, they waste a lot of energy as <u>heat</u>.

## *If an appliance is efficient it wastes less energy*

All this energy wasted as heat can get a little <u>depressing</u> — but there is a solution.

1) When you buy electrical appliances you can choose to buy ones that are more <u>energy efficient</u>.

2) These appliances transfer more of their <u>total electrical energy output to useful energy</u>.

3) For example, less energy is wasted as heat in power-saving lamps such as <u>compact fluorescent lamps</u> (CFLs) and <u>light-emitting diodes</u> (p.104) than in ordinary filament bulbs.

4) Unfortunately, they do <u>cost more to buy</u>, but over time the money you <u>save</u> on your electricity bills pays you back for the initial investment.

# Energy and Power in Circuits

Power ratings tell you how much energy a device transfers per second.

## Appliances *have* power ratings

1) The total energy transferred by an appliance depends on
   how long the appliance is on and its power rating.
2) The power of an appliance is the energy that it uses per second.

$$\textbf{Energy Transferred = Power rating} \times \textbf{time}$$

### Example

> A 2.5 kW kettle is on for 5 minutes.  Calculate the energy transferred by the kettle in this time.
>
> ANSWER:  2500 × 300 = 750 000 J = __750 kJ__. (5 minutes = 300 s).

## *Electrical power* and *fuse ratings*

1) The formula for electrical power is:

$$\textbf{POWER = CURRENT} \times \textbf{POTENTIAL DIFFERENCE}$$

$$\textbf{P = I} \times \textbf{V}$$

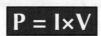 

2) Most electrical goods show their power rating and voltage rating.  To work out the size of
   the fuse needed, you need to work out the current that the item will normally use.

### Example

> A hair dryer is rated at 230 V, 1 kW.  Find the fuse needed.
>
> ANSWER:  I = P/V = 1000/230 = 4.3 A.  Normally, the fuse should be rated just a
>          little higher than the normal current, so a 5 amp fuse is ideal for this one.

## *Use fuses with a rating just above the usual current*

In the UK, you can usually get fuses rated at 3 A, 5 A or 13 A, and that's about it.
You should bear that in mind when you're working out fuse ratings.
If you find you need a 10.73 A fuse — tough.  You'll have to use a 13A one.

# Power and Energy Change

You can think about <u>electrical circuits</u> in terms of <u>energy transfer</u> — the charge carriers take charge around the circuit, and when they go through an electrical component energy is transferred to make the component work. Read on for more...

## *Potential difference is the energy transferred per charge passed*

1) When an electrical <u>charge</u> (Q) goes through a <u>change</u> in potential difference (V), then <u>energy</u> (E) is <u>transferred</u>.

2) Energy is <u>supplied</u> to the charge at the <u>power source</u> to 'raise' it through a potential.

3) The charge <u>gives up</u> this energy when it '<u>falls</u>' through any <u>potential drop</u> in <u>components</u> elsewhere in the circuit.

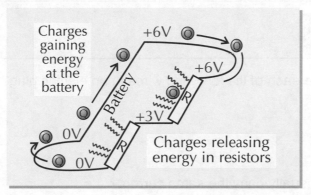

4) The formula is simple:

## Energy transformed = Charge × Potential difference

5) The <u>bigger</u> the <u>change</u> in P.D. (or voltage.), the <u>more energy</u> is transferred for a <u>given amount of charge</u> passing through the circuit.

6) That means that a battery with a <u>bigger voltage</u> will supply <u>more energy</u> to the circuit for every <u>coulomb</u> of charge which flows round it, because the charge is raised up "<u>higher</u>" at the start — and as the diagram shows, <u>more energy</u> will be <u>dissipated</u> in the circuit too.

### Example

> The motor in an electric toothbrush is attached to a 3 V battery.
> If a current of 0.8 A flows through the motor for 3 minutes:
>
> a) Calculate the total charge passed.
>
> b) Calculate the energy transformed by the motor.
>
> c) Explain why the kinetic energy output of the motor will be less than your answer to b).

ANSWER: a) Use the formula (p.100) $Q = I \times t = 0.8 \times (3 \times 60) = \underline{144 \text{ C}}$

b) Use $E = Q \times V = 144 \times 3 = \underline{432 \text{ J}}$

c) The motor won't be 100% efficient.
Some of the energy will be transformed into <u>sound and heat</u>.

# Warm-Up and Exam Questions

Check you can do the straightforward stuff with this warm-up, then have a go at the exam questions...

## Warm-Up Questions

1) What is the frequency of UK mains electricity supply?
2) Which of the live, neutral or earth wires is always at 0 volts?
3) Why is the case of a plug usually made out of plastic?
4) Appliances with double insulation don't need which type of wire?
5) What energy transformation occurs when electric current flows through a resistor?
6) What is the equation linking Q, V and E?

## Exam Questions

1   (a)   What colour(s) are each of the following wires in an electric plug?
     (i)   live
     (ii)  neutral
     (iii) earth

*(3 marks)*

  (b)   Which two wires usually carry the same current?

*(1 mark)*

  (c)   What type of safety device contains a wire that is designed to melt when the current passing through it goes above a certain value?

*(1 mark)*

2   *In this question you will be assessed on the quality of your English, the organisation of your ideas and your use of appropriate specialist vocabulary.*

   A domestic appliance has a plug containing live, neutral and earth wires and a fuse.
The appliance has a metal case.

   Describe how the earth wire and fuse work together to protect the appliance and to prevent the user getting an electric shock if there is a fault.

*(6 marks)*

3   A current of 0.5 A passes through a torch bulb.  The torch is powered by a 3 V battery.
  (a)   Calculate the power of the torch.

*(2 marks)*

  (b)   In half an hour, 900 C of charge pass through the battery.
Calculate how much electrical energy the bulb transfers in half an hour.

*(2 marks)*

4   The diagram on the right shows a trace on a CRO.
  (a)   Is the trace displaying the output from the mains or a battery?  Explain your answer.

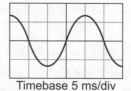
Timebase 5 ms/div

*(1 mark)*

  (b)   What is the time period of the wave?

*(1 mark)*

  (c)   What is the frequency of the wave?

*(2 marks)*

  (d)   What will happen to the CRO trace if the voltage of the supply is reduced?

*(1 mark)*

# Atomic Structure

Ernest Rutherford didn't just pick the nuclear model of the atom out of thin air. It all started with a Greek fella called Democritus in the 5th Century BC. He thought that all matter, whatever it was, was made up of identical lumps called "atomos". And that's about as far as the theory got until the 1800s...

## *Rutherford scattering and the demise of the plum pudding*

1) In 1804 John Dalton agreed with Democritus that matter was made up of tiny spheres ("atoms") that couldn't be broken up, but he reckoned that each element was made up of a different type of "atom".

2) Nearly 100 years later, J J Thomson discovered that electrons could be removed from atoms. So Dalton's theory wasn't quite right (atoms could be broken up). Thomson suggested that atoms were spheres of positive charge with tiny negative electrons stuck in them like plums in a plum pudding.

3) That "plum pudding" theory didn't last very long though. In 1909 Rutherford and Marsden tried firing a beam of alpha particles (see p.124) at thin gold foil. They expected that the positively charged alpha particles would be slightly deflected by the electrons in the plum pudding model.

4) However, most of the alpha particles just went straight through, but the odd one came straight back at them, which was frankly a bit of a shocker for Rutherford and his pal.

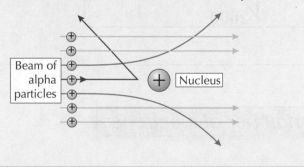

5) Being pretty clued-up guys, Rutherford and Marsden realised this meant that most of the mass of the atom was concentrated at the centre in a tiny nucleus. They also realised that the nucleus must have a positive charge, since it repelled the positive alpha particles.

6) It also showed that most of an atom is just empty space, which is also a bit of a shocker when you think about it.

# Atomic Structure

Rutherford and Marsden used the results from their scattering experiment (see previous page) to produce a model for the atom.

## Rutherford and Marsden came up with

### the nuclear model of the atom

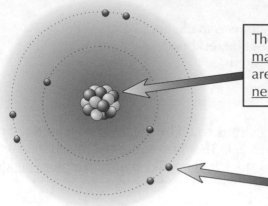

The nucleus is tiny but it makes up most of the mass of the atom. It contains protons (which are positively charged) and neutrons (which are neutral) — which gives it an overall positive charge.

The rest of the atom is mostly empty space.

The negative electrons whizz round the outside of the nucleus really fast. They give the atom its overall size — the radius of the atom's nucleus is about 10 000 times smaller than the radius of the atom.

## We can use relative charges and masses to compare particles

Learn the relative charges and masses of each particle:

| PARTICLE | MASS | CHARGE |
|---|---|---|
| Proton | 1 | +1 |
| Neutron | 1 | 0 |
| Electron | $\frac{1}{2000}$ | -1 |

## Number of protons equals number of electrons

1) Atoms have no charge overall.

2) The charge on an electron is the same size as the charge on a proton — but opposite.

3) This means the number of protons always equals the number of electrons in a neutral atom.

4) If some electrons are added or removed, the atom becomes a charged particle called an ion.

## The nuclear model is just one way of thinking about the atom

Rutherford and Marsden's nuclear model works really well for explaining a lot of physical properties of different elements — but it's certainly not the whole story. Other bits of science are explained using different models of the atom. The beauty of it though is that no one model is more right than the others.

# Radioactivity and Background Radiation

You have just entered the <u>subatomic</u> realm — now stuff starts to get real interesting...

## *Isotopes are different forms of the same element*

1) <u>Isotopes</u> are atoms with the <u>same</u> number of <u>protons</u> but a <u>different</u> number of <u>neutrons</u>.
2) Hence they have the <u>same atomic number</u>, but <u>different mass numbers</u>.
3) Atomic number is the <u>number of protons</u> in an atom.
4) Mass number is the <u>number of protons</u> + the <u>number of neutrons</u> in an atom.
5) <u>Carbon-12</u> and <u>carbon-14</u> are good examples of isotopes:

6) <u>Most elements</u> have different isotopes, but there's usually only one or two <u>stable</u> ones.
7) The other isotopes tend to be <u>radioactive</u>, which means they <u>decay</u> into <u>other elements</u> and <u>give out radiation</u>.

## *Radioactivity is a totally random process*

1) <u>Radioactive substances</u> give out radiation from the nuclei of their atoms — <u>no matter what is done to them</u>.
2) This process is entirely <u>random</u>. This means that if you have 1000 unstable nuclei, you can't say when <u>any one of them</u> is going to decay, and neither can you do anything at all <u>to make a decay happen</u>.
3) It's completely unaffected by <u>physical</u> conditions like <u>temperature</u> or by any sort of <u>chemical bonding</u> etc.
4) Radioactive substances <u>spit out</u> one or more of the three types of radiation, <u>alpha</u>, <u>beta</u> or <u>gamma</u> (see next page).

## *Background radiation comes from many sources*

<u>Background radiation</u> is radiation that is present at all times, all around us, wherever you go. The background radiation we receive comes from:

1) Radioactivity of naturally occurring <u>unstable isotopes</u> which are <u>all around us</u> — in the <u>air</u>, in <u>food</u>, in <u>building materials</u> and in the <u>rocks</u> under our feet.
2) Radiation from <u>space</u>, which is known as <u>cosmic rays</u>. These come mostly from the <u>Sun</u>.
3) Radiation due to <u>man-made sources</u>, e.g. <u>fallout</u> from <u>nuclear weapons tests</u>, <u>nuclear accidents</u> (such as Chernobyl) or <u>dumped nuclear waste</u>.

The <u>RELATIVE PROPORTIONS</u> of <u>background radiation</u>:

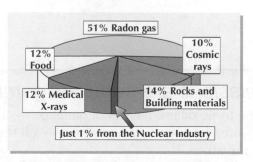

# Ionising Radiation

Alpha (α) Beta (β) Gamma (γ) — there's a short alphabet of radiation for you to learn. And it's all <u>ionising</u>.

## Alpha particles are helium nuclei

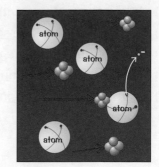

1) An <u>alpha</u> particle is <u>two neutrons</u> and <u>two protons</u> — the same as a <u>helium nucleus</u>.

2) They are relatively <u>big</u> and <u>heavy</u> and <u>slow moving</u>.

3) They therefore <u>don't</u> penetrate very far into materials and are <u>stopped quickly</u>, even when travelling through <u>air</u>.

4) Because of their size they are <u>strongly ionising</u>, which just means they <u>bash into</u> a lot of atoms and <u>knock electrons off them</u> before they slow down, which creates lots of ions — hence the term "<u>ionising</u>".

## Beta particles are electrons

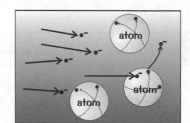

1) Beta particles are <u>in between</u> alpha and gamma in terms of their <u>properties</u>.

2) They move <u>quite</u> fast and they are <u>quite</u> small (they're electrons).

3) They <u>penetrate moderately</u> into materials before colliding, have a <u>long range</u> in air, and are <u>moderately ionising</u> too.

4) For every β-particle emitted, a <u>neutron</u> turns to a <u>proton</u> in the nucleus.

5) A <u>β-particle</u> is simply an <u>electron</u>, with virtually no mass and a charge of –1.

## Gamma rays are very short wavelength EM waves

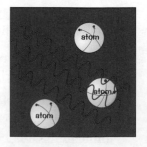

1) Gamma rays are the <u>opposite</u> of alpha particles in a way.

2) They <u>penetrate far into materials</u> without being stopped and pass <u>straight through air</u>.

3) This means they are <u>weakly</u> ionising because they tend to <u>pass through</u> rather than collide with atoms. Eventually they <u>hit something</u> and do <u>damage</u>.

4) Gamma rays have <u>no mass</u> and <u>no charge</u>.

---

## Alpha and beta emissions are particles, gamma emissions are rays

Learn <u>all the details</u> about the three different types of radiation — alpha, beta and gamma. You need to know what they are, their ionising power, how well they penetrate through materials and their range in the air.

# Ionising Radiation

When nuclei decay by <u>alpha</u> or <u>beta</u> emission, they change from one element into a different one.

## You need to be able to **balance nuclear equations**

1) You can write alpha and beta decays as <u>nuclear equations</u>.
2) Watch out for the <u>mass and atomic numbers</u> — they have to <u>balance up</u> on both sides.

### *Alpha decay:*

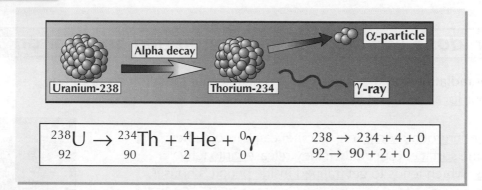

$$^{238}_{92}U \rightarrow \, ^{234}_{90}Th + \, ^{4}_{2}He + \, ^{0}_{0}\gamma$$

$$238 \rightarrow 234 + 4 + 0$$
$$92 \rightarrow 90 + 2 + 0$$

### *Beta decay:*

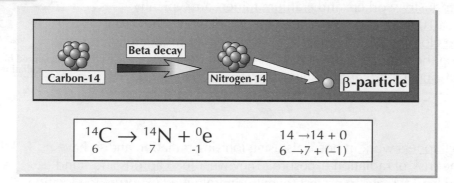

$$^{14}_{6}C \rightarrow \, ^{14}_{7}N + \, ^{0}_{-1}e$$

$$14 \rightarrow 14 + 0$$
$$6 \rightarrow 7 + (-1)$$

## *Alpha* and *beta* are **deflected** by *electric* and *magnetic fields*

1) Alpha particles have a <u>positive charge</u>, beta particles have a <u>negative charge</u>.

2) When travelling through a <u>magnetic</u> or <u>electric field</u>, both alpha and beta particles will be <u>deflected</u>.

3) They're deflected in <u>opposite directions</u> because of their <u>opposite charge</u>.

4) Alpha particles have a <u>larger charge</u> than beta particles, and feel a <u>greater force</u> in magnetic and electric fields. But they're <u>deflected less</u> because they have a <u>much greater mass</u>.

5) <u>Gamma radiation</u> is an electromagnetic (EM) wave and has <u>no charge</u>, so it <u>doesn't get</u> <u>deflected</u> by electric or magnetic fields.

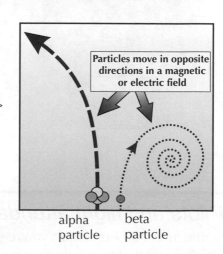

Particles move in opposite directions in a magnetic or electric field

alpha particle     beta particle

# Radiation Dose

This page is all about what <u>affects</u> the amount of <u>radiation</u> we're <u>exposed</u> to, and the damage it does.

## *The **damage** caused by **radiation depends** on the **radiation dose***

How likely you are to <u>suffer damage</u> if you're exposed to nuclear radiation depends on the <u>radiation dose</u>.

1) Radiation dose depends on the <u>type</u> and <u>amount of radiation</u> you've been exposed to.

2) The <u>higher</u> the radiation dose, the <u>more at risk</u> you are of <u>developing cancer</u>.

## *Radiation dose can depend on **location** and **occupation***

The amount of radiation you're exposed to (and hence your radiation dose) can be affected by your <u>location</u> and <u>occupation</u>:

1) Certain <u>underground rocks</u> (e.g. granite) can cause higher levels at the <u>surface</u>, especially if they release <u>radioactive radon gas</u>, which tends to get <u>trapped inside people's houses</u>.

**Coloured bits indicate more radiation from rocks**

2) <u>Nuclear industry</u> workers and <u>uranium miners</u> are typically exposed to <u>10 times</u> the normal amount of radiation. They wear <u>protective clothing</u> and <u>face masks</u> to stop them from <u>touching</u> or <u>inhaling</u> the radioactive material, and <u>monitor</u> their radiation doses with <u>special radiation badges</u> and <u>regular check-ups</u>.

3) <u>Radiographers</u> work in hospitals using ionising radiation and so have a higher risk of radiation exposure. They wear <u>lead aprons</u> and stand behind <u>lead screens</u> to protect them from <u>prolonged exposure</u> to radiation.

4) At <u>high altitudes</u> (e.g. in <u>jet planes</u>) the background radiation <u>increases</u> because of more exposure to <u>cosmic rays</u>. That means <u>commercial pilots</u> have an increased risk of getting some types of cancer.

5) <u>Underground</u> (e.g. in <u>mines</u>, etc.) it increases because of the <u>rocks</u> all around, posing a risk to <u>miners</u>.

## *Pilots and flight attendants have a greater exposure to cosmic rays*

So the amount of radiation you're <u>exposed</u> to depends on your <u>job</u> and your <u>location</u>.
Don't forget that some places have higher levels of background radiation than others
— so the people there'll get a <u>higher radiation dose</u>.

# Warm-Up and Exam Questions

It's time again to test what you've learnt from the last few pages. Have a go at these...

## Warm-Up Questions

1) In the 'plum pudding' model of the atom, what are the 'plums'?
2) Give one man-made source of background radiation.
3) Which are the most ionising — alpha particles or gamma rays?
4) Give two factors that affect a person's average yearly radiation dose.
5) Which type of background radiation are pilots more exposed to than the average person?

## Exam Questions

1   (a)   Give the relative charge of the following particles:
    (i)   electron
    (ii)   proton
    (iii)   neutron
*(3 marks)*

  (b)   Name the two types of particle that the nucleus of an atom contains.
*(2 marks)*

  (c)   Describe how the atomic number of a nucleus changes when a
beta particle is emitted.
*(1 mark)*

  (d)   Describe how the mass number of a nucleus changes after alpha emission.
*(1 mark)*

  (e)   The table below contains information about three atoms.

| | Mass number | Atomic number |
|---|---|---|
| Atom A | 32 | 17 |
| Atom B | 33 | 17 |
| Atom C | 32 | 16 |

    (i)   What is meant by the mass number of an atom?
*(1 mark)*

    (ii)   Which of the two atoms are isotopes of the same element? Explain your answer.
*(2 marks)*

  (f)   Alpha and beta particles are deflected in electric and magnetic fields.
    (i)   Explain why alpha and beta particles are deflected in opposite directions.
*(1 mark)*

    (ii)   Explain why alpha particles are deflected less than beta particles.
*(1 mark)*

2   Rutherford and Marsden's scattering experiment led to their nuclear model of the atom.
  (a)   Describe what Rutherford and Marsden saw when they fired a beam of alpha
particles at thin gold foil.
*(2 marks)*

  (b)   Describe the main features of their nuclear model of the atom.
*(4 marks)*

# Half-Life

The <u>unit</u> for measuring <u>radioactivity</u> is the <u>becquerel</u> (Bq). 1 Bq means <u>one nucleus decaying per second</u>.

## *The **radioactivity** of a sample always **decreases** over time*

1) This is <u>pretty obvious</u> when you think about it. Each time a <u>decay</u> happens and an alpha, beta or gamma is given out, it means one more <u>radioactive nucleus</u> has <u>disappeared</u>.

2) Obviously, as the <u>unstable nuclei</u> all steadily disappear, the <u>activity</u> (the number of nuclei that decay per second) will <u>decrease</u>. So the <u>older</u> a sample becomes, the <u>less radiation</u> it will emit.

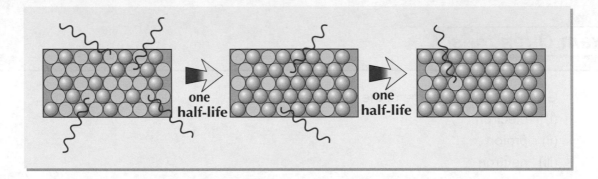

3) <u>How quickly</u> the activity <u>drops off</u> varies a lot. For <u>some</u> substances it takes <u>just a few microseconds</u> before nearly all the unstable nuclei have <u>decayed</u>, whilst for others it can take <u>millions of years</u>.

4) The problem with trying to <u>measure</u> this is that <u>the activity never reaches zero</u>, which is why we have to use the idea of <u>half-life</u> to measure how quickly the activity <u>drops off</u>.

5) Learn this <u>definition</u> of <u>half-life</u>:

> **HALF-LIFE is the AVERAGE TIME it
> takes for the NUMBER OF NUCLEI in a
> RADIOACTIVE ISOTOPE SAMPLE to HALVE.**

6) In other words, it is the <u>time it takes</u> for the <u>count rate</u> (the number of radioactive emissions detected per unit of time) from a sample containing the isotope to <u>fall to half its initial level</u>.

7) A <u>short half-life</u> means the <u>activity falls quickly</u>, because <u>lots</u> of the nuclei decay <u>quickly</u>.

8) A <u>long half-life</u> means the activity <u>falls more slowly</u> because <u>most</u> of the nuclei don't decay <u>for a long time</u> — they just sit there, <u>basically unstable</u>, but kind of <u>biding their time</u>.

---

## *Half-life measures how quickly the activity of a source drops off*

For <u>medical applications</u>, you need to use isotopes that have a <u>suitable half-life</u>.
A radioactive tracer needs to have a short half-life to minimise the risk of damage to the patient.
A radioactive source for sterilising equipment needs to have a long half-life, so you don't have to replace it too often (see page 130 for more). Don't forget that some places have higher levels of background radiation than others — so the people there'll get a <u>higher radiation dose</u>.

# Half-Life

Calculating half-life is bound to come up on the exam. So this page is about <u>how to tackle</u> the two main types of half-life questions.

## *Do half-life questions step by step*

Half-life is maybe a little confusing, but exam calculations are <u>straightforward</u> so long as you do them slowly, <u>STEP BY STEP</u>. Like this one:

> The activity of a radioisotope is 640 cpm (counts per minute).
> Two hours later it has fallen to 80 cpm. Find the half-life of the sample.

<u>ANSWER</u>: You must go through it in <u>short simple steps</u> like this:

| INITIAL count: | (÷2)→ | after ONE half-life: | (÷2)→ | after TWO half-lives: | (÷2)→ | after THREE half-lives: |
|---|---|---|---|---|---|---|
| 640 | | 320 | | 160 | | 80 |

Notice the careful <u>step-by-step method</u>, which tells us it takes <u>three half-lives</u> for the activity to fall from 640 to 80. Hence <u>two hours</u> represents three half-lives, so the <u>half-life</u> is 120 mins ÷ 3 = <u>40 minutes</u>.

## *Finding the half-life of a sample using a graph*

1) The data for the graph will usually be <u>several readings</u> of <u>count rate</u> taken with a <u>G-M tube and counter</u>.

2) The <u>graph</u> will always be <u>shaped</u> like the one shown.

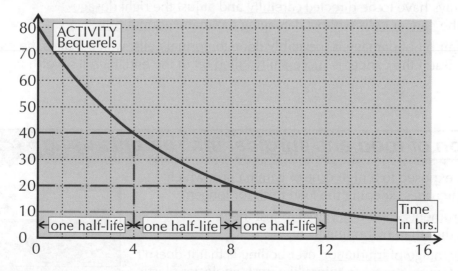

The <u>half-life</u> is found from the graph by finding the <u>time interval</u> on the <u>bottom axis</u> corresponding to a <u>halving</u> of the <u>activity</u> on the <u>vertical axis</u>. Easy peasy really.

*So the half-life of the sample is 4 hours.*

# Uses of Radiation

Radiation gets a lot of bad press, but the fact is it's essential for things like <u>modern medicine</u>.

## Smoke *detectors* — *use* α-*radiation*

1) A <u>weak</u> source of <u>alpha</u> radiation is placed in the detector, close to <u>two electrodes</u>.

2) The source causes <u>ionisation</u>, and a <u>current</u> flows between the electrodes.

3) If there is a fire then smoke will <u>absorb</u> the radiation — so the current stops and the <u>alarm sounds</u>.

## *Tracers* in *medicine* — *always* **short half-life** β *or* γ *-emitters*

1) Certain <u>radioactive isotopes</u> can be <u>injected</u> into people (or they can just <u>swallow</u> them) and their progress <u>around the body</u> can be followed using an external <u>detector</u>. A computer converts the reading to a <u>display</u> showing where the <u>strongest reading</u> is coming from.

2) A well-known example is the use of <u>iodine-131</u>, which is absorbed by the <u>thyroid gland</u> just like normal iodine-127, but it gives out <u>radiation</u> which can be <u>detected</u> to indicate whether the thyroid gland is <u>taking in iodine</u> as it should.

3) <u>All isotopes</u> which are taken <u>into the body</u> must be <u>GAMMA or BETA</u> emitters (never alpha), so that the radiation <u>passes out of the body</u> — and they should only last <u>a few hours</u>, so that the radioactivity inside the patient <u>quickly disappears</u> (i.e. they should have a <u>short half-life</u>).

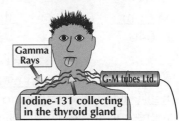

Gamma Rays

G-M tubes Ltd.

**Iodine-131 collecting in the thyroid gland**

## *Radiotherapy* — *the* **treatment** *of* **cancer** *using* γ-**rays**

1) Since high doses of gamma rays will <u>kill all living cells</u>, they can be used to <u>treat cancers</u>.

2) The gamma rays have to be <u>directed carefully</u> and at just the right <u>dosage</u> so as to kill the <u>cancer cells</u> without damaging too many <u>normal cells</u>.

3) However, a <u>fair bit of damage</u> is <u>inevitably</u> done to <u>normal cells</u>, which makes the patient feel <u>very ill</u>. But if the cancer is <u>successfully killed off</u> in the end, then it's worth it.

## *Sterilisation* of **food** and **surgical instruments** using γ -**rays**

1) <u>Food</u> can be exposed to a <u>high dose</u> of <u>gamma rays</u> which will <u>kill</u> all <u>microbes</u>, keeping the food <u>fresh for longer</u>.

2) <u>Medical instruments</u> can be <u>sterilised</u> in just the same way, rather than by <u>boiling them</u>.

3) The great <u>advantage</u> of <u>irradiation</u> over boiling is that it doesn't involve <u>high temperatures</u>, so things like <u>fresh apples</u> or <u>plastic instruments</u> can be totally <u>sterilised</u> without <u>damaging</u> them.

4) The food is <u>not</u> radioactive afterwards, so it's <u>perfectly safe</u> to eat.

5) The isotope used for this needs to be a <u>very strong</u> emitter of <u>gamma rays</u> with a <u>reasonably long half-life</u> (at least several months) so that it doesn't need <u>replacing</u> too often.

unsterilised | Gamma source | sterilised

# Radioactivity Safety

When <u>Marie Curie</u> discovered the radioactive properties of <u>radium</u> in 1898, nobody knew about its dangers. Radium was used to make glow-in-the-dark watches and many <u>watch dial painters</u> developed cancer as a result. We now know lots more about the dangers of radiation...

## Radiation harms living cells

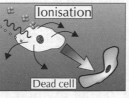

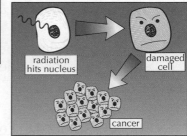

1) <u>Alpha</u>, <u>beta</u> and <u>gamma</u> radiation will cheerfully <u>enter living cells</u> and <u>collide with molecules</u>.

2) These collisions cause <u>ionisation</u>, which <u>damages or destroys</u> the <u>molecules</u>.

3) <u>Lower doses</u> tend to cause <u>minor damage</u> without <u>killing</u> the cell.

4) This can give rise to <u>mutant cells</u> which <u>divide uncontrollably</u>. This is <u>cancer</u>.

5) <u>Higher doses</u> tend to <u>kill cells completely</u>, which causes <u>radiation sickness</u> if a lot of body cells <u>all get hit at once</u>.

6) The <u>extent</u> of the harmful effects depends on <u>two things</u>:

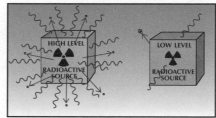

   a) <u>How much exposure</u> you have to the radiation.

   b) The <u>energy and penetration</u> of the radiation, since <u>some types</u> are <u>more hazardous</u> than others, of course.

## Outside the body, β and γ–sources are the most dangerous

This is because <u>beta and gamma</u> can get <u>inside</u> to the delicate <u>organs</u>, whereas alpha is much less dangerous because it <u>can't penetrate the skin</u>.

## Inside the body, an α-source is the most dangerous

<u>Inside the body</u> alpha sources do all their damage in a <u>very localised area</u>. Beta and gamma sources on the other hand are <u>less dangerous</u> inside the body because they mostly <u>pass straight out</u> without doing much damage.

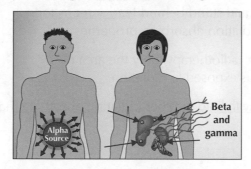

## Nuclear radiation + living cells = cell damage, cell death or cancer

Sadly, much of our knowledge of the harmful effects of radiation has come as a result of devastating events such as the <u>atomic bombing</u> of Japan in 1945. In the months following the bombs, <u>thousands</u> suffered from <u>radiation sickness</u> — the symptoms of which include nausea, fatigue, skin burns, hair loss and, in serious cases, death. In the long term, the area has experienced <u>increased rates</u> of cancer.

# Radioactivity Safety

The last page was all about the damage that radiation can do to your body.  Now here are some ways you can <u>protect</u> yourself <u>against exposure</u> to radiation.

## You need to **learn** about these **safety precautions**

Obviously radioactive materials need to be handled <u>carefully</u>.
But in the exam they might ask you to <u>evaluate some specific precautions</u> that should be taken when <u>handling radioactive materials</u>.

1) When conducting experiments, use radioactive sources for as <u>short a time</u> as possible so your <u>exposure</u> is kept to a <u>minimum</u>.

2) <u>Never</u> allow <u>skin contact</u> with a source.
Always handle with <u>tongs</u>.

3) Hold the source at <u>arm's length</u> to keep it <u>as far</u> from the body <u>as possible</u>.
This will decrease the amount of radiation that hits you, especially for alpha particles as they <u>don't travel far in air</u>.

4) Keep the source <u>pointing away</u> from the body and <u>avoid looking directly at it</u>.

## Lead can help **protect** us from **exposure** to **radiation**

1) <u>Lead</u> absorbs all three types of radiation (though a lot of it is needed to stop gamma radiation completely).  <u>Always</u> store radioactive sources in a <u>lead box</u> and put them away <u>as soon</u> as the experiment is <u>over</u>.

2) Medical professionals who work with radiation <u>every day</u> (such as radiographers) wear <u>lead aprons</u> and stand behind <u>lead screens</u> for extra protection because of its radiation absorbing properties.

3) When someone needs an X-ray or radiotherapy, only the area of the body that <u>needs to be treated</u> is exposed to radiation.

4) The rest of the body is <u>protected with lead</u> or other <u>radiation absorbing</u> materials.

## Radiation's dangerous stuff — safety precautions are crucial

Radiation can be harmful to us (see previous page) but following the safety precautions above can <u>minimise</u> our exposure to radiation.  Learn all the points above about how to <u>protect</u> yourself in the laboratory, and make sure you can give examples of how <u>medical workers</u> can protect themselves from radiation too.

# Warm-Up and Exam Questions

There's no point in skimming through the section and glancing over the questions. Do the warm-up questions and go back over any bits you don't know. Then try the exam questions — without cheating.

## Warm-Up Questions

1) How do smoke detectors work?
2) Why is nuclear radiation dangerous?
3) Which type of radiation is most dangerous inside the body — alpha particles or beta particles?
4) Describe two precautions that should be taken when handling radioactive sources in the lab.
5) Give one way in which people who work with radiation can be protected from it.

## Exam Questions

1   Which of the following is not a use of gamma radiation?  Circle the correct answer.

| treatment of cancer | smoke detectors | sterilising machines | medical tracers |

*(1 mark)*

2   Nuclear radiation has many uses within medicine.

(a)   Suggest **two** reasons why alpha sources aren't used as medical tracers.

*(2 marks)*

(b)   Suggest **one** reason why it is important that radioactive sources used in hospital sterilising machines have a long half-life.

*(1 mark)*

(c)   Explain why the dose of radiation given in radiotherapy is directed only at the tumour.

*(1 mark)*

3   Nuclear radiation can have harmful effects on the human body.

(a)   Briefly explain how a low dose of nuclear radiation can cause cancer.

*(2 marks)*

(b)   Describe what can happen to the body if it receives a very high dose of nuclear radiation.

*(1 mark)*

4   A sample of a highly ionising radioactive gas has a half-life of two minutes.

(a)   Describe what is meant by the term 'half-life'.

*(1 mark)*

(b)   The sample contains a number of unstable atoms.
Calculate the fraction of these atoms that will be present after four minutes.

*(1 mark)*

(c)   A worker holds a sample of the gas in a container using tongs.
Suggest **two** other ways she could protect herself against exposure to radiation from the gas.

*(2 marks)*

# Nuclear Fission

Unstable isotopes aren't just good for medicine — with the right set-up you can generate some serious energy.  Read on for how we can use that energy in power stations...

## Nuclear fission — the splitting up of big atomic nuclei

1) Nuclear power stations generate electricity using nuclear reactors.

2) In a nuclear reactor, a controlled chain reaction takes place in which atomic nuclei split up and release energy in the form of heat.  This heat is then simply used to heat water to make steam, which is used to drive a steam turbine connected to an electricity generator.

3) The "fuel" that's split is usually uranium-235, though sometimes it's plutonium-239 (or both).

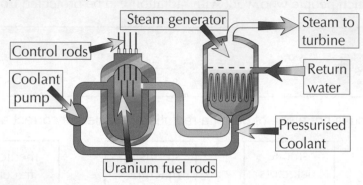

## The chain reactions:

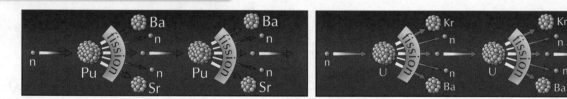

1) For nuclear fission to happen, a slow moving neutron must be absorbed into a uranium or plutonium nucleus.  This addition of a neutron makes the nucleus unstable, causing it to split.

2) Each time a uranium or plutonium nucleus splits up, it spits out two or three neutrons, one of which might hit another nucleus, causing it to split also, and thus keeping the chain reaction going.

3) When a large atom splits in two it will form two new smaller nuclei.  These new nuclei are usually radioactive because they have the "wrong" number of neutrons in them.

4) A nucleus splitting (called a fission) gives out a lot of energy — lots more energy than you get from any chemical reaction.  Nuclear processes release much more energy than chemical processes do.  That's why nuclear bombs are so much more powerful than ordinary bombs (which rely on chemical reactions).

5) The main problem with nuclear power is with the disposal of waste.  The products left over after nuclear fission are highly radioactive, so they can't just be thrown away.  They're very difficult and expensive to dispose of safely.

6) Nuclear fuel is cheap but the overall cost of nuclear power is high due to the cost of the power plant and final decommissioning.  Dismantling a nuclear plant safely takes decades.

7) Nuclear power also carries the risk of radiation leaks from the plant or a major catastrophe like Chernobyl.

# Nuclear Fusion

Scientists have been looking into producing energy the same way stars do — through <u>fusion</u>.

## Nuclear fusion — the *joining* of small atomic nuclei

1) Two <u>light nuclei</u> (e.g. hydrogen) can <u>join</u> to create a larger nucleus — this is called <u>nuclear fusion</u>.

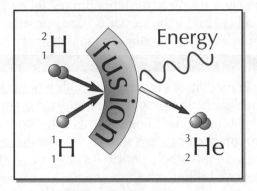

$^2_1$H  fusion  Energy

$^1_1$H  $^3_2$He

2) Fusion releases <u>a lot</u> of energy (<u>more</u> than fission for a given mass) — all the energy released in <u>stars</u> comes from fusion (see next page). So people are trying to develop <u>fusion reactors</u> to generate <u>electricity</u>.

3) Fusion <u>doesn't</u> leave behind a lot of radioactive <u>waste</u> like fission, and there's <u>plenty</u> of hydrogen knocking about to use as <u>fuel</u>.

4) The <u>big problem</u> is that fusion can only happen at <u>really high temperatures</u> — about <u>10 000 000 °C</u>.

5) You can't hold the hydrogen at the <u>high temperatures</u> and <u>pressures</u> required for fusion in an ordinary container — you need an <u>extremely strong magnetic field</u>.

6) There are a few <u>experimental</u> reactors around, but none of them are generating electricity yet. At the moment it takes <u>more power</u> to get up to temperature than the reactor can <u>produce</u>.

## Ten million degrees — that's hot...

It'd be great if we could get nuclear fusion to work — there's loads of fuel available and it doesn't create much radioactive waste compared with fission. It's a shame that at the moment we need to use more energy to create the conditions for fusion than we can get out of it. Make sure you know the <u>pros</u> and <u>cons</u> of fission and fusion.

# The Life Cycle of Stars

Stars go through <u>many traumatic stages</u> in their lives — just like teenagers.

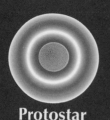

**Protostar**

1) Stars <u>initially form</u> from <u>clouds of DUST AND GAS</u>. The <u>force of gravity</u> makes the gas and dust <u>spiral in together</u> to form a <u>protostar</u>.

2) <u>Gravitational energy</u> is converted into <u>heat energy</u>, so the <u>temperature rises</u>. When the temperature gets <u>high enough</u>, <u>hydrogen nuclei</u> undergo <u>nuclear fusion</u> to form <u>helium nuclei</u> and give out massive amounts of <u>heat and light</u>. A star is born. Smaller masses of gas and dust may also pull together to make <u>planets</u> that orbit the star.

**Main Sequence Star**

3) The star immediately enters a <u>long stable period</u>, where the <u>heat created</u> by the nuclear fusion provides an <u>outward pressure</u> to <u>balance</u> the <u>force of gravity</u> pulling everything <u>inwards</u>. The star maintains its energy output for <u>millions of years</u> due to the <u>massive amounts of hydrogen</u> it consumes. In this <u>stable</u> period it's called a <u>MAIN SEQUENCE STAR</u> and it lasts <u>several billion years</u>. (The Sun is in the middle of this stable period — or to put it another way, the <u>Earth</u> has already had <u>half its innings</u> before the Sun <u>engulfs</u> it!)

**Stars much bigger than the Sun**

**Stars about the same size as the Sun**

4) Eventually the <u>hydrogen</u> begins to <u>run out</u>. <u>Heavier elements</u> such as iron are made by nuclear fusion of <u>helium</u>. The star then <u>swells</u> into a <u>RED GIANT</u>, if it's a small star, or a <u>RED SUPER GIANT</u> if it's a big star. It becomes <u>red</u> because the surface <u>cools</u>.

**Red Giant**

**Red Super Giant**

**White Dwarf**

5) A <u>small-to-medium</u>-sized star like the Sun then becomes unstable and <u>ejects</u> its <u>outer layer</u> of <u>dust and gas</u> as a <u>PLANETARY NEBULA</u>.

6) This leaves behind a hot, dense solid core — a <u>WHITE DWARF</u>, which just cools down to a <u>BLACK DWARF</u> and eventually disappears.

**Neutron Star...**

**...or Black Hole**

**Supernova**

7) <u>Big stars</u>, however, start to <u>glow brightly again</u> as they undergo more <u>fusion</u> and <u>expand and contract several times</u>, forming elements as <u>heavy as iron</u> in various <u>nuclear reactions</u>. Eventually they <u>explode</u> in a <u>SUPERNOVA</u>, forming elements <u>heavier than iron</u> and ejecting them into the universe to <u>form new planets and stars</u>.

8) The <u>exploding supernova</u> throws the outer layers of <u>dust and gas</u> into space, leaving a <u>very dense core</u> called a <u>NEUTRON STAR</u>. If the star is <u>big enough</u> this will become a <u>BLACK HOLE</u>.

## Only big stars become black holes

The early universe contained <u>only hydrogen</u>, the simplest and lightest element. It's only thanks to nuclear fusion inside stars that we have any of the other <u>naturally occurring elements</u>. Remember — the heaviest element produced in stable stars is iron, but it takes a <u>supernova</u> (or a lab) to create <u>the rest</u>.

# Warm-Up and Exam Questions

The end of another section — they just go far too quickly. Make sure you've understood it all by doing these questions (and the revision summary on the next page) before you whizz on to the next section.

## Warm-Up Questions

1) Name two elements often used as nuclear fuel.
2) What does nuclear fission produce in addition to energy? Why is this a problem?
3) What are stars formed from?
4) Will our Sun become a black hole? Explain your answer.
5) At the end of its main sequence phase, what does a small star become?

## Exam Questions

1   Nuclear reactors often use uranium-235.

(a) Describe how a chain reaction is set up in a nuclear reactor.

*(4 marks)*

(b) Describe how the heat energy released by nuclear fission is used to generate electricity.

*(2 marks)*

2   The table shows some information about various elements and isotopes.

| Element/isotope | Deuterium | Hydrogen | Krypton | Plutonium | Thorium | Tin |
|---|---|---|---|---|---|---|
| Relative mass | 2 | 1 | 84 | 239 | 232 | 119 |

(a) Name the **two** substances in the table that would be most likely to be used in a fusion reaction.

*(2 marks)*

(b) Explain why scientists are interested in developing fusion power.

*(2 marks)*

(c) Explain why fusion is not used to generate electricity at present.

*(1 mark)*

3   Stars go through many stages in their lives.

(a) Describe how a star is formed.

*(3 marks)*

(b) The stable period of a main sequence star can last millions of years.
Explain why main sequence stars undergo a stable period.

*(2 marks)*

(c) When main sequence stars begin to run out of hydrogen in their core, they swell and become either a red giant or a super red giant depending on their size.

(i)  Describe what happens to small stars after their red giant phase.

*(3 marks)*

(ii) Describe what happens to big stars after their super red giant phase.

*(3 marks)*

# Revision Summary for Physics 2b

There's some pretty heavy physics in this section. But just take it one page at a time and it's really not so bad. You're even allowed to go back through the pages for a sneaky peak if you get stuck on any of the questions below...

1)* An AC supply of electricity has a time period of 0.08 s. What is its frequency?

2)  Name the three wires in a three-core cable.

3)  Sketch and label a properly wired three-pin plug.

4)  Explain fully how a fuse and earth wire work together.

5)  How does an RCCB stop you from getting electrocuted?

6)* Which uses more energy, a 45 W pair of hair straighteners used for 5 minutes, or a 105 W hair dryer used for 2 minutes?

7)* Find the appropriate fuse (3 A, 5 A or 13 A) for these appliances:
    a) a toaster rated at 230 V, 1100 W        b) an electric heater rated at 230 V, 2000 W

8)* Calculate the energy transformed by a torch using a 6 V battery when 530 C of charge pass through.

9)  Explain how the experiments of Rutherford and Marsden led to the nuclear model of the atom.

10) Draw a table stating the relative mass and charge of the three basic subatomic particles.

11) True or false: radioactive decay can be triggered by certain chemical reactions?

12) What type of subatomic particle is a beta particle?

13) Sketch the paths of an alpha particle and a beta particle travelling through an electric field.

14) List two places where the level of background radiation is increased and explain why.

15) Name three occupations that have an increased risk of exposure to radiation.

16) What is the definition of half-life?

17) Give an example of how gamma radiation can be used in medicine.

18) Which is the most dangerous form of radiation if you eat it? Why?

19) Draw a diagram to illustrate the fission of uranium-235 and explain how the chain reaction works.

20) What is the main environmental problem associated with nuclear power?

21) What is nuclear fusion? Why is it difficult to construct a working fusion reactor?

22) Describe the steps that lead to the formation of a main sequence star (like our Sun).

# X-rays in Medicine

X-rays are <u>ionising</u> and can damage living cells (see p.131), but they can be very useful if <u>handled carefully</u>.

## X-ray images are used in hospitals for medical diagnosis

1) <u>X-rays</u> are <u>high frequency</u>, <u>short wavelength electromagnetic waves</u> (see p.62).
   Their wavelength is roughly the same size as the <u>diameter of an atom</u>.

2) They are <u>transmitted</u> by (pass through)
   <u>healthy tissue</u>, but are absorbed by
   <u>denser materials</u> like <u>bones</u> and <u>metal</u>.

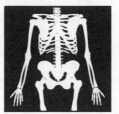

*The brighter bits are where fewer X-rays get through. This is a negative image. The plate starts off all white.*

3) They affect <u>photographic</u> film in the same way as <u>light</u>,
   which means they can be used to take photographs.

4) <u>X-ray photographs</u> can be used to diagnose many medical conditions such
   as <u>bone fractures</u> or <u>dental problems</u> (problems with your teeth).

5) X-ray images can be formed <u>electronically</u> using <u>charge-coupled devices</u> (CCDs).
   CCDs are <u>silicon chips</u> about the size of a postage stamp, divided up into a grid of millions
   of identical <u>pixels</u>.  CCDs detect X-rays and produce <u>electronic signals</u> which are used to
   form <u>high resolution</u> images.  The same technology is used to take photographs in <u>digital cameras</u>.

## CT scans use X-rays

<u>Computerised axial tomography</u> (CT) scans use X-rays to
produce <u>high resolution images</u> of soft and hard tissue.

The patient is put inside the cylindrical
scanner, and an X-ray beam is fired through
the body from an <u>X-ray tube</u> and picked up by
<u>detectors</u> on the opposite side.  The X-ray tube
and detectors are <u>rotated</u> during the scan.

A computer interprets the signals from the
detectors to form an image of a <u>two-dimensional
slice</u> through the body.  Multiple two-dimensional
CT scans can be put together to make a <u>three-
dimensional image</u> of the inside of the body.

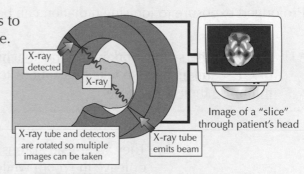

X-ray detected

X-ray

X-ray tube and detectors are rotated so multiple images can be taken

X-ray tube emits beam

Image of a "slice" through patient's head

*Soft tissue can absorb a small amount of X-ray radiation.  CT scans use lots of X-rays (more than normal X-ray photographs) to distinguish between the tiny variations in tissue density.*

## X-rays — short wavelength electromagnetic waves

X-rays were actually discovered by accident by German physicist Wilhem Röntgen in 1895.
Wilhem didn't just discover this amazingly useful type of radiation — he also discovered that they
could be used to produce an image of the bones in his own hand if it got in the way of the X-ray beam.

# X-rays in Medicine

X-rays aren't only useful to doctors as a method of medical imaging —
they can also be used as a <u>treatment</u> for illnesses like <u>cancer</u>.

## *X-rays can be used to* **treat cancer**

X-rays can cause <u>ionisation</u> — high doses of X-rays will <u>kill living cells</u>.
They can therefore be used to <u>treat cancers</u>, just like gamma radiation (see p.130).
The X-rays have to be <u>carefully focused</u> and at just the right <u>dosage</u> to
kill the <u>cancer cells</u> without damaging too many <u>normal cells</u>.

TO TREAT CANCER:

1) The X-rays are <u>focused</u> on the tumour
   using a <u>wide beam</u>.

2) This beam is <u>rotated</u> round the patient
   with the tumour at the centre.

3) This <u>minimises</u> the exposure of <u>normal cells</u>
   to radiation, and so <u>reduces</u> the chances of
   damaging the rest of the body.

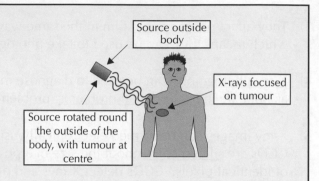

## *Radiographers take* **precautions** *to* **minimise radiation dose**

Prolonged exposure to ionising radiation can be very dangerous to your health.

1) <u>Radiographers</u> who work with <u>X-ray machines</u>
   or <u>CT scanners</u> need to take precautions to
   <u>minimise</u> their <u>X-ray dose</u>.

2) They wear <u>lead aprons</u>, stand behind a <u>lead screen</u>,
   or <u>leave the room</u> while scans are being done.

3) Lead is used to <u>shield</u> areas of the patient's body
   that aren't being scanned, and the <u>exposure time</u> to
   the X-rays is always kept to an absolute minimum.

## *Ionising radiation can be used to treat cancer*

As well as having lead aprons and screens to stand behind, radiographers wear special <u>badges</u>
that record the amount of radiation they are exposed to. This means that their <u>radiation dose</u>
can be <u>monitored</u> and <u>regulated</u>, so that changes can be made if they are being put in danger.

# Ultrasound

There's sound, and then there's <u>ultrasound</u>.

## *Ultrasound is sound with a higher frequency than we can hear*

Electrical systems can be made which produce <u>electrical oscillations</u> of <u>any frequency</u>.
These can easily be converted into <u>mechanical vibrations</u> to produce <u>sound</u> waves of a <u>higher frequency than the upper limit of human hearing</u> (the range of human hearing is 20 to 20 000 Hz).
This is called <u>ultrasound</u>.

## *Ultrasound waves get partially reflected at a boundary between media*

1) When a wave passes from one medium into another, <u>some</u> of the wave is <u>reflected</u> off the boundary between the two media, and some is transmitted (and refracted).  This is <u>partial reflection</u>.

2) What this means is that you can point a pulse of ultrasound at an object, and wherever there are <u>boundaries</u> between one substance and another, some of the ultrasound gets <u>reflected back</u>.

3) The time it takes for the reflections to reach a <u>detector</u> can be used to measure <u>how far away</u> the boundary is.

4) This is how <u>ultrasound imaging</u> works (see p.143).

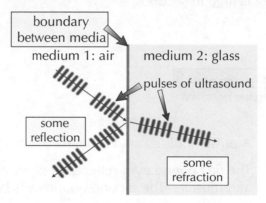

## *Ultrasound waves can be used in medicine*

<u>Ultrasound</u> has a variety of uses in medicine, from investigating <u>blood flow</u> in organs, to diagnosing <u>heart problems</u>, to checking on <u>fetal development</u>.  The examples below are two of the <u>most common</u>.

### *Breaking down kidney stones*

<u>Kidney stones</u> are <u>hard masses</u> that can <u>block</u> the <u>urinary tract</u>.  An ultrasound beam concentrates <u>high-energy waves</u> at the kidney stone and turns it into <u>sand-like particles</u>.
These particles then pass out of the body in the <u>urine</u>.  It's a good method because the patient <u>doesn't need surgery</u> and it's relatively <u>painless</u>.

### *Pre-natal scanning of a fetus*

<u>Ultrasound waves</u> can pass through the body, but whenever they reach a <u>boundary</u> between <u>two different media</u> (like fluid in the womb and the skin of the fetus) some of the wave is <u>reflected back</u> and <u>detected</u> (see p.142).  The exact <u>timing and distribution</u> of these <u>echoes</u> are <u>processed by a computer</u> to produce a <u>video image</u> of the fetus.

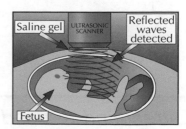

# Ultrasound

This page is all about how ultrasound can be used to <u>calculate distances</u> — which means using the equation that links <u>distance</u>, <u>speed</u> and <u>time</u>. It also means doing some maths, so prepare yourself...

## *You can use **oscilloscope traces** to find boundaries*

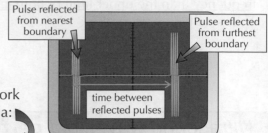

Pulse reflected from nearest boundary

Pulse reflected from furthest boundary

time between reflected pulses

1) The oscilloscope trace below shows an ultrasound pulse reflecting off <u>two separate boundaries</u>.

2) Given the "seconds per division" setting of the oscilloscope (see p.112), you can work out the <u>time</u> between the pulses by measuring on the screen.

3) If you know the <u>speed of sound</u> in the medium, you can work out the <u>distance</u> between the boundaries, using this formula:

s is <u>distance</u> in metres, m.
v is <u>speed</u> in metres per second, m/s.
t is <u>time</u> in seconds, s.

$$s = v \times t$$

### *Example:*

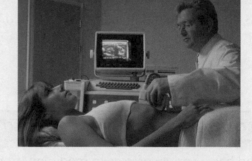

A pulse of ultrasound is beamed into a patient's abdomen.

The first boundary it reflects off is between fat and muscle. The second boundary is between muscle and a body cavity.

An oscilloscope trace shows that the <u>time between the reflected pulses</u> is <u>10 μs</u>.

The ultrasound travels at a <u>speed</u> of <u>1500 m/s</u>.

Calculate the <u>distance</u> between the fat/muscle boundary and the muscle/cavity boundary.

*1 μs = 0.000001 s*

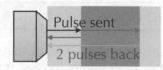

Pulse sent

2 pulses back

So, you'll need to find the distance using s = v × t.

BUT, the reflected pulses have travelled <u>there and back</u>, so the distance you calculate will be <u>twice the distance between boundaries</u> (think about it).

s = v × t = 1500 × 0.00001 = 0.015 m.

So the distance between boundaries = 0.015 ÷ 2 = 0.0075 m = <u>7.5 mm</u>.

## *Ultrasound — used for the imaging of soft tissue*

It's crazy to think that you can use sound waves to make a image — but that's the basis of ultrasound scanning. And it all comes down to simple reflection and distance = speed × time.

# Medical Imaging

## *Medical imaging is full of compromises*

Doctors have to make a <u>compromises</u> between getting a <u>good enough</u> image to be able to diagnose problems, whilst putting the patient at <u>as low a risk</u> as possible. X-ray and ultrasound imaging both have their advantages and disadvantages...

---

<u>IS IT SAFE?</u>

1) Ultrasound waves are <u>non-ionising</u> and, as far as anyone can tell, <u>safe</u>.

2) X-rays are <u>ionising</u>. They can cause <u>cancer</u> if you're exposed to too high a dose, and are definitely <u>NOT</u> safe to use on developing babies (see p.131).

3) CT scans use a lot <u>more X-ray radiation</u> than standard X-ray photographs, so the patient is exposed to <u>even more</u> ionising radiation. Generally CT scans aren't taken unless they are really needed because of the <u>increased radiation dose</u>.

---

<u>WHAT ABOUT IMAGE QUALITY?</u>

1) Ultrasound images are typically <u>fuzzy</u> — which can make it harder to diagnose some conditions using these images.

2) X-ray photographs produce <u>clear images</u> of <u>bones</u> and <u>metal</u>, but not a lot else.

3) CT scans produce <u>detailed</u> images and can be used to diagnose <u>complicated</u> illnesses, as the <u>high resolution</u> images can make it easier to work out the problem. High quality 3D images can also be used in the <u>planning of complicated surgery</u>.

---

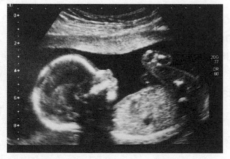

*Ultrasound scans are safe for the fetus, but they do give a fuzzy image.*

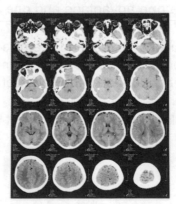

*CT scans of the brain are very detailed and clear.*

---

## *You need to match the medical imaging technique to the problem*

It's important that you're able to compare and contrast the different imaging techniques. Sit down with a pen and paper and write yourself a <u>mini essay</u> all about medical imaging and all the <u>advantages</u> and <u>disadvantages</u> that doctors have to consider when deciding which technique to use.

# Warm-Up and Exam Questions

There's a knack to passing exams — applying all the facts you've got stored in your brain to get as many marks as possible. These exam questions will help you to practise that.

## Warm-Up Questions

1) What are X-ray photographs typically used to diagnose?
2) What type of radiation is used to take CT scans?
3) What property of X-rays makes them a suitable cancer treatment?
4) How can parts of a patient's body not being scanned be protected during an X-ray procedure?
5) What is partial reflection? Why is it important for ultrasound scanning?
6) Give two medical uses of ultrasound.

## Exam Questions

1   Jamie has an X-ray taken to see if he has broken his arm.

   (a)   Explain why X-rays are not very useful for looking at soft tissue injuries.

*(1 mark)*

   (b)   X-ray images can be formed using a charge-coupled device (CCD).

      (i)   Explain how a CCD forms an image.

*(3 marks)*

      (ii)   Suggest **one** reason why CCDs are increasingly being used in medical imaging.

*(1 mark)*

   (c)   Give **two** ways in which radiographers can minimise their exposure to X-rays.

*(2 marks)*

2   Ultrasound is used to produce an image of a fetus in pre-natal scans.

   (a)   Give **one** advantage and **one** disadvantage of using ultrasound for pre-natal scans.

*(2 marks)*

   (b)   A pulse of ultrasound is emitted and returns two signals with a time difference of 20 μs between them. Calculate the distance between the two boundaries if the speed of sound through tissue is 1550 m/s.

*(3 marks)*

   (c)   Explain why X-rays would not be used for prenatal scans.

*(2 marks)*

3   CT scans are typically used to diagnose head injuries.

   (a)   Explain why CT scans are particularly suited to medical imaging of the head.

*(2 marks)*

   (b)   Explain why doctors should avoid performing multiple CT scans on a patient.

*(2 marks)*

# Refractive Index

You might remember <u>refraction</u> from when you did Physics 1b (see p.60). Here it is again in a bit more depth.

## *Refraction is caused by the* **waves changing speed**

<u>Refraction</u> is when waves <u>change direction</u> as they <u>enter a different medium</u>.  This is caused by the change in density from one medium to the other — which <u>changes the speed</u> of the waves.

1)  When waves <u>slow down</u> they bend <u>towards</u> the normal.

2)  When <u>light</u> enters <u>glass</u> or plastic it <u>slows down</u> — to about <u>2/3</u> of its speed in <u>air</u>.

3)  If a wave hits a <u>boundary</u> at 90° (i.e. along the <u>normal</u>) it will <u>not change direction</u> — but it'll still slow down.

4)  When light hits a <u>different medium</u> (e.g. plastic or glass) <u>some</u> of the light will <u>pass through</u> the new medium but some will be <u>reflected</u> — it all depends on the <u>angle of incidence</u> (the angle it hits the medium).

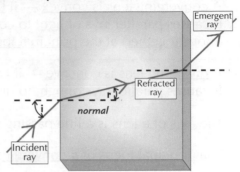

## *Every transparent material has a* **refractive index**

1)  <u>Refractive index</u> of a medium is the <u>ratio</u> of speed of light in a vacuum to speed of light in that medium.

2)  The <u>angle of incidence</u>, i, <u>angle of refraction</u>, r, and <u>refractive index</u>, n, are all <u>linked</u>.

3)  When an <u>incident ray</u> passes from air into another material, the angle of <u>refraction</u> of the ray depends on the <u>refractive index</u> of the material:

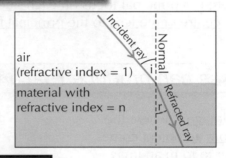

$$\text{refractive index (n)} = \frac{\sin i}{\sin r}$$

*Most of the time, we can assume that the refractive index of air = 1.*

4)  So if you know any two of n, i or r, you can work out the missing one.

### Example 1

Jacob does an experiment to find out the refractive index of jelly. He finds that when the angle of incidence for a light beam travelling into jelly is <u>42°</u>, the angle of refraction is <u>35°</u>.  What is the <u>refractive index</u> of this particular type of jelly?

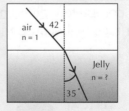

$$n = \frac{\sin i}{\sin r} \qquad \begin{array}{l} \sin i = \sin 42 = 0.67 \\ \sin r = \sin 35 = 0.57 \end{array} \implies \text{so } n_{jelly} = \frac{0.67}{0.57} = \underline{1.18}$$

### Example 2

A beam of light travels from air into water (refractive index <u>n = 1.33</u>).  The angle of incidence is <u>23°</u>. Calculate the angle of refraction to the nearest degree.

$$\sin r = \frac{\sin i}{n} = \frac{\sin 23}{1.33} = 0.29 \implies \text{so } r = \sin^{-1}(0.29) = \underline{17°}$$

# Lenses and Images

This bit is about <u>how light acts</u> when it hits a <u>lens</u>. Be ready for lots of diagrams on the next few pages.

## *Different lenses* produce *different* kinds of *image*

Lenses form images by <u>refracting</u> light and changing its direction. There are <u>two main types</u> of lens — <u>converging</u> and <u>diverging</u>. They have different shapes and have <u>opposite effects</u> on light rays.

1) A <u>converging</u> lens is <u>convex</u> — it <u>bulges outwards</u>. It causes parallel rays of <u>light</u> to converge (move <u>together</u>) at the <u>principal focus</u>.

2) A <u>diverging</u> lens is <u>concave</u> — it <u>caves inwards</u>. It causes parallel rays of <u>light</u> to diverge (<u>spread out</u>).

3) The <u>axis</u> of a lens is a line passing through the <u>middle</u> of the lens.

4) The <u>principal focus</u> of a <u>converging lens</u> is where rays hitting the lens parallel to the axis all <u>meet</u>.

5) The <u>principal focus</u> of a <u>diverging lens</u> is the point where rays hitting the lens parallel to the axis <u>appear</u> to all <u>come from</u> — you can trace them back until they all appear to <u>meet up</u> at a point behind the lens.

6) There is a principal focus on <u>each side</u> of the lens. The <u>distance</u> from the <u>centre of the lens</u> to the <u>principal focus</u> is called the <u>focal length</u>.

## *Lenses can produce* real *and* virtual *images*

A <u>real image</u> is where the <u>light from an object</u> comes together to form an <u>image on a 'screen'</u> — like the image formed on an eye's <u>retina</u> (the 'screen' at the back of an <u>eye</u>).

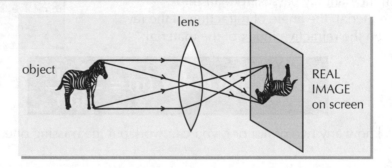

A <u>virtual image</u> is when the rays are diverging, so the light from the object <u>appears</u> to be coming from a completely <u>different place</u>. When you look in a <u>mirror</u> (see p.59) you see a <u>virtual image</u> of your face — because the <u>object</u> (your face) <u>appears</u> to be <u>behind the mirror</u>.

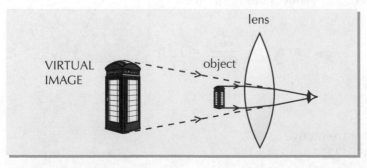

You can get a virtual image when looking at an object through a <u>magnifying lens</u> (see p.149) — the virtual image looks <u>bigger</u> than the object <u>actually</u> is.

To describe an image properly, you need to say <u>3 things</u>:

1) <u>How big it is</u> compared to the object.

2) Whether it's <u>upright or inverted</u> (upside down) relative to the object.

3) Whether it's <u>real or virtual</u>.

# Converging Lenses

You might have to draw a ray diagram of refraction through a lens.
Follow the instructions very carefully.

## There are **three rules** for refraction in a **converging lens**

1) An incident ray <u>parallel to the axis</u> refracts through the lens
   and passes through the <u>principal focus</u> on the other side.

2) An incident ray passing <u>through the principal focus</u>
   refracts through the lens and travels <u>parallel to the axis</u>.

3) An incident ray passing through the <u>centre</u> of the lens carries on in the <u>same direction</u>.

*The neat thing about these rules is that they allow you to draw ray diagrams without
bending the rays as they go into the lens and as they leave the lens. You can draw the
diagrams as if each ray only changes direction once, in the middle of the lens.*

## Draw a **ray diagram** for an **image** through a **converging lens**

1) Pick a point on the <u>top</u> of the object. Draw a ray going
   from the object to the lens <u>parallel</u> to the axis of the lens.

2) Draw another ray from the <u>top</u> of the object
   going right through the <u>middle</u> of the lens.

3) The incident ray that's <u>parallel</u> to the axis is
   <u>refracted</u> through the <u>principal focus</u> (F). Draw a
   <u>refracted ray</u> passing through the <u>principal focus</u>.

4) The ray passing through the <u>middle</u>
   of the lens doesn't bend.

5) Mark where the rays <u>meet</u>. That's the <u>top of the image</u>.

6) Repeat the process for a point on the bottom of the
   object. When the bottom of the object is on the
   <u>axis</u>, the bottom of the image is <u>also</u> on the axis.

*In ray diagrams,
this represents a
convex lens.*

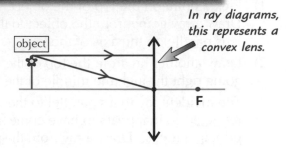

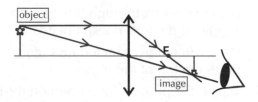

*If you really want to draw a third incident ray passing through the principal focus
on the way to the lens, you can (refract it so that it goes parallel to the axis).
In the exam, you can get away with two rays, so no need to bother with three.*

## **Distance** from the lens affects the **image**

1) An object <u>at 2F</u> will
   produce a <u>real</u>, <u>inverted</u>
   (upside down) image
   the <u>same size</u> as the
   object, and <u>at 2F</u>.

2) <u>Between F and 2F</u> it'll
   make a <u>real</u>, <u>inverted</u>
   image <u>bigger</u> than the
   object, and <u>beyond 2F</u>.

3) An object <u>nearer than F</u>
   will make a <u>virtual</u> image
   the <u>right way up</u>, <u>bigger</u>
   than the object, on the
   <u>same side</u> of the lens.

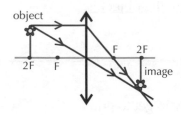

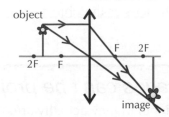

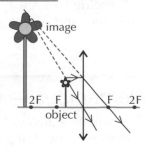

# Diverging Lenses

This page is all about drawing <u>ray diagrams</u> for <u>diverging lenses</u>.

## There are **three rules** for refraction in a **diverging lens**

1) An incident ray <u>parallel to the axis</u> refracts through the lens, and travels in line with the <u>principal focus</u> (so it appears to have come from the principal focus).

2) An incident ray passing through the lens <u>towards the principal focus</u> refracts through the lens and travels <u>parallel to the axis</u>.

3) An incident ray passing through the <u>centre</u> of the lens carries on in the <u>same direction</u>.

## Draw a **ray diagram** for an **image** through a **diverging lens**

1) Pick a point on the <u>top</u> of the object. Draw a ray going from the object to the lens <u>parallel</u> to the axis of the lens.

2) Draw another ray from the <u>top</u> of the object going right through the <u>middle</u> of the lens.

3) The incident ray that's <u>parallel</u> to the axis is <u>refracted</u> so it appears to have come from the <u>principal focus</u>. Draw a <u>ray</u> from the principal focus. Make it <u>dotted</u> before it reaches the lens.

4) The ray passing through the <u>middle</u> of the lens doesn't bend.

5) Mark where the refracted rays <u>meet</u>. That's the top of the image.

6) Repeat the process for a point on the bottom of the object. When the bottom of the object is on the <u>axis</u>, the bottom of the image is <u>also</u> on the axis.

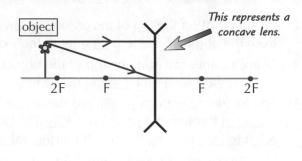

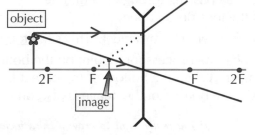

*Again, if you really want to draw a third incident ray in the direction of the principal focus on the far side of the lens, you can. Remember to refract it so that it goes parallel to the axis. In the exam, you can get away with two rays. Choose whichever two are easiest to draw — don't try to draw a ray that won't actually pass through the lens.*

## The **image** is always **virtual**

A diverging lens always produces a <u>virtual image</u>. The image is <u>right way up</u>, <u>smaller</u> than the object and on the <u>same side of the lens as the object</u> — <u>no matter where the object is</u>.

---

## *Remember — virtual images can't be projected*

Ray diagrams always look a lot scarier than they actually are. The best way to get to grips with them is by doing them, so get busy practising. Make sure you know how the distance between the object and a lens, and the type of lens, affects the image produced.

# Magnification and Power

Converging lenses are used in magnifying glasses and in cameras.

## Magnifying glasses use converging lenses

Magnifying glasses work by creating a magnified virtual image (see p.146).

1) The object being magnified must be closer to the lens than the focal length.

2) Since the image produced is a virtual image, the light rays don't actually come from the place where the image appears to be.

3) Remember "you can't project a virtual image onto a screen" — that's a useful phrase to use in the exam if they ask you about virtual images.

## Learn the magnification formula

You can use the magnification formula to work out the magnification produced by a lens at a given distance:

$$\text{Magnification} = \frac{\text{image height}}{\text{object height}}$$

> EXAMPLE: A coin with diameter 14 mm is placed a certain distance behind a magnifying lens. The virtual image produced has a diameter of 35 mm. What is the magnification of the lens at this distance?
>
> ANSWER: magnification = 35 ÷ 14 = **2.5**

In the exam you might have to draw a ray diagram to show where an image would be, and then measure the image so that you can work out the magnification of the lens or mirror. Another reason to draw those ray diagrams carefully.

## A powerful lens has a short focal length

1) Focal length is related to the power of the lens. The more powerful the lens, the more strongly it converges rays of light, so the shorter the focal length (see p.146).

2) The power of a lens is given by the formula:

$$\text{Power (D)} = \frac{1}{\text{Focal length (m)}} \qquad P = \frac{1}{f}$$

E.g. for a lens with focal length f = 0.2 m, power = 1 ÷ 0.2 = 5 D.
(D stands for dioptres, the unit for lens power.)

3) For a converging lens, the power is positive. For a diverging lens, the power is negative.

4) The focal length of a lens is determined by two factors:

> a) the refractive index of the lens material,
> b) the curvature of the two surfaces of the lens.

5) To make a more powerful lens from a certain material like glass, you just have to make it with more strongly curved surfaces.

6) For a given focal length, the greater the refractive index of the material used to make the lens, the flatter the lens will be.

7) This means powerful lenses can be made thinner by using materials with high refractive indexes (see p.145).

# Warm-Up and Exam Questions

Lots of questions on lenses here.  Go on, answer them, you know you want to...

## Warm-Up Questions

1) Name the two main types of lens.
2) Of the two types of lens, which bulges outwards at the centre and which curves inwards?
3) Of the two types of lens, which always creates a virtual image
   and which can create both real and virtual images?
4) Of the two types of lens, which has a negative power?
5) State the magnification formula.

## Exam Questions

1   (a)   Edward is trying to start a campfire by focussing sunlight through his spectacle lens
          onto the firewood.  The lens is diverging.  Explain why he cannot focus the sunlight
          onto the wood using this lens.

                                                                                    *(2 marks)*

    (b)   Edward finds a slug and uses a magnifying glass to look at it.

          (i)   Complete the ray diagram below to show how the image of the slug is formed.

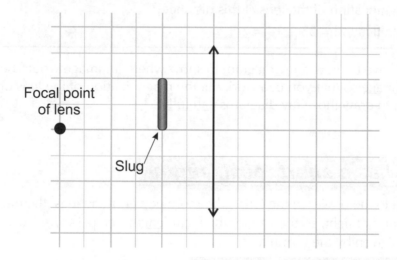

                                                                                    *(3 marks)*

          (ii)  Calculate the magnification of the lens for the slug at this distance.

                                                                                    *(2 marks)*

2   A lens maker is producing lenses with a focal length of 0.3 m.

    (a)   Calculate the power of the lenses.

                                                                                    *(2 marks)*

    (b)   The lens maker wants to start using a material with a higher refractive index.
          If he keeps the size and shape of the lenses the same, describe how the focal
          length and power of the new lenses will change with the new material.

                                                                                    *(2 marks)*

# The Eye

## You need to know the **basic structure of the eye**

1) The <u>cornea</u> is a transparent 'window' with a <u>convex shape</u>, and a <u>high refractive index</u>. The cornea does most of the eye's <u>focusing</u>.

2) The <u>iris</u> is the <u>coloured</u> part of the eye. It's made up of muscles that <u>control</u> the size of the <u>pupil</u> — the hole in the middle of the iris. This <u>controls</u> the <u>intensity of light</u> entering the eye.

3) The <u>lens</u> changes shape to focus light from objects at <u>varying distances</u>. It's connected to the <u>ciliary muscles</u> by the <u>suspensory ligaments</u> and when the ciliary muscles <u>contract</u>, tension is released and the lens takes on a <u>fat</u>, more <u>spherical shape</u>. When they relax, the <u>suspensory ligaments</u> pull the lens into a thinner, <u>flatter shape</u>.

4) Images are formed on the <u>retina</u>, which is covered in <u>light-sensitive cells</u>. These cells <u>detect light</u> and send signals to the <u>brain</u> to be interpreted.

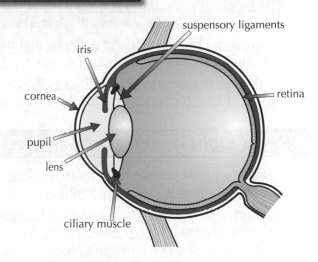

## A **camera** forms images in a similar way to the eye

When you take a <u>photograph</u> of a flower, light from the object (flower) travels to the camera and is <u>refracted</u> by the lens, forming an <u>image</u> on the film.

- The image on the film is a <u>real image</u> because light rays actually meet there.
- The image is <u>smaller</u> than the object, because the object's a lot <u>further away</u> than the <u>focal length</u> of the lens.
- The image is <u>inverted</u> (see p.146).

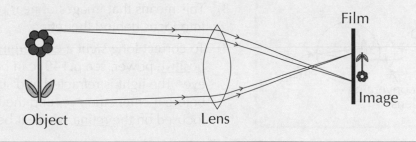

The <u>same</u> thing happens in our <u>eye</u> — a <u>real, inverted image</u> forms on the <u>retina</u>. Our very clever brains <u>flip</u> the image so that we see it right way up.

The <u>film</u> in a camera, or the <u>CCD</u> in a digital camera, are the <u>equivalent</u> of the <u>retina</u> in the eye — they all detect the light focused on them and record it.

## The eye — your window on the world

The <u>light-sensitive cells</u> in the retina at the back of the eye send signals to the brain depending on the <u>amount</u> and <u>colour</u> of the light they've been exposed to. Then your <u>brain</u> works out all the different signals, forms an image, puts the image the right way up and figures out what it is.

# Correcting Vision

## The **eye** can **focus** on objects between the **near** and **far points**

1) The <u>far point</u> is the <u>furthest distance</u> that the eye can focus <u>comfortably</u>. For normally-sighted people, that's <u>infinity</u>.

2) The <u>near point</u> is the <u>closest distance</u> that the eye can focus on. For adults, the near point is approximately <u>25 cm</u>.

3) As the eye focuses on <u>closer objects</u>, its <u>power increases</u> — the lens <u>changes shape</u> and the <u>focal length decreases</u>. But the distance between the lens and the image <u>stays the same</u>.

## **Short sight** is corrected with **diverging lenses**

1) Short-sighted people can't focus on <u>distant objects</u> — their <u>far point is closer than infinity</u>.

2) Short sight is caused by the <u>eyeball being too long</u>, or by the <u>cornea</u> and <u>lens system</u> being too <u>powerful</u> — this means the eye lens <u>can't produce</u> a focused image on the <u>retina</u> where it is supposed to.

3) Images of distant objects are brought into focus <u>in front of</u> the retina instead.

4) To <u>correct</u> short sight you need to put a <u>diverging lens</u> (with a <u>negative</u> power, see p.149) in front of the eye. This diverges light <u>before</u> it enters the eye, which means the lens can focus it on the retina.

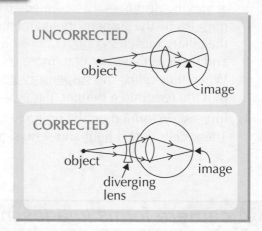

## **Long sight** is corrected with **converging lenses**

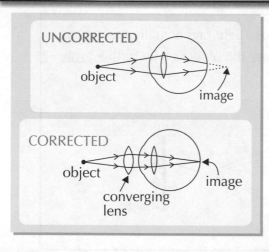

1) Long-sighted people can't focus clearly on <u>near objects</u> — their <u>near point</u> is <u>further away than normal</u> (25 cm or more).

2) Long sight happens when the <u>cornea and lens are too weak</u> or the <u>eyeball is too short</u>.

3) This means that images of <u>near objects</u> are brought into focus <u>behind the retina</u>.

4) To correct long sight a <u>converging</u> lens (with a <u>positive</u> power, see p.149) can be put in front of the eye. The light is refracted and starts to converge before it enters the eye, and the image can be focused on the <u>retina</u> where it belongs.

## **Lasers** are used to **surgically correct eye problems**

A laser is an <u>narrow, intense beam</u> of <u>light</u>.
The light waves that come from a laser all have the same <u>wavelength</u>.

1) Lasers can be used in surgery to <u>cut through body tissue</u>, instead of using a scalpel.

2) Lasers <u>cauterise</u> (burn and seal shut) small <u>blood vessels</u> as they cut through the tissue. This <u>reduces</u> the amount of <u>blood</u> the patient loses and helps to protect against <u>infection</u>.

3) Lasers are used to treat <u>skin conditions</u> such as <u>acne scars</u>. Lasers can be used to <u>burn off</u> the top layers of <u>scarred skin</u> revealing the less-scarred lower layers.

4) One of the most common types of laser surgery is <u>eye surgery</u>. A laser can be used to <u>vaporise</u> some of the cornea to change its <u>shape</u> — which changes its <u>focusing ability</u>. This can <u>increase</u> or <u>decrease</u> the <u>power</u> of the cornea so that the eye can focus images properly on the <u>retina</u>.

# Total Internal Reflection

Total internal reflection is a really clever bit of physics that has loads of uses
— medicine is just one of them.

## *Light can be sent along **optical fibres** using **total internal reflection***

1) Optical fibres can carry visible light over long distances.

2) They work by bouncing waves off the sides of a thin inner core of glass or plastic. The wave enters one end of the fibre and is reflected repeatedly until it emerges at the other end.

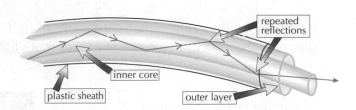

*Remember, angle of reflection, r, equals the angle of incidence, i.*

3) Optical fibres work because of total internal reflection.

4) Total internal reflection can only happen when a wave travels through a dense substance like glass or water towards a less dense substance like air.

5) It all depends on whether the angle of incidence is bigger than the critical angle.

---

If the angle of incidence (i) is...

*The angle of incidence (i) and the angle of reflection (r) are always measured from the normal (a line at right angles to the surface).*

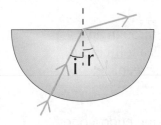

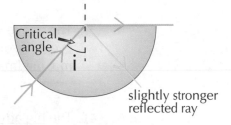

slightly stronger reflected ray

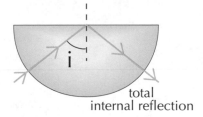

total internal reflection

...LESS than Critical Angle:-
Most of the light passes out but a little bit of it is internally reflected.

...EQUAL to Critical Angle:-
The emerging ray comes out along the surface. There's quite a bit of internal reflection.

...GREATER than Critical Angle:-
No light comes out. It's all internally reflected, i.e. total internal reflection.

---

## *Remember — the critical angle is measured from the normal*

The glass in optical fibres has to be of very high quality — otherwise some of the light could be absorbed each time it is reflected. This might not affect the signal much if it's only reflected a few times, but over hundreds of miles it can have a big effect on the signal quality.

# Total Internal Reflection

## The value of the **critical angle** depends on the **refractive index**

1) A <u>dense material</u> with a <u>high refractive index</u> (see p.145) has a <u>low critical angle</u>.

2) If a material has a high refractive index, it will <u>totally internally reflect more light</u> — more light will be incident at an angle <u>bigger</u> than the critical angle.

3) For example, the critical angle of <u>glass</u> is around 42°, but for <u>diamond</u> the critical angle is just 24°, so <u>more light</u> is totally internally reflected — which is why diamonds are so <u>sparkly</u>.

4) Refractive index and critical angle (c) are related by <u>this formula</u>:

$$\text{Refractive index} = \frac{1}{\sin c}$$

## **Endoscopes** use bundles of **optical fibres**

1) An <u>endoscope</u> is a thin tube containing <u>optical fibres</u> that lets surgeons examine <u>inside</u> the body.

2) Endoscopes consist of <u>two bundles</u> of optical fibres — one to carry <u>light</u> to the area of interest and one to carry an <u>image</u> back so that it can be viewed.

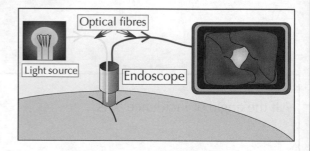

Optical fibres

Light source

Endoscope

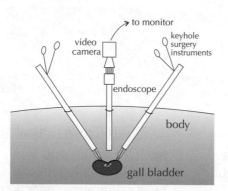

to monitor

video camera

keyhole surgery instruments

endoscope

body

gall bladder

3) The <u>image</u> can be seen through an <u>eyepiece</u> or displayed as a <u>full-colour moving image</u> on a TV screen.

4) The <u>big advantage</u> of using endoscopes is that surgeons can now perform many <u>operations</u> by only cutting <u>tiny holes</u> in people — this is called <u>keyhole surgery</u>, and it wasn't possible before optical fibres.

## The smaller the critical angle, the more total internal reflection

Endoscopes aren't just for keyhole surgery — they are a useful <u>diagnostic tool</u>, particularly for problems with the <u>lungs</u>, <u>stomach</u> or <u>intestines</u>. Endoscopes are also commonly used to perform a <u>biopsy</u>. This is when a doctor cuts out a small piece of tissue to <u>test it</u> for diseases (such as cancer). The use of an endoscope <u>removes the need</u> for <u>major surgery</u>, reducing the likelihood of <u>infection</u>.

# Warm-Up and Exam Questions

There were lots of new ideas for you to tackle in that section.  Try these questions and see what has stuck.

## Warm-Up Questions

1) Where are the light sensitive cells in the eye located?
2) Is the image on a camera film real or virtual?
3) What type of lens can be used to correct long sight?
4) Name one application of lasers in medicine.
5) What two conditions are needed for total internal reflection to occur?

## Exam Questions

1   The diagram shows a light ray entering an optical fibre.

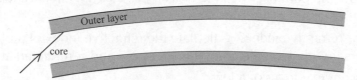

(a)   Complete the diagram to show the path taken by the light ray.

*(1 mark)*

(b)   Explain why the light ray follows this path.

*(1 mark)*

(c)   An optical fibre has a core refractive index of 1.65.
Calculate the critical angle for light sent through this optical fibre.

*(2 marks)*

2   The diagram on the right shows the different parts of the eye.

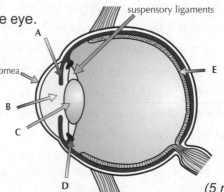

(a)   For each of the following parts of the eye, give the
corresponding letter, A-E, from the diagram:

   (i)   retina

   (ii)   lens

   (iii)   iris

   (iv)   pupil

   (v)   ciliary muscle

*(5 marks)*

(b)   Describe how the eye focuses on objects at various distances.

*(3 marks)*

(c)   The cornea forms part of the eye's focusing system.

   (i)   What eye condition can be caused by the cornea being too powerful?

*(1 mark)*

   (ii)   Suggest **two** ways in which this eye condition can be corrected.

*(2 marks)*

(d)   The eye can focus between the near and far points.
Describe what is meant by the near point.

*(1 mark)*

# Revision Summary for Physics 3a

Another section conquered — congratulations. Now all you need to do is just answer a few more questions to see how much you've learnt. I bet it's loads.

1) What are X-rays? Name two materials X-rays are absorbed by.
2) What is a charge-coupled device?
3) How do CT scans form images of the body?
4) Describe how X-rays can be used to treat cancer.
5) What is ultrasound?
6) * Ultrasound travels through fat at a velocity of 1000 m/s. A pulse of ultrasound is sent into a person and is partially reflected off a layer of fat and a layer of muscle. The time between two reflected pulses of ultrasound is 0.00004 s. How thick is the layer of fat?
7) Explain why ultrasound waves rather than X-rays are used to take images of a fetus.
8) What are the advantages of using CT scans over ultrasound scans?
9) What is refraction?
10) Draw a diagram to show the path of a ray of light as it passes from air → block of glass → air, meeting the block of glass at an angle.
11)*What is the formula for refractive index? Calculate the refractive index of a block of clear plastic if a beam of light enters it with an angle of incidence of 27° and is refracted at an angle of 18°.
12) What is meant by the principal focus of a lens?
13) Draw a ray diagram for light from a distant object being focused by a converging lens. What type of image is formed?
14) What type of lenses are used to make magnifying glasses?
15)*Peter measures the length of a seed to be 1.5 cm. When he looks at the seed through a converging lens at a certain distance, the seed appears to have a length of 4.5 cm. What is the magnification of this lens at this distance?
16)*What is the power of a lens with focal length of 10 cm?
17) What two things affect the focal length of a lens?
18) Draw a labelled diagram of the eye. Describe how the eye forms a focused image on the retina.
19) What is the far point of vision?
20) Give an approximate value of the near point for adults.
21) Describe two causes of short sight. How can short sight be corrected using lenses?
22) Describe two causes of long sight. How can long sight be corrected using lenses?
23) Describe how lasers can be used to correct vision problems.
24) a) What is total internal reflection?
    b) What happens if the angle of incidence is less than the critical angle?
    c) What happens if it is more than the critical angle?
25) a) What is an endoscope?
    b) Explain how an endoscope uses total internal reflection.
    c) Name one medical technique made possible by endoscopy.

# Turning Forces and Centre of Mass

Turning forces — all about spanners and levers. You should have a good idea about calculating moments, pivots and centres of mass by the time you've finished these pages.

## A *moment* is the *turning effect* of a force

The <u>size</u> of the <u>moment</u> of the force is given by:

**MOMENT = FORCE ×** **perpendicular DISTANCE from the line of action of the force to the pivot**

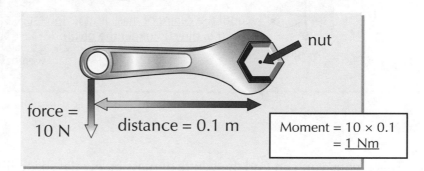

*Moment of the force in newton-metres (Nm).* → **M = F × d** ← *Distance in metres (m).*

*Force in newtons (N).*

1) The <u>force</u> on the spanner causes a <u>turning effect</u> or <u>moment</u> on the nut (which acts as pivot). A <u>larger</u> force would mean a <u>larger</u> moment.

nut

force = 10 N

distance = 0.1 m

Moment = 10 × 0.1
= <u>1 Nm</u>

2) Using a longer spanner, the same force can exert a <u>larger</u> moment because the <u>distance</u> from the pivot is <u>greater</u>.

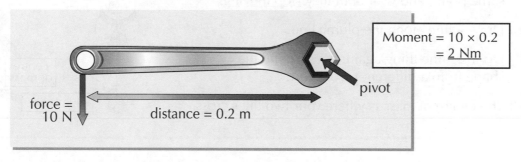

Moment = 10 × 0.2
= <u>2 Nm</u>

pivot

force = 10 N

distance = 0.2 m

3) To get the <u>maximum</u> moment (or turning effect) you need to push at <u>right angles</u> (<u>perpendicular</u>) to the spanner.

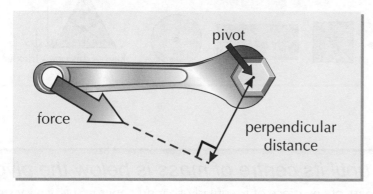

pivot

force

perpendicular distance

4) Pushing at <u>any other angle</u> means a smaller moment because the <u>perpendicular</u> distance between the line of action and the pivot is <u>smaller</u>.

# Turning Forces and Centre of Mass

## *The centre of mass hangs **directly below** the **point of suspension***

1) You can think of the <u>centre of mass</u> of an object as the point at which the <u>whole</u> mass is concentrated.

2) A freely suspended object will <u>swing</u> until its centre of mass is <u>vertically below</u> the <u>point of suspension</u>.

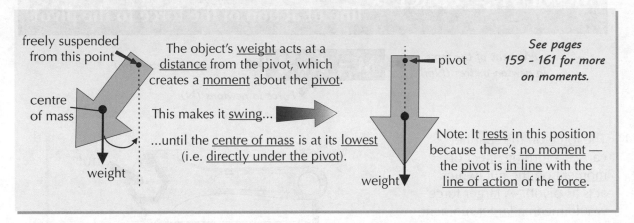

freely suspended from this point

centre of mass

weight

The object's <u>weight</u> acts at a <u>distance</u> from the pivot, which creates a <u>moment</u> about the <u>pivot</u>.

This makes it <u>swing</u>...

...until the <u>centre of mass</u> is at its <u>lowest</u> (i.e. <u>directly under the pivot</u>).

pivot

weight

*See pages 159 - 161 for more on moments.*

Note: It <u>rests</u> in this position because there's <u>no moment</u> — the <u>pivot</u> is <u>in line</u> with the <u>line of action</u> of the <u>force</u>.

3) This means you can find the <u>centre of mass</u> of any flat shape like this:

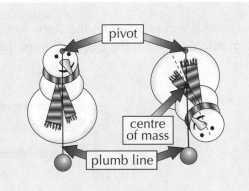

a) Suspend the shape and a <u>plumb line</u> from the same point, and wait until they <u>stop moving</u>.

b) <u>Draw</u> a line along the plumb line.

c) Do the same thing again, but suspend the shape from a <u>different</u> pivot point.

d) The centre of mass is where your two lines <u>cross</u>.

pivot

centre of mass

plumb line

4) But you don't need to go to all that trouble for <u>symmetrical</u> shapes. You can quickly guess where the centre of mass is by looking for <u>lines of symmetry</u>.

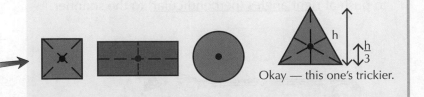

h

$\frac{h}{3}$

Okay — this one's trickier.

## *A suspended object swings until its centre of mass is below the pivot*

So there you go, how to find the centre of mass of any piece of irregularly-shaped paper in a few easy steps — why not practise finding it for lots of different shapes. Coming up next, some more about moments.

# Balanced Moments and Levers

Once you can calculate moments, you can work out if a <u>seesaw is balanced</u>. Useful thing, physics.

## A question of **balance** — are the **moments equal**?

If the <u>anticlockwise moments</u> are equal to the <u>clockwise moments</u>, the object <u>won't turn</u>.

### Example 1

Your younger brother weighs 300 N and sits 2 m from the pivot of a seesaw.
If you weigh 700 N, where should you sit to balance the seesaw?

For the seesaw to <u>balance</u>:

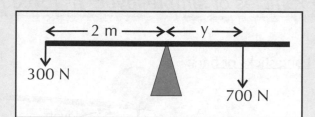

**Total Anticlockwise Moments = Total Clockwise Moments**

anticlockwise moment = clockwise moment
$300 \times 2 = 700 \times y$
$y = \underline{0.86\ m}$

*Ignore the weight of the seesaw —
its centre of mass is on the pivot,
so it doesn't have a turning effect.*

### Example 2

A 6 m long steel girder weighing 1000 N rests horizontally on a pole 1 m from one end.
What is the tension in a supporting cable attached vertically to the other end?

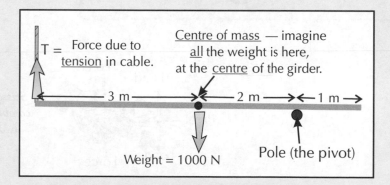

The '<u>tension in the cable</u>' bit makes it sound harder than it actually is.
But the girder's <u>weight</u> is <u>balanced</u> by the tension <u>force</u> in the cable, so...

anticlockwise moment  =  clockwise moment
(due to weight)           (due to tension in cable)

$1000 \times 2 = T \times 5$

$2000 = 5T$

and so $\underline{T = 400\ N}$

# Balanced Moments and Levers

You'll find examples of different kinds of levers all around you — <u>door handles</u> for example.
Levers help make it <u>easier</u> for you to do stuff by <u>multiplying</u> the <u>force</u> you apply.

## *Simple levers use balanced moments*

<u>Levers</u> use the idea of <u>balanced moments</u> to make it <u>easier</u> for us <u>to do work</u> (e.g. <u>lift</u> an object):

1)  The <u>moment needed to do work</u> = <u>force x distance from the pivot</u> (see page 157).  So the
    <u>amount of force</u> needed to do work <u>depends</u> on the <u>distance</u> the <u>force</u> is applied from the <u>pivot</u>.

2)  Levers <u>increase</u> the <u>distance</u> from the pivot at which the <u>force</u> is applied
    — so this means <u>less force</u> is needed to get the <u>same moment</u>.

3)  That's why levers are known as <u>force multipliers</u> — they <u>reduce</u> the amount of
    <u>force</u> that's needed to get the <u>same moment</u> by <u>increasing</u> the distance.

## *Examples of simple levers as force multipliers*

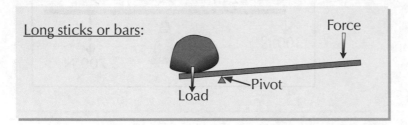
Long sticks or bars:

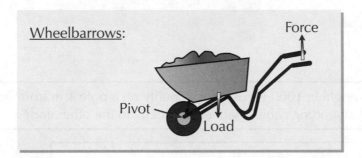
Wheelbarrows:

Scissors:

*Scissors use a combination of two levers.*

These levers make it <u>easier</u> to do <u>work</u> by moving the
<u>distance</u> the <u>force</u> is applied <u>further</u> from the pivot.

## *Get the same moment by applying less force further from the pivot*

Think of the extra force you need to open a door by pushing it <u>near the hinge</u> compared to <u>at the handle</u>
— the <u>distance from pivot</u> is <u>less</u>, so you need <u>more force</u> to get the <u>same moment</u>.  The best way to
understand it is to do <u>loads of practice</u>.  And learn the examples of some <u>simple levers</u> from above too.

# Moments and Stability

We've already met situations where total clockwise moments are <u>balanced</u> by total anticlockwise moments (see page 159) — but what happens if that isn't the case...

## *If the **moments acting** on an **object aren't equal** the object will **turn***

### If the Total <u>Anticlockwise</u> Moments <u>do not equal</u> the Total <u>Clockwise</u> Moments, there will be a <u>Resultant Moment</u>

...so the object will turn.

## *Low and wide objects are most stable*

<u>Unstable</u> objects tip over easily — <u>stable</u> ones don't.
The position of the centre of mass (p.158) is <u>all-important</u>.

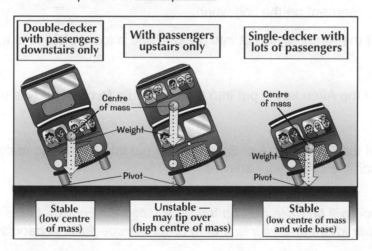

1) The most <u>stable</u> objects have a <u>wide base</u> and a <u>low centre of mass</u>.

2) An object will begin to <u>tip over</u> if its centre of mass moves <u>beyond</u> the edge of its base.

3) Again, it's because of <u>moments</u> — if the <u>line</u> of action of the <u>weight</u> of the object lies <u>outside</u> of the <u>base</u> of the object, it'll cause a <u>resultant moment</u>. This will <u>tip</u> the object over.

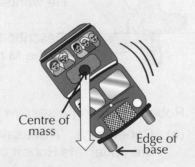

4) Lots of objects are specially designed to give them <u>as much stability</u> as possible. For example, a Bunsen burner has a <u>wide</u>, <u>heavy</u> base to give it a <u>low</u> centre of mass — this makes it harder to knock over.

---

*You can often tell just by looking what will tip easily and what won't*

<u>Learn</u> the factors that make an object hard to tip over — a <u>low centre of mass</u> and a <u>wide base</u>.

# Warm-Up and Exam Questions

Now, to wake you up, some nice warm-up questions followed by a trio of delightful exam style questions. If anything doesn't seem perfectly familiar, go back and read the relevant pages again.

## Warm-Up Questions

1) How do you calculate the moment of a force around a pivot?
2) What unit is used to describe the moment of a force?
3) What is meant by the centre of mass of an object?
4) What happens to an object if the clockwise and anticlockwise moments on it are not equal?
5) Why will an object begin to tip over if its centre of mass moves beyond the edge of its base?

## Exam Questions

1   Bolts are often secured using an Allen key, as shown in the diagram. One end of the Allen key is put into the bolt and the other is turned to tighten the bolt.

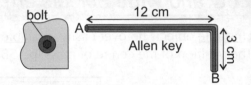

(a)   Calculate the moment on the bolt when:

    (i)   End A of the Allen key is put into the bolt and a force of 15 N is applied to end B.

*(2 marks)*

    (ii)   End B of the Allen key is put into the bolt and a force of 15 N is applied to end A.

*(2 marks)*

(b)   Which end of the Allen key (A or B) should be put into the bolt to make it easier to tighten the bolt? Explain your answer.

*(2 marks)*

2   *In this question you will be assessed on the quality of your English, the organisation of your ideas and your use of appropriate specialist vocabulary.*

Maurice has made a window decoration, as shown in the diagram. He wants to attach a string to it so that it hangs with the M the right way up.

Describe the method Maurice should use to find out where to place the string so the M hangs the right way up.

*(6 marks)*

3   Robert is making a seesaw from a plank and a pivot.

(a)   Robert says, "A seesaw will only balance if the masses on either side of the pivot are equal." Is Robert correct? Explain your answer.

*(2 marks)*

(b)   Robert rests the plank on a pivot as shown in the diagram below. End B is supported by a cord so that the plank is horizontal. The plank weighs 50 N.

Calculate the tension in the cord.

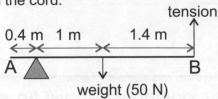

*(3 marks)*

# Pendulums

Hear the word pendulum, and you might think of <u>hypnotists</u> swinging their watches back and forth. But pendulums crop up in <u>lots of places</u> — there are some examples on this page. But first, some theory about the <u>swing</u> of a pendulum.

## *The **time** for one **pendulum swing** depends on its **length***

1) A simple <u>pendulum</u> is made by suspending a <u>weight</u> from a piece of <u>string</u>. When you pull back a pendulum and let it go, it will <u>swing</u> back and forth.

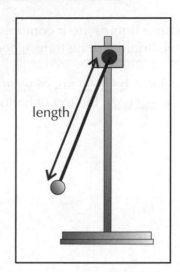
length

2) The time taken for the pendulum to swing from one side to the other and back again is called the <u>time period</u>.

3) The time period for <u>each swing</u> of a given pendulum is the always the <u>same</u> — this is what makes pendulums perfect for <u>keeping time</u> in clocks.

4) The time period can be calculated using this <u>formula</u>:

$$\text{Time period} = \frac{1}{\text{Frequency}}$$

$$T = \frac{1}{f}$$

*Where:*
*T = the period time in seconds (s)*
*f = frequency of the pendulum in hertz (Hz)*

5) The time period of a pendulum depends on its <u>length</u>. The <u>longer</u> the pendulum, the <u>greater</u> the time period. So the <u>shorter</u> the length, the <u>shorter</u> the time period.

6) As well as being using in old-style clocks, pendulums have many other (more fun) uses. For example, playground <u>swings</u> are pendulums. Any <u>fairground rides</u> that swing you back and forth are pendulums too.

## *The time for one swing of a pendulum depends on its length*

The formula above isn't too tricky to use — just make sure you're happy with how to <u>rearrange</u> it. And don't forget that the <u>longer</u> the <u>length</u> of the pendulum, the <u>longer</u> the <u>time period</u> of its swing will be.

# Hydraulics

The word hydraulics sounds a <u>little</u> scary, but it's not all that bad really.
It's just about how we can use the <u>properties of liquids</u> to our advantage.

## *Liquids* are virtually *incompressible*

1) <u>Liquids</u> are virtually <u>incompressible</u> — you can't <u>squash</u>
them, their <u>volume</u> and <u>density</u> stay the <u>same</u>.

*See page 19 for more on liquids.*

2) Because liquids are incompressible and can <u>flow</u>, a <u>force</u> applied to one point
in the liquid will be <u>transmitted</u> (passed) to <u>other points</u> in the liquid.

3) Imagine a <u>balloon</u> full of <u>water</u> with a <u>few holes</u> in it.
If you <u>squeeze</u> the <u>top</u> of balloon, the water will <u>squirt</u> out of the holes.

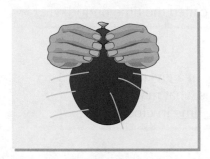

4) This shows that <u>force applied</u> to the <u>water</u> at the <u>top</u> of the
balloon is transmitted to the <u>water</u> in <u>other parts</u> of the balloon.

5) This also shows that <u>pressure</u> can be <u>transmitted</u> throughout a liquid.

<u>Pressure</u> in a liquid is <u>transmitted</u>
<u>equally</u> in <u>all directions</u>

*Pressure and force are linked —
see formula below.*

## *Pressure* is the *force per unit area*

$$\text{Pressure} = \frac{\text{Force}}{\text{Cross-sectional Area}}$$

newtons (N)
metres² (m²)
pascals (Pa)

## *Pressure can be transmitted through a liquid...*

...which turns out to be very useful, as you'll see on the next page. Make sure you're happy with the
formula above, and learn the correct units for pressure, force and cross-sectional area too.

# Hydraulics

Time to put the formula $P = F \div A$ (see previous page) to good use...

## The **pressure** in **liquids** can be used in **hydraulic systems**

1) Hydraulic systems are used as <u>force multipliers</u> — they use a <u>small force</u> to produce a <u>bigger force</u>. They do this using <u>liquid</u> and a sneaky trick with <u>cross-sectional areas</u>.

2) The diagram below shows a <u>simple hydraulic system</u>.

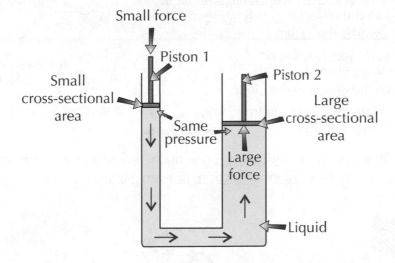

3) The system has <u>two pistons</u>, one with a <u>smaller cross-sectional area</u> than the other. Pressure is transmitted <u>equally</u> through a liquid — so the pressure at <u>both</u> pistons is the <u>same</u>.

4) <u>Pressure = force ÷ area</u>, so at the <u>1st</u> piston, a pressure is exerted on the liquid using a <u>small force</u> over a <u>small area</u>. This pressure is <u>transmitted</u> to the <u>2nd</u> piston.

5) The <u>2nd</u> piston has a <u>larger area</u>, and so as <u>force = pressure × area</u>, there will be a <u>larger force</u>.

6) Hydraulic systems are used in all sorts of things, e.g. <u>car braking</u> systems, hydraulic <u>car jacks</u>, <u>manufacturing</u> and deployment of <u>landing gear</u> on some aircraft.

### Example

To the right is a diagram showing a simple hydraulic system. A force of 15 N is applied to the first piston which has a cross-sectional area of 0.0005 m².

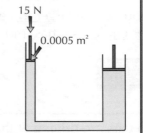

a) Calculate the pressure created on the first piston.

b) Calculate the force acting on the second piston if its cross-sectional area is 0.0012 m².

<u>ANSWER</u>:  a)   $P = F \div A = 15 \div 0.0005 = $ <u>30 000 Pa</u> (or 30 000 N/m²)

b)   Pressure at first piston = pressure at second piston, so
$F = P \times A = 30\,000 \times 0.0012 = $ <u>36 N</u>

# Circular Motion

If it wasn't for <u>circular</u> motion our little planet would just be wandering aimlessly around the universe. And as soon as you launched a <u>satellite</u>, it'd just go flying off into space. Hardly ideal.

## Circular motion — *velocity* is *constantly changing*

1) <u>Velocity</u> is both the <u>speed</u> and <u>direction</u> of an object (p.72).

2) If an object is travelling in a circle it is <u>constantly changing direction</u>. This means its <u>velocity</u> is <u>constantly changing</u> (but not its speed) — so the object is <u>accelerating</u> (p.73). This acceleration is <u>towards</u> the <u>centre</u> of the circle.

3) There must be a <u>resultant force</u> acting on the object causing this acceleration (p.79). This force acts towards the <u>centre</u> of the circle.

4) This force that keeps something moving in a circle is called a <u>centripetal force</u>.

*Pronounced sen-tree-pee-tal*

The object's acceleration changes the direction of motion but not the speed.

The force causing the acceleration is always towards the centre of the circle.

In the exam, you could be asked to say <u>which force</u> is actually providing the centripetal force in a given situation. It can be <u>tension</u>, or <u>friction</u>, or even <u>gravity</u>.

<u>A car going round a bend</u>:
1) Imagine the bend is part of a <u>circle</u> — the centripetal force is towards the <u>centre</u> of the circle.
2) The force is from <u>friction</u> between the car's tyres and the road.

<u>A bucket whirling round on a rope</u>:
The centripetal force comes from <u>tension in the rope</u>. Break the rope, and the bucket flies off at a tangent.

<u>A spinning fairground ride</u>:
The centripetal force comes from <u>tension</u> in the <u>spokes of the ride</u>.

## Centripetal force depends on *mass*, *speed* and *radius*

1) The <u>faster</u> an object's moving, the <u>bigger</u> the centripetal force has to be to keep it moving in a <u>circle</u>.

2) The <u>larger</u> the <u>mass</u> of the object, the <u>bigger</u> the centripetal force has to be to keep it moving in a <u>circle</u>.

3) And you need a <u>larger force</u> to keep something moving in a <u>smaller circle</u> — it has 'more turning' to do.

### Example

Two cars are driving at the same speed around the same circular track. One has a mass of 900 kg, the other has a mass of 1200 kg. Which car has the larger centripetal force?

The <u>three things</u> that mean you need a <u>bigger centripetal force</u> are:
<u>more speed</u>, <u>more mass</u>, <u>smaller radius</u> of circle.

In this example, the speed and radius of circle are the same — the <u>only difference</u> is the <u>masses</u> of the cars. So you don't need to calculate anything — you can confidently say:

The <u>1200 kg car</u> (the heavier one) must have the <u>larger centripetal force</u>.

# Warm-Up and Exam Questions

You guessed it — it's time again to see if you've learnt all the stuff from the last few pages. See how you get on with these questions — and don't forget to go back and re-read anything you struggle with.

## Warm-Up Questions

1) Give the formula that links time period and frequency for a pendulum.
2) What would happen to the time period of a pendulum if you shortened its length?
3) Give one use of hydraulic systems.
4) Why are hydraulic systems called force multipliers?
5) What's the general name for a force that keeps an object moving in a circle?

## Exam Questions

1    A car is driving round a circular track at constant speed.

(a)    Explain why the car is said to be accelerating when its speed is constant.

*(1 mark)*

(b)    The force that keeps the car moving in a circle is known as the centripetal force.
Complete the following sentences.

(i)    The centripetal force acting on the car would be .................................... if the car was travelling at the same constant speed but with three extra passengers in the car.

*(1 mark)*

(ii)    The centripetal force acting on the car would be ................................ if the car was travelling at the same constant speed but on a track with a smaller radius.

*(1 mark)*

2    The diagram below shows a simple hydraulic system containing a liquid.

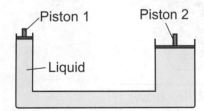

(a)    A force of 175 N is applied to piston 1, which has a cross-sectional area of 0.25 m².
Calculate the pressure created at the first piston.
Write down the equation you use, and then show clearly how you work out your answer.

*(2 marks)*

(b)    Piston 2 has a cross-sectional area of 1.3 m².
Calculate the force acting on piston 2.

*(3 marks)*

# Magnetic Fields

Electric currents can create magnetic fields.  This turns out to be quite useful...

## *Magnetic fields are areas where a magnetic force acts*

There's a proper definition of a magnetic field which you really ought to learn:

A MAGNETIC FIELD is a region where MAGNETIC MATERIALS (like iron and steel) and also WIRES CARRYING CURRENTS experience A FORCE acting on them.

Magnetic fields can be represented by field diagrams.

The arrows on the field lines always point FROM THE NORTH POLE of the magnet TO THE SOUTH POLE.

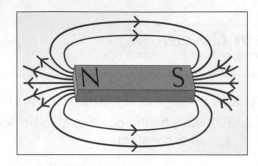

## *The magnetic field round a current-carrying wire*

1) When a current flows through a wire, a magnetic field is created around the wire.

2) The field is made up of concentric circles with the wire in the centre.

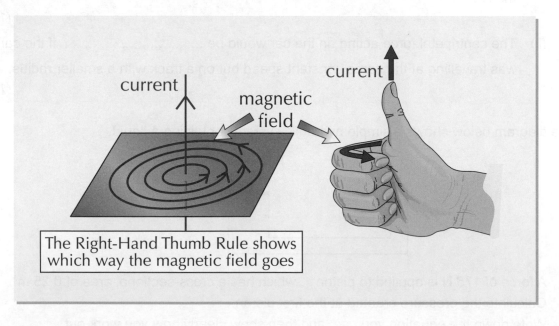

The Right-Hand Thumb Rule shows which way the magnetic field goes

## *Just point your thumb in the direction of the current...*

...and your fingers show the direction of the field.  Remember, it's always your right thumb.  Not your left, but your right thumb.  You'll use your left hand on page 170 though, so it shouldn't feel left out...

# Magnetic Fields

Some strong magnets are a bit like a dog with a stick — once they grab hold of some iron or steel, they're reluctant to give it up. Luckily, there's a way of creating magnets that can be <u>switched on and off</u>.

## *The magnetic field round a **coil** of **wire***

1) The magnetic field <u>inside</u> a coil of wire (a solenoid) is <u>strong</u> and <u>uniform</u>.

2) <u>Outside</u> the coil, the magnetic field is just like the one round a <u>bar magnet</u>.

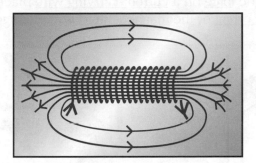

3) You can increase the <u>strength</u> of the magnetic field around a solenoid by adding a <u>magnetically "soft" iron core</u> through the middle of the coil. It's then called an <u>ELECTROMAGNET</u>.

> A <u>magnetically soft</u> material <u>magnetises</u> and <u>demagnetises</u> very easily. So, as soon as you <u>turn off</u> the current through the solenoid, the magnetic field <u>disappears</u> — the iron doesn't stay magnetised. This is what makes it <u>useful</u> for something that needs to be able to <u>switch</u> its magnetism <u>on</u> and <u>off</u> (see below).

## *Electromagnets* are *useful* as their *magnetism* can be *turned off*

An electromagnet must be <u>constantly supplied</u> with current — as that's what produces the <u>magnetic field</u>. So if the current <u>stops</u>, then it <u>stops</u> being magnetic. Magnets you can <u>switch off</u> at your whim can be really <u>useful</u>...

### *Example: **cranes** used for **lifting iron** and **steel***

1) <u>Magnets</u> can be used to <u>attract</u> and <u>pick up</u> things made from <u>magnetic materials</u> like <u>iron</u> and <u>steel</u>.

2) Electromagnets are used in <u>some cranes</u>, e.g. in <u>scrap yards</u> and <u>steel works</u>.

3) If an <u>ordinary magnet</u> was used, the crane would be able to pick up the cars etc., but then <u>wouldn't</u> let it go. Which isn't very helpful.

4) Using an electromagnetic means the magnet can be <u>switched on</u> when you want to and <u>attract</u> and <u>pick stuff up</u>, then <u>switched off</u> when you want to <u>drop it</u>. Which is far <u>more useful</u>.

## *Fields around electromagnets and bar magnets are the same shape*

Electromagnets pop up in lots of different places — they're used in <u>electric bells</u>, <u>car ignition circuits</u> and some <u>security doors</u>. Electromagnets aren't all the same strength though — how <u>strong</u> they are depends on stuff like the number of <u>turns</u> of wire there are and the <u>size</u> of <u>current</u> going through the wire.

# The Motor Effect

Passing an electric current through a wire produces a magnetic field around the wire (p.168).
If you put that wire into a magnetic field, you have <u>two magnetic fields combining</u>, which puts
a force on the wire (generally).

## A *current* in a *magnetic field* experiences a *force*

The <u>force</u> experienced by a <u>current-carrying wire</u> in a <u>magnetic field</u> is known as the <u>motor effect</u>.

The two tests below demonstrate the <u>force</u> on a <u>current-carrying wire</u> placed in a <u>magnetic field</u>.
The <u>force</u> gets <u>bigger</u> if either the <u>current</u> or the <u>magnetic field</u> is made bigger.

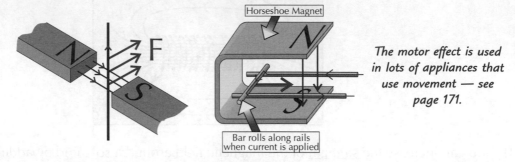

*The motor effect is used in lots of appliances that use movement — see page 171.*

Horseshoe Magnet

Bar rolls along rails when current is applied

1) Note that in <u>both cases</u> the <u>force</u> on the wire is at <u>90°</u> to both the <u>wire</u> and to the <u>magnetic field</u>.
2) If the <u>direction</u> of the <u>current</u> or <u>magnetic field</u> is <u>reversed</u>, then the <u>direction</u> of the <u>force is reversed</u> too. You can always <u>predict</u> which way the <u>force</u> will act using <u>Fleming's left hand rule</u> (see below).
3) To experience the <u>full force</u>, the <u>wire</u> has to be at <u>90°</u> to the <u>magnetic field</u>.
4) If the wire runs <u>along parallel</u> to the <u>magnetic field</u> it won't experience <u>any force at all</u>.
5) At angles in between it'll feel <u>some</u> force.

## *Fleming's left hand rule* tells you *which way* the force acts

1) They could test if you can do this, so <u>practise it</u>.
2) Using your <u>left hand</u>, point your <u>First finger</u> in the direction of the <u>Field</u> and your <u>seCond finger</u> in the direction of the <u>Current</u>.
3) Your <u>thuMb</u> will then point in the direction of the <u>force</u> (Motion).

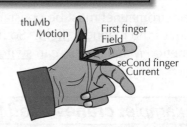

### Example

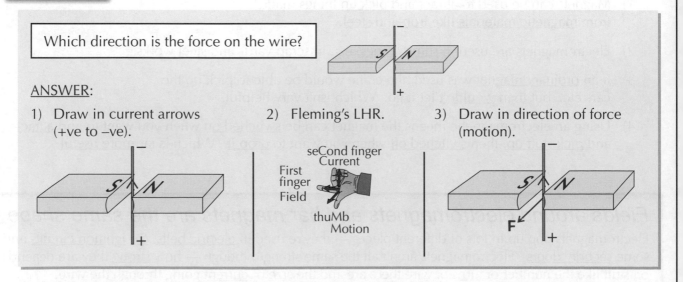

Which direction is the force on the wire?

ANSWER:
1) Draw in current arrows (+ve to –ve).
2) Fleming's LHR.
3) Draw in direction of force (motion).

# The Simple Electric Motor

Electric motors use the motor effect (see previous page) to get them (and keep them) moving. This is one of the favourite exam topics of all time. Read it. Understand it. Learn it. Lecture over.

## The simple **electric motor**

1) The diagram shows the forces acting on the two side arms of the coil of wire.

2) These forces are just the usual forces which act on any current in a magnetic field.

3) Because the coil is on a spindle and the forces act one up and one down, it rotates.

4) The split-ring commutator is a clever way of "swapping the contacts every half turn to keep the motor rotating in the same direction". (Learn that statement because they might ask you.)

5) The direction of the motor can be reversed either by swapping the polarity of the direct current (DC) supply or swapping the magnetic poles over.

6) There are two factors which speed it up:

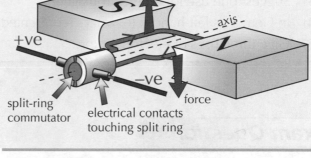

*Direct current is current that only flows in one direction.*

> 1) More <u>CURRENT</u>
> 2) <u>STRONGER MAGNETIC FIELD</u>

## Example

| Is the coil turning clockwise or anticlockwise? |  |
|---|---|

ANSWER:

1) Draw in current arrows (+ve to –ve).

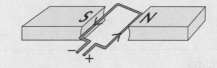

2) Fleming's LHR on one side arm (I've used the right hand arm).

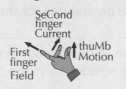

SeCond finger Current
thuMb Motion
First finger Field

3) Draw in direction of force (motion).

So — the coil is turning anticlockwise.

## Electric motors *are used in:* CD players, food mixers, printers...

## ...fan heaters, fans, drills, hair dryers, cement mixers, *etc.*

1) Link the coil to an axle, and the axle spins round.

2) In the diagram there's a fan attached to the axle, but you can stick almost anything on a motor axle and make it spin round.

3) For example, in a food mixer, the axle's attached to a blade or whisks. In a CD player the axle's attached to the bit you sit the CD on. Fan heaters and hair dryers have an electric heater as well as a fan.

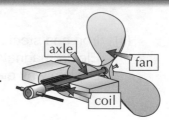

*PHYSICS 3b — FORCES AND ELECTROMAGNETISM*

# Warm-Up and Exam Questions

It's time for another page of questions to check your knowledge retention. If you can do the warm-up questions without breaking into a sweat, then see how you get on with the exam questions below.

## Warm-Up Questions

1) What does the right-hand thumb rule show?
2) Describe the magnetic field around a current-carrying wire.
3) Suggest one use for an electromagnet.
4) In Fleming's left-hand rule, what's represented by the first finger? the second finger? the thumb?
5) Give three uses of electric motors.

## Exam Questions

1    Arnold is making an electromagnet using a current-carrying solenoid and a core.

(a)    Complete the following diagram of the solenoid to show the magnetic field around it.

*(2 marks)*

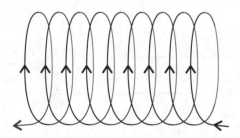

(b)    Suggest a material that would be suitable for the core.

*(1 mark)*

(c)    Arnold uses his electromagnet to pick up some paper clips.
He turns off the current to the solenoid and the paper clips fall.

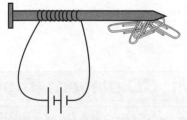

(i)    Explain why the paper clips fall.

*(2 marks)*

(ii)    Iron and steel are magnetic.
Electromagnets are often used in scrap yards to lift iron and steel.
Explain why electromagnets are used, rather than ordinary magnets.

*(1 mark)*

# Exam Questions

2   The diagram below shows an aerial view of a current-carrying wire in a magnetic field.
    The circle represents the wire carrying current out of the page, towards you.

N        ○        S

(a)   Describe the direction of the magnetic field of the magnet.

*(1 mark)*

(b)   On the diagram, draw an arrow to show the direction of the force acting on the
      current-carrying wire.

*(1 mark)*

(c)   Describe what would happen to the force acting on the current-carrying wire if the
      direction of the current was reversed.

*(1 mark)*

(d)   Describe how the size of the force acting on the wire would change if:
      (i)    the wire was at 30° to the magnetic field.

*(1 mark)*

      (ii)   the wire ran parallel to the magnetic field.

*(1 mark)*

3   Julia is designing a toy car with a small electric motor to drive the wheels.
    The diagram shows a simplified version of Julia's motor.

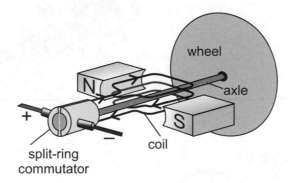

(a)   In which direction will the wheel turn?

*(1 mark)*

(b)   Explain the purpose of the split-ring commutator.

*(1 mark)*

(c)   Julia is testing her car and wants it to go faster.
      Suggest **one** change Julia can make to the motor to make the car go faster.

*(1 mark)*

(d)   Julia wants to make the car able to travel both forwards and backwards.
      Give **one** way she can reverse the direction of the wheels.

*(1 mark)*

# Electromagnetic Induction

Sounds terrifying. Well, sure it's quite mysterious, but it isn't that complicated:

> ## ELECTROMAGNETIC INDUCTION:
> The creation of a POTENTIAL DIFFERENCE
> across a conductor which is experiencing
> a CHANGE IN MAGNETIC FIELD.

*Remember —
potential difference
is just another name
for voltage.*

For some reason they use the word "induction" rather than "creation", but it amounts to the same thing.

## Moving a magnet in a coil of wire induces a voltage

1) Electromagnetic induction means creating a potential difference across the ends of a conductor (e.g. a wire).

   *If the conductor is part of a complete circuit, a current will flow.*

2) You can do this by moving a magnet in a coil of wire or moving an electrical conductor in a magnetic field ("cutting" magnetic field lines). Shifting the magnet from side to side creates a little "blip" of current.

3) Here are a few examples of electromagnetic induction:

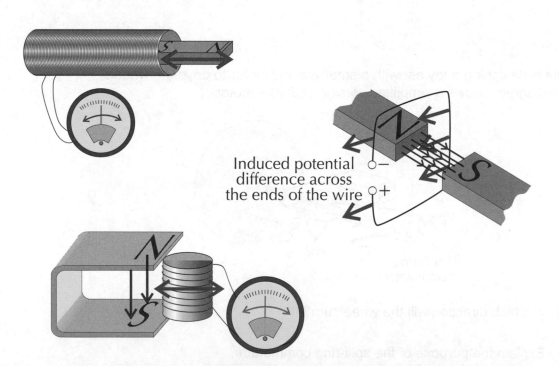

Induced potential difference across the ends of the wire

4) If you move the magnet in the opposite direction, then the potential difference/current will be reversed too. Likewise, if the polarity of the magnet is reversed, then the potential difference/current will be reversed too.

5) If you keep the magnet (or the coil) moving backwards and forwards, you produce a potential difference that keeps swapping direction — and this is how you produce an alternating current (AC) — see p.112.

# Electromagnetic Induction

## A magnet *turning* end to end in a coil also *creates* a *current*

You can also create a potential difference by <u>turning</u> a magnet <u>end to end</u> in a coil, which lasts as long as you spin the magnet.

This is how generators work (see below for an example).

1) As you <u>turn</u> the magnet, the <u>magnetic field</u> through the <u>coil</u> changes — this <u>change</u> in the magnetic field induces a <u>potential difference</u>, which can make a <u>current</u> flow in the wire.

2) When you've turned the magnet through half a turn, the <u>direction</u> of the <u>magnetic field</u> through the coil <u>reverses</u>. When this happens, the <u>potential difference reverses</u>, so the <u>current</u> flows in the <u>opposite direction</u> around the coil of wire.

3) If you keep turning the magnet in the <u>same direction</u> — always clockwise, say — then the potential difference will keep on reversing every half turn and you'll get an <u>AC current</u>.

## Some *appliances* use *electromagnetic induction*

Electromagnetic induction is used by some appliances to generate a <u>current</u>.

### Example: dynamos

1) <u>Dynamos</u> are often used on <u>bikes</u> to power the <u>lights</u>.
2) The <u>cog wheel</u> at the top is positioned so that it <u>touches</u> one of the <u>wheels</u>.
3) As the wheel moves round, it <u>turns</u> the cog which is attached to the <u>magnet</u>.
4) This creates an <u>AC current</u> to power the lights.

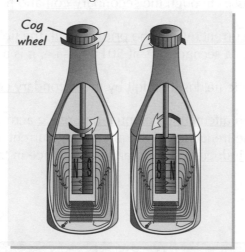

Cog wheel

## *EM induction — works whether the coil or the field is moving*

"Electromagnetic Induction" gets my vote for "Definitely Most Headache Inducing Topic". If it wasn't so important maybe you wouldn't have to bother learning it, but this is how most of our electricity is generated, whether it's in a coal-fired power station or a wind turbine.

# Transformers

Transformers use <u>electromagnetic induction</u> to change potential difference (p.d.).
So they will <u>only</u> work on <u>AC</u>.

## *Transformers change the p.d. — but only AC p.d.*

There are a few different types of transformer. The <u>two</u> you need to know
about are <u>step-up transformers</u> and <u>step-down transformers</u>.

They both have two coils, the <u>primary</u> and the <u>secondary</u>, joined with an <u>iron core</u>.

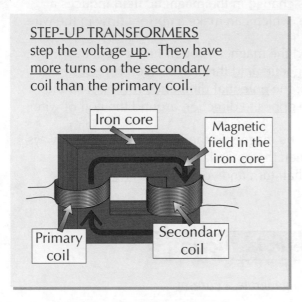

STEP-UP TRANSFORMERS
step the voltage <u>up</u>. They have
<u>more</u> turns on the <u>secondary</u>
coil than the primary coil.

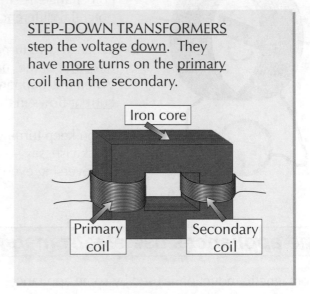

STEP-DOWN TRANSFORMERS
step the voltage <u>down</u>. They
have <u>more</u> turns on the <u>primary</u>
coil than the secondary.

## *Transformers work by **electromagnetic induction***

1)  The primary coil <u>produces a magnetic field</u> which stays <u>within the iron core</u>.
    This means <u>nearly all</u> of it passes through the <u>secondary coil</u> and hardly any is lost.

2)  Because there is <u>alternating current</u> (AC) in the <u>primary coil</u>, the field in the iron core is constantly
    <u>changing direction</u> (100 times a second if it's at 50 Hz) — i.e. it is a <u>changing</u> magnetic field.

3)  This <u>rapidly changing</u> magnetic field is then felt by the <u>secondary coil</u>.

4)  The changing field <u>induces</u> an <u>alternating potential difference</u> across the
    secondary coil (with the same frequency as the alternating current in the
    primary) — <u>electromagnetic induction</u> of a potential difference in fact.

## *The **iron core** carries **magnetic field, not current***

1)  The <u>iron core</u> is purely for transferring the <u>changing magnetic
    field</u> from the primary coil to the secondary.

2)  No <u>electricity</u> flows round the <u>iron core</u>.

# Transformers

Ah, more about transformers. And as per usual, some <u>equations</u> to learn too.

## *Transformers have more turns on one coil than another*

1) The <u>relative number of turns</u> on the two coils determines whether the potential difference induced in the secondary coil is <u>greater</u> or <u>less</u> than the potential difference in the primary.

2) In a <u>step-up transformer</u>, the <u>p.d.</u> across the <u>secondary coil</u> is <u>greater</u> than the p.d. across the <u>primary coil</u>.

3) In a <u>step-down transformer</u>, the <u>p.d.</u> across the <u>secondary coil</u> is <u>less</u> than the p.d. across the <u>primary coil</u>.

4) If you supplied DC to the primary, you'd get <u>nothing</u> out of the secondary at all. Sure, there'd still be a magnetic field in the iron core, but it wouldn't be <u>constantly changing</u>, so there'd be no <u>induction</u> in the secondary because you need a <u>changing field</u> to induce a potential difference. So don't forget it — transformers only work with <u>AC</u>. They won't work with DC <u>at all</u>.

## *The transformer equation — use it either way up*

You can calculate the <u>output</u> potential difference from a transformer if you know the <u>input</u> potential difference and the number of turns on each coil.

$$\frac{\text{Potential Difference across Primary Coil}}{\text{Potential Difference across Secondary Coil}} = \frac{\text{Number of turns on Primary Coil}}{\text{Number of turns on Secondary Coil}}$$

Well, it's <u>just another formula</u>. You stick in the numbers <u>you've got</u> and work out the one <u>that's left</u>.

It's really useful to remember you can write it <u>either way up</u> — this example's much trickier algebra-wise if you start with $V_S$ on the bottom...

$$\frac{V_P}{V_S} = \frac{n_P}{n_S}$$

or

$$\frac{V_S}{V_P} = \frac{n_S}{n_P}$$

### Example

A transformer has 40 turns on the primary and 800 on the secondary. If the input potential difference is 1000 V, find the output potential difference.

<u>ANSWER:</u> $V_S/V_P = n_S/n_P$ so $V_S/1000 = 800/40$ $V_S = 1000 \times (800/40) = \underline{20\,000\,V}$

## *Transformers only work with AC*

I'll say that again. Transformers only work with AC. Prevent disaster in the exam by remembering that fact. Now that's out of the way — make sure you <u>practise</u>, <u>practise</u>, <u>practise</u> using that tricky equation.

# Transformers

## Transformers are nearly 100% efficient so "power in = power out"

The formula for power supplied is:  Power = Current × Potential Difference or:  P = I × V (see page 118).

So you can write electrical power input = electrical power output as:

$$V_p I_p = V_s I_s$$

$V_p$ = p.d. across primary coil (V)          $V_s$ = p.d. across secondary coil (V)
$I_p$ = current in the primary coil (A)          $I_s$ = current in the secondary coil (A)

### Example

A transformer in a travel adaptor steps up a 110 V AC mains electricity supply to the 230 V needed for a hair dryer.  The current through the hair dryer is 5 A.  If the transformer is 100% efficient, calculate how much current is drawn by the transformer from the mains supply.

ANSWER:  $V_p \times I_p = V_s \times I_s$  so  $110 \times I_p = 230 \times 5$    $I_p = (230 \times 5) \div 110 = \underline{10.5 \text{ A}}$

## Switch mode transformers are used in chargers

1) Switch mode transformers are a type of transformer that operate at higher frequencies than traditional transformers.

2) They usually operate at between 50 kHz and 200 kHz.

3) Because they work at higher frequencies, they can be made much lighter and smaller than traditional transformers that work from a 50 Hz mains supply.

4) This makes them more useful in things like mobile phone chargers and power supplies, e.g. for laptops.

5) Switch mode transformers are more efficient than other types of transformer.  They use very little power when they're switched on but no load (the thing you're charging or powering) is applied, e.g. if you've left your phone charger plugged in but haven't attached your phone.

---

## Switch mode transformers are more efficient than regular transformers

Another formula to learn — the transformer equations are all unusual because they can't be put into formula triangles.  Other than that the method is the same — just stick in the numbers.

# Warm-Up and Exam Questions

Time to test your knowledge — as usual, check you can do the basics, then get stuck into some lovely exam questions. Don't forget to go back and check up on any niggling bits you can't do.

## Warm-Up Questions

1) What is meant by electromagnetic induction?

2) Do step-up transformers have more turns on their primary or secondary coil?

3) Write down the transformer equation.

4) Explain why switch mode transformers are used instead of traditional transformers in mobile phone chargers.

## Exam Questions

1 Gordon fits a dynamo to his bicycle, to power its lights.
The cog wheel of the dynamo is placed so that it touches the top of one of his wheels.

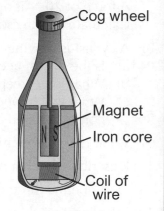

(a) Describe how the dynamo is used to power the lights.

*(3 marks)*

(b) (i) Describe what happens to the dynamo's output when it is not rotating.

*(1 mark)*

(ii) Explain why this is a disadvantage when a dynamo is used to power bicycle lights.

*(1 mark)*

2 A transformer is used to reduce the potential difference from a mains electricity supply.

(a) Will the transformer have more turns on its primary or secondary coil? Explain your answer.

*(1 mark)*

(b) Describe how a potential difference is induced in the secondary coil of the transformer.

*(3 marks)*

3 A student is trying to test a transformer using a battery.

(a) Explain why the voltmeter connected to the secondary coil reads 0 V.

*(2 marks)*

(b) The student finds an AC power supply and reconnects the transformer.
Her results are: $V_P = 12$ V, $I_P = 2.5$ A, $V_S = 4$ V (where $V_P$ is the voltage across the primary coil, etc.).

(i) Calculate the power input to the transformer.

*(2 marks)*

(ii) Calculate the current in the secondary coil, $I_S$.

*(3 marks)*

(iii) The primary coil has 15 turns.
How many turns must be on the secondary coil?

*(2 marks)*

# Revision Summary for Physics 3b

There's only one way to check you know it all.  Sorry.

1)  Sarah is levering the lid off a can of paint using a screwdriver.  She places the tip of the 20 cm long
    screwdriver under the can's lid and applies a force of 10 N on the end of the screwdriver's handle.
    Suggest two ways that Sarah could increase the moment about the pivot point (the side of the can).

2)  Describe two different ways of finding the centre of mass of a rectangular playing card.

3) * Arthur weighs 600 N and is sitting on a seesaw 1.5 m from the pivot point.
    His friend Caroline weighs 450 N and sits on the seesaw so that it
    balances.  How far from the pivot point is Caroline sitting?

4)  Give three situations where you use a simple lever.

5)  Give two features of a Bunsen burner that make it difficult to tip over.

6) * Calculate the time period of a pendulum swinging with a frequency of 10 Hz.

7) * A force of 20 N is applied to a piston in a hydraulic system with a cross-sectional area 0.25 m².
    Calculate the pressure applied to the piston.

8)  A cyclist is moving at a constant speed of 5 m/s around a circular track.
    a)  Is the cyclist accelerating?  Explain your answer.
    b)  What force keeps the cyclist travelling in a circle?  Where does this force come from?
    c)  What will happen to the size of this force if the same cyclist travels at a
        constant speed of 5 m/s around a different circular track that has a larger radius?

9)  What is an electromagnet?

10) Describe what happens to a current-carrying wire when it is placed in a magnetic field.

11) Describe the three details of Fleming's left hand rule.  What is it used for?

12) The diagrams show a simple electric motor.  The coil is turning clockwise.
    Which diagram, A or B, shows the correct polarity of the magnets?

13) Describe two ways in which you could induce a
    potential difference using a wire and a magnet.

14) Describe how a dynamo works.

15) Sketch two types of transformer and explain the differences between them.

16) An engineering executive is travelling from the USA to Italy and taking a computer
    monitor with him.  In the USA, domestic electricity is 110 V AC, and in Italy it's 230 V AC.
    What kind of transformer would the engineering executive need to plug his monitor into?

17) Explain how a transformer works and why transformers only work on AC voltage.

18)*A transformer has 20 turns on the primary coil and 600 on the secondary coil.
    If the input potential difference is 9 V, find the output potential difference.

19)*A transformer steps down 230 V from the mains supply to the 130 V
    needed for an appliance.  If the transformer draws 2 A from the mains
    supply, calculate how much current goes through the appliance.

## Practice Exams

Once you've been through all the questions in this book, you should feel pretty confident about the exam. As final preparation, here is a **practice exam** to really get you set for the real thing. The total time allowed for each paper is 60 minutes. These papers are designed to give you the best possible preparation for your exams.

# GCSE AQA Science

# Unit Physics 1

## *Higher Tier*

CGP  Practice Exam Paper
GCSE Physics

In addition to this paper you should have:
- A ruler.
- A calculator.

| Centre name | | | | |
|---|---|---|---|---|
| Centre number | | | | |
| Candidate number | | | | |

**Time allowed:**
- 60 minutes

| Surname |
|---|
| Other names |
| Candidate signature |

**Instructions to candidates**
- Write your name and other details in the spaces provided above.
- Answer **all** questions in the spaces provided.
- Do all rough work on the paper.

**Information for candidates**
- The marks available are given in brackets at the end of each question.
- There are 9 questions in this paper.
- There are 60 marks available for this paper.
- You are allowed to use a calculator.
- You should answer Questions 5 and 9(c) with continuous prose. You will be assessed on the quality of your English, the organisation of your ideas and your use of appropriate specialist vocabulary.

**Advice to candidates**
- In calculations show clearly how you worked out your answers.

## For examiner's use

| Q | Attempt Nº | | | Q | Attempt Nº | | |
|---|---|---|---|---|---|---|---|
| | 1 | 2 | 3 | | 1 | 2 | 3 |
| 1 | | | | 6 | | | |
| 2 | | | | 7 | | | |
| 3 | | | | 8 | | | |
| 4 | | | | 9 | | | |
| 5 | | | | | | | |
| | | | | Total | | | |

Answer **all** questions in the spaces provided

**1** A survey shows all the places where a house 'loses' energy, and how much energy is transferred from the inside to the outside of the house through each place. The results are shown in the diagram.

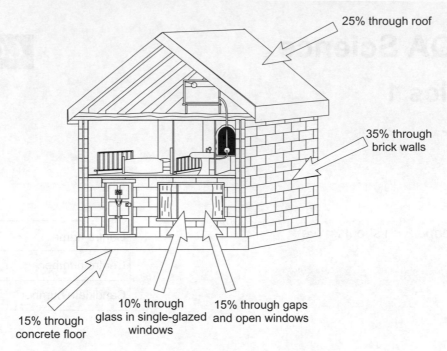

25% through roof

35% through brick walls

15% through concrete floor

10% through glass in single-glazed windows

15% through gaps and open windows

**1 (a)** The house has cavity walls — two layers of bricks with an air gap between them. Explain how the gap in a cavity wall helps to insulate the house.

.................................................................................................................................

.................................................................................................................................
*(1 mark)*

**1 (b)** Draughts are caused by convection. Explain why you often get cold draughts near single-glazed windows, even if there are no cracks in the window frame.

.................................................................................................................................

.................................................................................................................................
*(2 marks)*

**1 (c)** The owner wants to install double-glazed windows in his house to reduce energy loss. He is choosing between two different brands of windows that both cost the same amount to buy and install.

Brand A has a U-value of 1.85 W/m²K and brand B has a U-value of 1.75 W/m²K.

Which brand of window should he choose? Explain your answer.

.................................................................................................................................

.................................................................................................................................
*(2 marks)*

5

**2** A student did an experiment using the apparatus shown. He used identical electric heating coils to heat a beaker of water and a beaker of oil. He used 1 kg of each liquid.

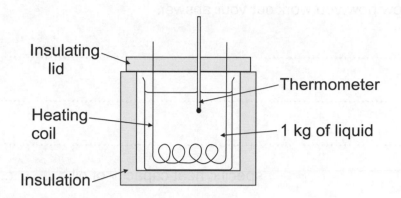

The student took the temperatures of both the liquids before heating, and then again after ten minutes of heating. His results are shown in the table.

|  | Water | Oil |
|---|---|---|
| Initial temperature (°C) | 18 | 16 |
| Final temperature (°C) | 48 | 93 |

**2 (a)** The student noticed that the temperatures of the liquids decreased after the heaters were switched off. Explain why this happened.

..........................................................................................................................
*(1 mark)*

**2 (b)** Which of the liquids has a lower specific heat capacity?

..........................................................................................................................
*(1 mark)*

**Question 2 continues on the next page**

**Turn over ▶**

**2 (c)** During the experiment, the heating coil transferred 126 kJ of energy to each liquid.

Use data from the experiment to calculate the specific heat capacity of oil.

Clearly show how you work out your answer.

.......................................................................................................................

.......................................................................................................................

.......................................................................................................................

specific heat capacity of oil = ....................... kJ/kg°C

*(4 marks)*

**2 (d)** Both oil and water can be used in heating systems.
Explain why most heating systems use water rather than oil.

.......................................................................................................................

.......................................................................................................................

.......................................................................................................................

*(2 marks)*

8

**3**      Light bulbs are designed to transform electrical energy into light energy. However, some of the electrical energy is wasted.

**3 (a)**      Here are some diagrams showing the energy transformations in four light bulbs.

Draw a ring around the energy transformation diagram which shows the least efficient light bulb.

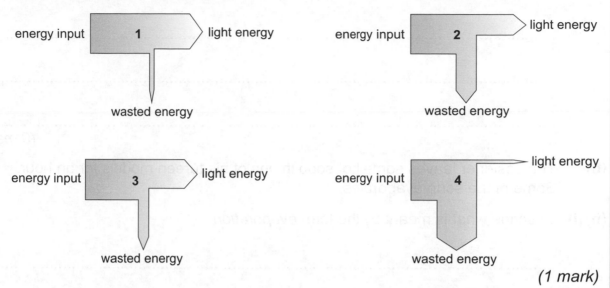

*(1 mark)*

**3 (b)**      A light bulb transforms 200 J of electrical energy into 150 J of heat energy and 50 J of light energy. Calculate the efficiency of the light bulb.

Clearly show how you work out your answer.

..........................................................................................................................

..........................................................................................................................

efficiency = ........................%

*(2 marks)*

**3 (c)**      The table gives some data about one type of high efficiency light bulb.

| Type of light bulb | Cost | Saving per hour (compared to a low efficiency bulb) |
|---|---|---|
| High efficiency | £3.75 | 0.75p |

Calculate the payback time of this type of high efficiency light bulb.

Clearly show how you work out your answer.

..........................................................................................................................

..........................................................................................................................

payback time = ........................ hours

*(2 marks)*

**Turn over for the next question**

5

**Turn over ▶**

**4**     A designer is designing a soup tureen — a big serving bowl used to serve soup at the table.  It is important that the tureen keeps the soup hot.

**4 (a)**     The designer creates a model of a tureen using thick metal for the body. He puts some hot soup into the model tureen.

Explain how energy from the soup is transferred through the metal body.

..................................................................................................................................

..................................................................................................................................

..................................................................................................................................

*(3 marks)*

**4 (b)**     The designer leaves some hot soup in one of his tureen models for an hour. Some of the soup evaporates.

**4 (b) (i)**  Describe what is meant by the term *evaporation*.

..................................................................................................................................

..................................................................................................................................

*(1 mark)*

**4 (b) (ii)** Explain why the evaporating soup causes the remaining soup to cool.

..................................................................................................................................

..................................................................................................................................

..................................................................................................................................

..................................................................................................................................

*(3 marks)*

7

**5** *In this question you will be assessed on the quality of your English, the organisation of your ideas and your use of appropriate specialist vocabulary.*

Below is a close-up of a metal cooling fin on a motorbike engine.

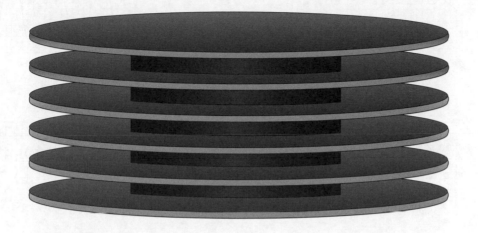

Explain how the design of the metal cooling fin helps it maximise energy transfer from the hot motorbike engine.

.................................................................................................................................

.................................................................................................................................

.................................................................................................................................

.................................................................................................................................

.................................................................................................................................

.................................................................................................................................

.................................................................................................................................

.................................................................................................................................

.................................................................................................................................

.................................................................................................................................

*(6 marks)*

6

**Turn over for the next question**

**Turn over ▶**

**6** Radio waves are one type of electromagnetic radiation. The diagram shows four electromagnetic waves that are all drawn to the same scale.

**1**

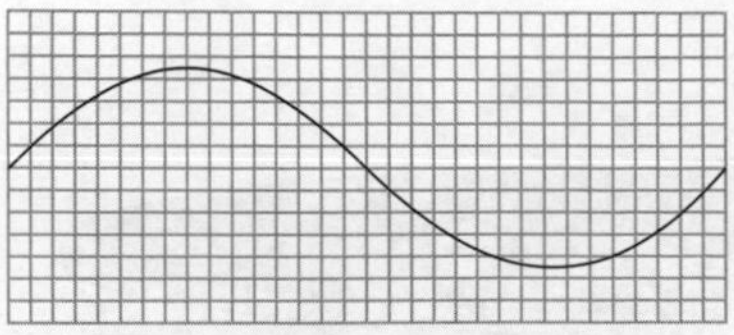

**2**

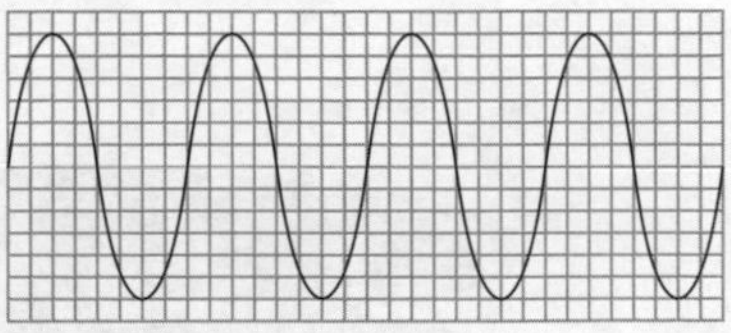

**3**

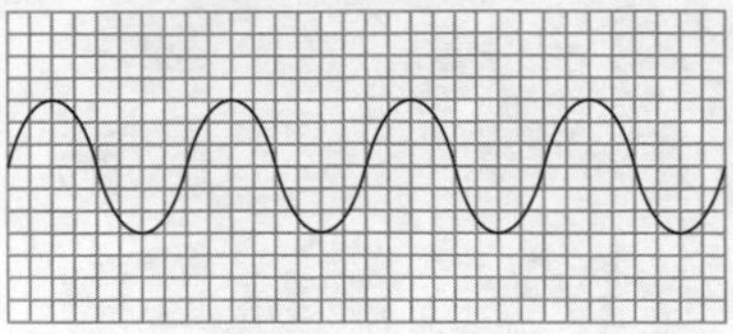

**4**

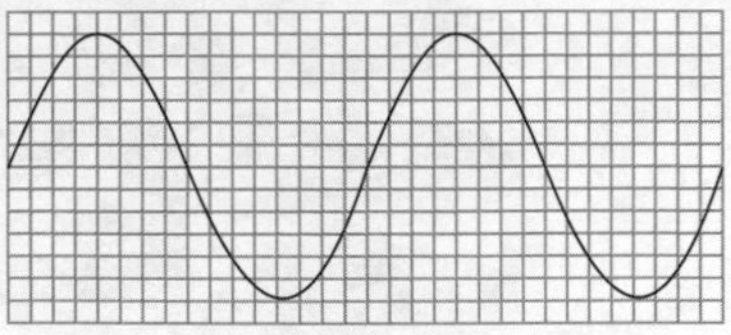

**6 (a) (i)** Give the numbers next to the **two** waves that are most likely to be the same type of electromagnetic radiation.

.................................................................................................................................
*(1 mark)*

**6 (a) (ii)** Which wave is most likely to be a radio wave? Give a reason for your answer.

.................................................................................................................................

.................................................................................................................................
*(1 mark)*

**6 (b)** Medium-wave radio waves can be used for communications.

Describe how the ionosphere allows radio waves to be transmitted from one side of the Earth and received on the other side.

.................................................................................................................................

.................................................................................................................................
*(1 mark)*

**6 (c)** The picture below shows a house near a hill.
On the other side of the hill is a long wavelength radio transmitter.

long wavelength
radio transmitter

House

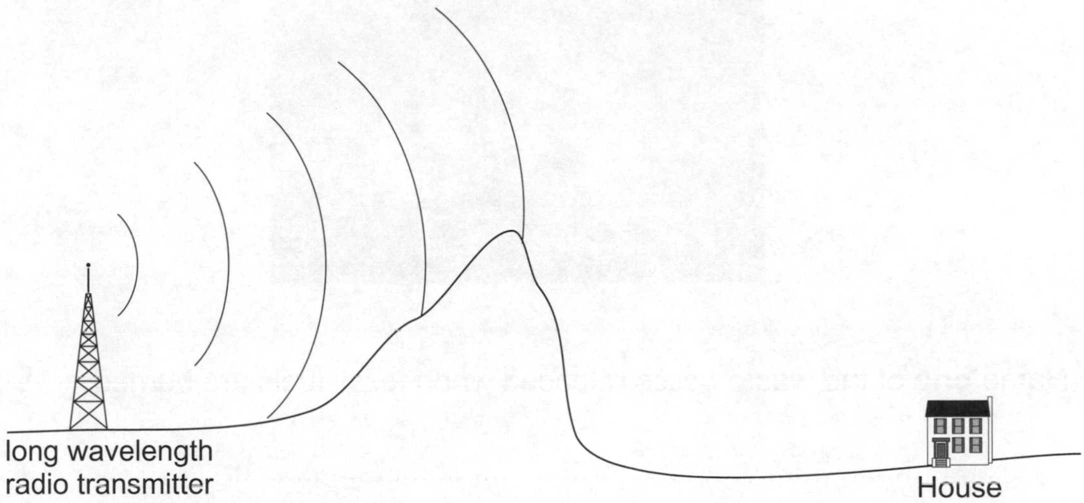

Explain why the people living in the house are able to receive radio programmes from the transmitter. Add to the diagram to help your explanation.

.............................................................................................................................

.............................................................................................................................

.............................................................................................................................

*(2 marks)*

5

**Turn over for the next question**

**Turn over ▶**

**7** Burning fossil fuels such as coal and oil in power stations releases waste gases.

**7 (a) (i)** Name **one** of the waste gases released when fossil fuels are burned.

.......................................................................................................................................................

*(1 mark)*

**7 (a) (ii)** Describe **one** advantage of using fossil fuels, rather than renewable alternatives, to generate electricity.

.......................................................................................................................................................

.......................................................................................................................................................

*(1 mark)*

**7 (a) (iii)** Explain how carbon capture and storage helps reduce the impact of burning fossil fuels on the environment.

.......................................................................................................................................................

.......................................................................................................................................................

.......................................................................................................................................................

*(2 marks)*

**7 (b)** The pie chart below shows what proportion of a country's electricity is generated by different energy sources.

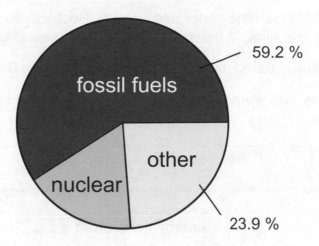

59.2 %

23.9 %

**7 (b)(i)** Calculate the proportion of the country's electricity that comes from nuclear power.

...........................................................................................................................

nuclear power = ........................................ %

*(1 mark)*

**7 (b)(ii)** Give **one** advantage and **one** disadvantage of using nuclear fuel to generate electricity.

Advantage: ......................................................................................................

...........................................................................................................................

Disadvantage: ................................................................................................

...........................................................................................................................

*(2 marks)*

7

**Turn over for the next question**

**8**     A farmer decides to generate some electricity for his farmhouse
using a small wind turbine mounted on the roof.

**8 (a)**     In a strong wind, the turbine generates enough electricity to power the farmer's
1.5 kW washing machine.  A wash cycle on the machine takes 90 minutes.

**8 (a) (i)** Calculate the energy transferred by the washing machine during one cycle.

Clearly show how you work out your answer.

..................................................................................................................

..................................................................................................................

energy transferred = ......................................... kWh

*(2 marks)*

**8 (a) (ii)** If electricity costs 18 pence per kilowatt-hour, calculate how much the farmer
saves each time he washes his clothes without mains electricity.

Clearly show how you work out your answer.

..................................................................................................................

..................................................................................................................

money saved = ......................................... p

*(2 marks)*

**8 (b)**     Explain how the wind turbine generates electricity.

..................................................................................................................

..................................................................................................................

..................................................................................................................

*(2 marks)*

**8 (c)**     The farmer's house is also connected to the National Grid.

Explain how step-up transformers are used to reduce energy loss from the cables
that make up the National Grid.

..................................................................................................................

..................................................................................................................

..................................................................................................................

*(2 marks)*

8

**9**     Jessica is reading about stars and how the universe began.

**9 (a)**   Jessica reads about light being detected from a distant star.  The detected light has a wavelength of $6.56 \times 10^{-7}$ m and a frequency of $4.57 \times 10^{14}$ Hz. Calculate the speed of the light.

Clearly show how you work out your answer.

.............................................................................................................

.............................................................................................................

speed = ......................................... m/s

*(2 marks)*

**9 (b)**   The Big Bang is the currently accepted theory of how the universe started. Describe how the universe began according to this theory.

.............................................................................................................

.............................................................................................................

*(1 mark)*

**9 (c)**   *In this question you will be assessed on the quality of your English, the organisation of your ideas and your use of appropriate specialist vocabulary.*

Jessica reads that: "Red-shift and cosmic microwave background radiation are both strong pieces of evidence in support of the Big Bang theory."

Explain how the evidence of red-shift and cosmic microwave background radiation have led to the Big Bang theory being the currently accepted theory of how the universe began.

.............................................................................................................

.............................................................................................................

.............................................................................................................

.............................................................................................................

.............................................................................................................

.............................................................................................................

.............................................................................................................

*(6 marks)*

## 9

**END OF QUESTIONS**

# GCSE AQA Science

## Unit Physics 2

## *Higher Tier*

CGP Practice Exam Paper GCSE Physics

In addition to this paper you should have:
- A ruler.
- A calculator.

| Centre name | | | |
|---|---|---|---|
| Centre number | | | |
| Candidate number | | | |

**Time allowed:**
- 60 minutes

| Surname | |
|---|---|
| Other names | |
| Candidate signature | |

## Instructions to candidates
- Write your name and other details in the spaces provided above.
- Answer **all** questions in the spaces provided.
- Do all rough work on the paper.
- You are allowed to use a calculator.

## Information for candidates
- The marks available are given in brackets at the end of each question.
- You may get marks for method, even if your answer is incorrect.
- There are 9 questions in this paper.
- There are 60 marks available for this paper.
- You should answer Questions 5(b) and 8(d) with continuous prose.
  You will be assessed on the quality of your English, the organisation
  of your ideas and your use of appropriate specialist vocabulary.

| **For examiner's use** | | | | | | |
|---|---|---|---|---|---|---|
| Q | Attempt Nº | | | Q | Attempt Nº | |
| | 1 | 2 | 3 | | 1 | 2 | 3 |
| 1 | | | | 6 | | | |
| 2 | | | | 7 | | | |
| 3 | | | | 8 | | | |
| 4 | | | | 9 | | | |
| 5 | | | | | | | |
| | | | Total | | | | |

## Advice to candidates
- In calculations show clearly how you worked out your answers.

Answer **all** questions in the spaces provided

**1** The diagram shows two children driving dodgem cars.

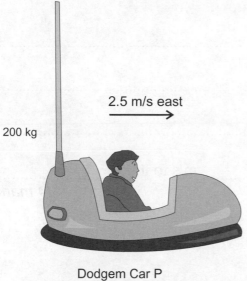

2.5 m/s east

200 kg

Dodgem Car P

Momentum = 500 kg m/s

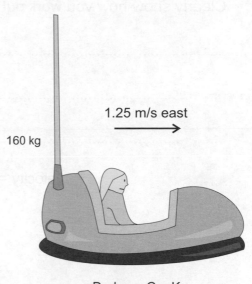

1.25 m/s east

160 kg

Dodgem Car K

Momentum = 200 kg m/s

**1 (a)** The two dodgem cars collide when **Car P** drives into the back of **Car K**. Calculate the total momentum of the two cars:

**1 (a) (i)** before the collision.

..............................................................................................................................

..............................................................................................................................

momentum = ............................. kg m/s to the east

*(1 mark)*

**1 (a) (ii)** immediately after the collision. Include units and a direction in your answer.

momentum = ........................................................................................

*(1 mark)*

**Question 1 continues on the next page**

**Turn over ▶**

**1 (b)** Immediately after the collision, **Car P** dodgem car travels with a momentum of 200 kg m/s to the east.

Calculate the velocity of **Car K** dodgem car after the collision.
Include the direction of travel in your answer.

Clearly show how you work out your answer.

......................................................................................................................................

......................................................................................................................................

......................................................................................................................................

velocity = ........................... m/s to the ...........................

*(4 marks)*

**2**  Terence drives along a flat, straight road before braking and stopping at a set of traffic lights.  The velocity-time graph below shows Terence's motion.

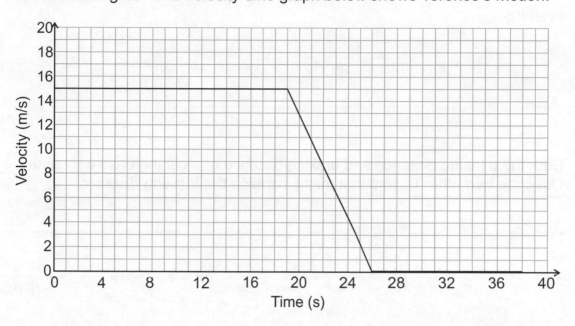

**2 (a)**  Use the graph to calculate Terence's acceleration between 19 s and 26 s.

.......................................................................................................................

.......................................................................................................................

acceleration = .............................. m/s²

*(2 marks)*

**2 (b)**  What happens to the temperature of the car brakes when they are applied to slow the car down?  Explain why this happens.

.......................................................................................................................

.......................................................................................................................

*(2 marks)*

**Question 2 continues on the next page**

**Turn over ▶**

**2 (c)**   Terence's friend drives a car that has a regenerative braking system.
Give **one** advantage of regenerative braking systems over traditional braking
systems.

.......................................................................................................................

.......................................................................................................................

*(1 mark)*

**2 (d)**   Both the thinking distance and braking distance of a car increase with speed.
Describe **two** other factors that might increase the thinking distance.

.......................................................................................................................

.......................................................................................................................

*(2 marks)*

7

**3** The diagram shows a shopper walking around a supermarket pushing a trolley.

To push her empty trolley at a constant speed, she needs a force of 20 N.

**3 (a)** Calculate how much work the shopper does if she pushes her empty trolley 300 m.

Clearly show how you work out your answer.

...................................................................................................................

...................................................................................................................

work done = .................................................. J

*(2 marks)*

**3 (b)** The shopper averages a power of 15 W.
Calculate how long it will take her to push the trolley 300 m.

Clearly show how you work out your answer.

...................................................................................................................

...................................................................................................................

time = .................................................. s

*(2 marks)*

$\boxed{4}$

**Turn over for the next question**

**Turn over ▶**

**4** Modern cars have many safety features.

**4 (a)** Air bags are one example of a safety feature found in many cars.
Explain how air bags help protect passengers during a crash.

.............................................................................................................................

.............................................................................................................................
*(2 marks)*

**4 (b)** Seat belts are made from an elastic material. They stretch slightly during a collision to reduce the risk of injury on the passengers.

The material used for one type of seat belt has a spring constant of 180 000 N/m. Calculate the extension of the seat belt if the force on a passenger in a crash is 13 500 N.

Clearly show how you work out your answer and give the unit.

.............................................................................................................................

.............................................................................................................................

.............................................................................................................................

extension = .......................................................
*(3 marks)*

**5**     A free-fall skydiver jumps from an aeroplane and his motion is recorded.
After his jump he looks at this velocity-time graph of his fall.

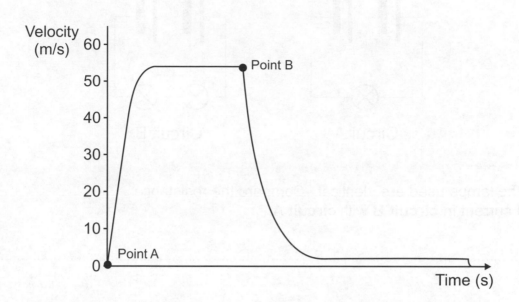

**5 (a)**   The skydiver has a mass of 83 kg.  Calculate his weight.
Use acceleration due to gravity = 10 N/kg.

Clearly show how you work out your answer.

.................................................................................................................................

.................................................................................................................................

weight = ............................................................... N

*(2 marks)*

**5 (b)**   *In this question you will be assessed on the quality of your English, the
organisation of your ideas and your use of appropriate specialist vocabulary.*

Describe the motion of the skydiver from **point A** to **point B** on the graph,
in terms of the forces acting on him.

.................................................................................................................................

.................................................................................................................................

.................................................................................................................................

.................................................................................................................................

.................................................................................................................................

.................................................................................................................................

*(6 marks)*

**Turn over for the next question**

8

**Turn over ▶**

**6**     Two electric circuits are shown in the diagram below.

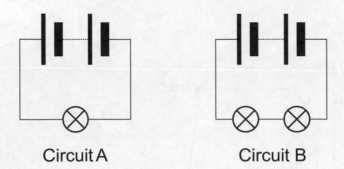

Circuit A          Circuit B

**6 (a)**     All the lamps used are identical.  Compare the resistance
and current in **circuit B** with **circuit A**.

.......................................................................................................................

.......................................................................................................................
*(2 marks)*

**6 (b)**     An ammeter and a voltmeter are added to **circuit A**.
They show readings of 0.5 A and 3 V respectively.

Calculate the power of the lamp.

Clearly show how you work out your answer.

.......................................................................................................................

.......................................................................................................................

power = ........................................................ W
*(2 marks)*

The following components are added to Circuit A.

A —————□———— B —————◿————

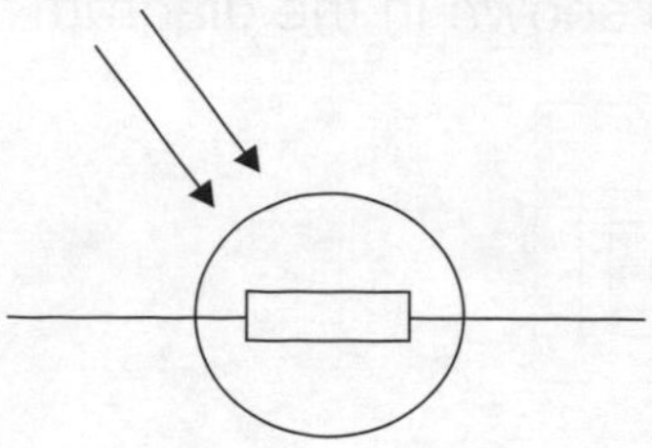

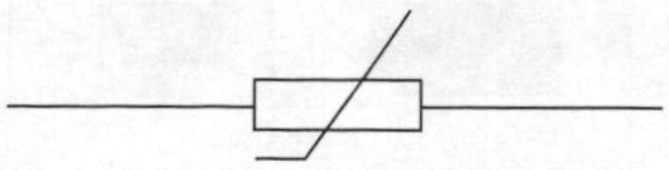

**6 (c) (i)** Name each of the components shown above.

A ..............................................................................................................................

B ..............................................................................................................................

*(2 marks)*

**6 (c) (ii)** Describe what happens to the resistance of component A as the intensity of the
light that falls on it increases.

..............................................................................................................................

*(1 mark)*

7

**Turn over for the next question**

**Turn over ▶**

**7**    Steven is carrying out an experiment to find out what types of radiation are emitted by a source.  He carries out three tests, as shown in the diagram.

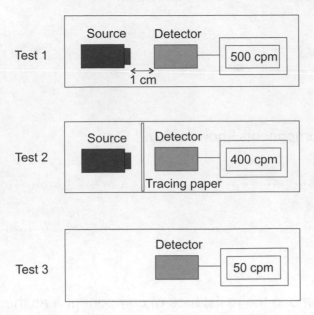

Steven's results show that the source is emitting more than one type of radiation.

**7 (a)**    What type of radiation is the source definitely emitting?
Give a reason for your answer.

.....................................................................................................................................
*(1 mark)*

**7 (b)**    Steven points the source into a uniform electric field.  He observes the paths of two types of nuclear radiation shown in the diagram below.

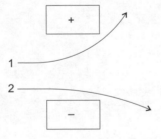

**7 (b)(i)**  Name the **two** types of radiation detected in this experiment.

.....................................................................................................................................
*(1 mark)*

**7 (b)(ii)** Explain why the two types of radiation are deflected in opposite directions and by different amounts as they travel through the electric field.

.....................................................................................................................................

.....................................................................................................................................

.....................................................................................................................................

.....................................................................................................................................
*(3 marks)*

**7 (c)** Explain why the detector registers radiation even when the radioactive source has been put away in a lead-lined box.

.......................................................................................................................................................

*(1 mark)*

## 6

**Turn over for the next question**

**8**     Nuclear reactors in power stations and submarines release energy through nuclear fission.

**8 (a)**     Describe what is meant by the term nuclear fission.

.................................................................................................................................

.................................................................................................................................

*(1 mark)*

**8 (b)**     Name **one** nuclear fuel commonly used in nuclear reactors.

.................................................................................................................................

*(1 mark)*

Scientists are trying to develop reactors in which
energy is released through nuclear fusion.

**8 (c)**     Describe what is meant by the term nuclear fusion.

.................................................................................................................................

.................................................................................................................................

*(1 mark)*

**8 (d)** *In this question you will be assessed on the quality of your English, the organisation of your ideas and your use of appropriate specialist vocabulary.*

Evaluate the advantages and disadvantages of nuclear fusion over nuclear fission as a method of generating electricity.

.......................................................................................................................

.......................................................................................................................

.......................................................................................................................

.......................................................................................................................

.......................................................................................................................

.......................................................................................................................

.......................................................................................................................

.......................................................................................................................

.......................................................................................................................

.......................................................................................................................

.......................................................................................................................

*(6 marks)*

9

**Turn over for the next question**

**Turn over ▶**

**9**   A student wanted to know how the current flowing through a filament lamp changes with the potential difference across it.  She set up this circuit.

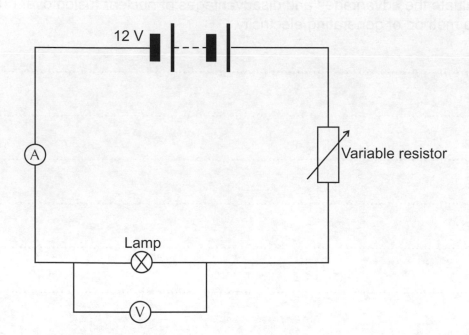

She used a variable resistor to change the potential difference across the lamp.

Here are the results the student got as she changed the potential difference across the lamp.

| Voltmeter (V) | Ammeter (A) |
|---|---|
| 0.0 | 0.0 |
| 3.0 | 1.0 |
| 5.0 | 1.4 |
| 7.0 | 1.7 |
| 9.0 | 1.9 |
| 11.0 | 2.1 |

**9 (a)** Use her results to draw a graph of current against potential difference for the lamp on the axes below. Draw a smooth curve through the points.

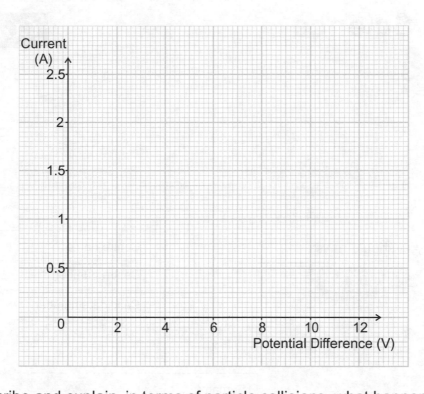

*(2 marks)*

**9 (b)** Describe and explain, in terms of particle collisions, what happens to the resistance of the lamp as the current through it increases.

.............................................................................................................................

.............................................................................................................................

.............................................................................................................................

.............................................................................................................................

*(3 marks)*

**9 (c)** Use your graph to find the current when the potential difference is 10 V.

current = ................................... A

*(1 mark)*

**9 (d)** Use your answer to **(c)** to calculate the resistance of the lamp when the potential difference is 10 V. Include units in your answer.

.............................................................................................................................

.............................................................................................................................

resistance = ...................................

*(2 marks)*

**END OF QUESTIONS**

# GCSE AQA Science

## Unit Physics 3

## *Higher Tier*

CGP Practice Exam Paper GCSE Physics

In addition to this paper you should have:
- A ruler.
- A calculator.

| Centre name | | | | |
|---|---|---|---|---|
| Centre number | | | | |
| Candidate number | | | | |

**Time allowed:**
- 60 minutes

| Surname | |
|---|---|
| Other names | |
| Candidate signature | |

### Instructions to candidates
- Write your name and other details in the spaces provided above.
- Answer **all** questions in the spaces provided.
- Do all rough work on the paper.
- You are allowed to use a calculator.

### Information for candidates
- The marks available are given in brackets at the end of each question.
- You may get marks for method, even if your answer is incorrect.
- There are 8 questions in this paper.
- There are 60 marks available for this paper.
- You should answer Question 8(d) with continuous prose.
  You will be assessed on the quality of your English,
  the organisation of your ideas and your use of
  appropriate specialist vocabulary.

**For examiner's use**

| Q | Attempt Nº | | | Q | Attempt Nº | | |
|---|---|---|---|---|---|---|---|
| | 1 | 2 | 3 | | 1 | 2 | 3 |
| 1 | | | | 5 | | | |
| 2 | | | | 6 | | | |
| 3 | | | | 7 | | | |
| 4 | | | | 8 | | | |
| | | | | Total | | | |

### Advice to candidates
- In calculations show clearly how you worked out your answers.

Answer **all** questions in the spaces provided

1    A child is learning to ride a bicycle.  He pushes down on the pedal with a force of 100 N.

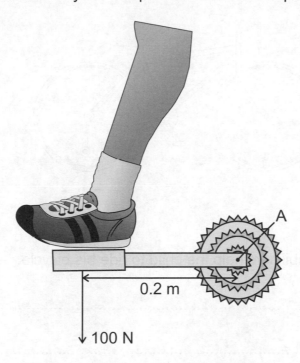

1 (a)   Calculate the moment, about point A, that the child exerts.
        Clearly show how you worked out your answer and give the unit.

..............................................................................................................................

..............................................................................................................................

moment = .............................................
*(3 marks)*

1 (b)   Explain what will happen to the moment about point **A** if the child continues to
        push on the pedal with the same force while the pedal moves downwards.

..............................................................................................................................

..............................................................................................................................

..............................................................................................................................
*(2 marks)*

**Question 1 continues on the next page**

**Turn over ▶**

The child has stabilisers fitted to the rear wheel of his bicycle.

**1 (c)** Explain how the stabilisers help the child to ride his bicycle.

..............................................................................................................................

..............................................................................................................................

..............................................................................................................................

..............................................................................................................................

*(3 marks)*

8

**2**    A lorry and a motorbike are driving around a bend in the road.
The diagram shows a view from above the road.

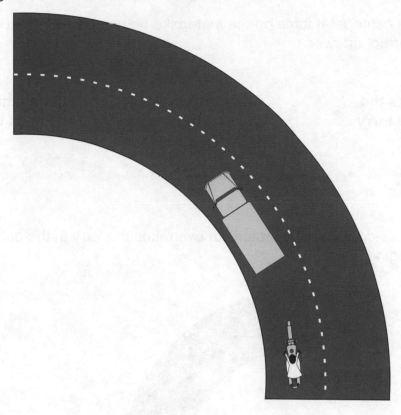

**2 (a)**    Name the force that allows the vehicles to travel around the bend.

............................................................................................................................

*(1 mark)*

**2 (b)**    Explain how you know that the motorbike is accelerating, without knowing its speed.

............................................................................................................................

............................................................................................................................

*(1 mark)*

**2 (c)**    Draw an arrow on the diagram to show the direction in which the motorbike is
accelerating.  Label the arrow with an **A**.

*(1 mark)*

**Question 2 continues on the next page**

**Turn over ▶**

**2 (d)**    The lorry has a mass of 8000 kg.  The bike and rider have a total mass of 200 kg.
Both the lorry and motorbike are travelling at the same speed.

What will the centripetal force on the motorbike be compared to that on the lorry?
Circle the correct answer.

| The same as the force on the lorry | Greater than the force on the lorry | Less than the force on the lorry |

*(1 mark)*

**2 (e)**    The lorry slows down, so the motorbike overtakes the lorry in the outside lane
without changing speed.

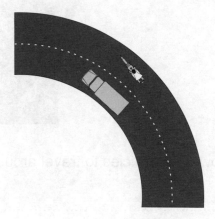

Will the centripetal force on the motorbike be different from the force that acted on
it when it was in the inside line?  Explain your answer.

.......................................................................................................................................

.......................................................................................................................................

*(1 mark)*

5

**3**　A student has made a simple electric motor.

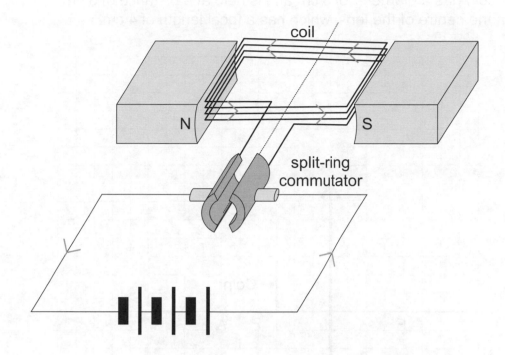

**3 (a)**　With the current and field as shown, describe how the coil will move.

....................................................................................................................

*(1 mark)*

**3 (b)**　The student decides to make some changes to his motor.

Describe what would happen if:

**3 (b)(i)**　he decreased the current.

....................................................................................................................

*(1 mark)*

**3 (b)(ii)**　he increased the strength of the magnetic field.

....................................................................................................................

*(1 mark)*

**3 (b)(iii)**　he reversed the direction of both the magnetic field and the current.

....................................................................................................................

*(1 mark)*

**Turn over for the next question**

4

**Turn over ▶**

**4**    An antiques dealer uses a converging lens to examine a coin.

The coin has a diameter of 3 cm and is held at a distance of 3 cm from the centre of the lens, which has a focal length of 4 cm.

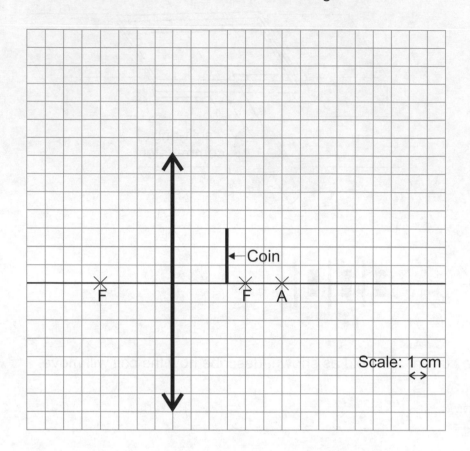

**4 (a)**    Complete the ray diagram above to show the image formed.

*(3 marks)*

**4 (b)**    Describe the size and distance from the lens (relative to the actual coin) of the image formed if the coin were placed 6 cm from the lens, at point **A**.

...................................................................................................................................

...................................................................................................................................

*(1 mark)*

**4 (c)**    Calculate the power of the lens.
Clearly show how you work out your answer and give the unit.

......................................................................................................................

......................................................................................................................

Power = .........................................
*(3 marks)*

**4 (d)**    Lens manufacturers can produce lenses with different focal lengths.
Give the **two** factors that determine the focal length of a lens.

1. ...................................................................................................................

2. ...................................................................................................................
*(2 marks)*

9

**Turn over for the next question**

**Turn over ▶**

**5**   A hydraulic system is shown in the diagram below.

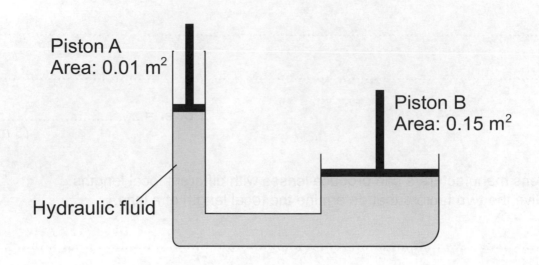

Piston A
Area: 0.01 m²

Piston B
Area: 0.15 m²

Hydraulic fluid

**5 (a)**   Explain why there is a force on **piston B** when a force is applied to **piston A**.

..................................................................................................................................

..................................................................................................................................

..................................................................................................................................

..................................................................................................................................

*(3 marks)*

**5 (b)**   Calculate the force on **piston B** when a force of 25 N is applied to piston A.
Clearly show how you worked out your answer.

..................................................................................................................................

..................................................................................................................................

..................................................................................................................................

..................................................................................................................................

..................................................................................................................................

Force on piston B = ......................................... N

*(5 marks)*

**6**    Amanda's fiancé has given her a diamond engagement ring.
The diagram below shows light entering Amanda's diamond ring.
The refractive index of the diamond is 2.4.

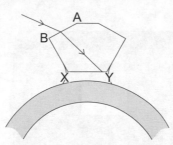

**6 (a)**    Light is refracted as it passes into the diamond.
Describe what is meant by refraction.

......................................................................................................................

......................................................................................................................
*(1 mark)*

**6 (b)**    Some light rays travelling through the diamond are **totally internally reflected**
at the boundary **XY**.  The rest of the light rays hitting this boundary pass out
of the diamond.

   **(i)** Explain why only **some** light rays are reflected at the boundary XY.

......................................................................................................................

......................................................................................................................
*(1 mark)*

   **(ii)** Explain why total internal reflection can happen at the bottom (**XY**) of the
diamond but **not** at the top (**AB**).

......................................................................................................................

......................................................................................................................

......................................................................................................................
*(2 marks)*

**6 (c)**    Amanda notices that her diamond ring sparkles more than a similar glass ring.
The refractive index of glass is 1.5.  Explain Amanda's observation using the
refractive indices of diamond and glass.

......................................................................................................................

......................................................................................................................

......................................................................................................................
*(2 marks)*

**Turn over for the next question**

**Turn over ▶**

**7** A student has made a simple transformer from an iron core and two lengths of wire, as shown in the diagram below. He connected a 12 V alternating power supply to one of the coils and a lamp and voltmeter to the other coil.

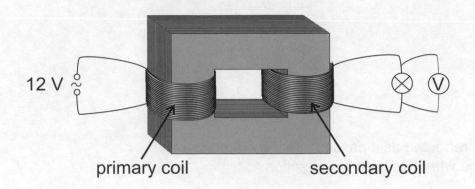

12 V

primary coil          secondary coil

**7 (a)** Explain how a potential difference is generated in the secondary coil.

..................................................................................................................................................

..................................................................................................................................................

..................................................................................................................................................

*(2 marks)*

**7 (b)** The student experimented with the transformer by changing the number of turns on the secondary coil and measuring the potential difference across the lamp each time. His results are shown below.

| Number of turns on secondary coil ($N_s$) | Potential difference induced in secondary coil ($V_s$) |
|:---:|:---:|
| 5 | 3.8 |
| 10 | 7.5 |
| 15 | 1.3 |
| 20 | 15 |
| 25 | 18.8 |

Plot the student's results on the axes given and draw a line of best fit.

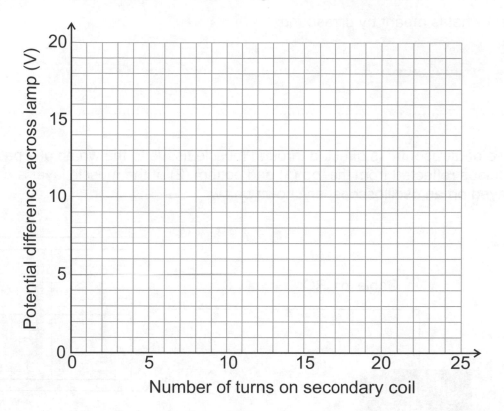

Number of turns on secondary coil

*(2 marks)*

**7 (c)**   The student thinks he may have read the voltmeter incorrectly on one of the trials and recorded an anomalous result.

**7 (c) (i)**   Circle the anomalous result on the graph.

*(1 mark)*

**(c) (ii)**   Use your graph to estimate the actual potential difference induced on this trial.

.......................................................................................................................................
*(1 mark)*

**(d)**   The student researches transformers on the internet.  He discovers that switch mode transformers are used in mobile phone chargers.  Explain why switch mode transformers are more suited to this use than traditional transformers.

.......................................................................................................................................

.......................................................................................................................................

.......................................................................................................................................

.......................................................................................................................................
*(3 marks)*

9

**Turn over for the next question**

**Turn over ▶**

**8**     Ultrasound is used in pre-natal scanning.

**8 (a)**   Explain what is meant by ultrasound.

..................................................................................................................................

..................................................................................................................................

*(1 mark)*

**8 (b)**   A pulse of ultrasound is directed through muscle tissue to the womb of a patient.
The pulses reflected from the top (1) and bottom (2) of the muscle layer are
displayed on an oscilloscope, as shown below.

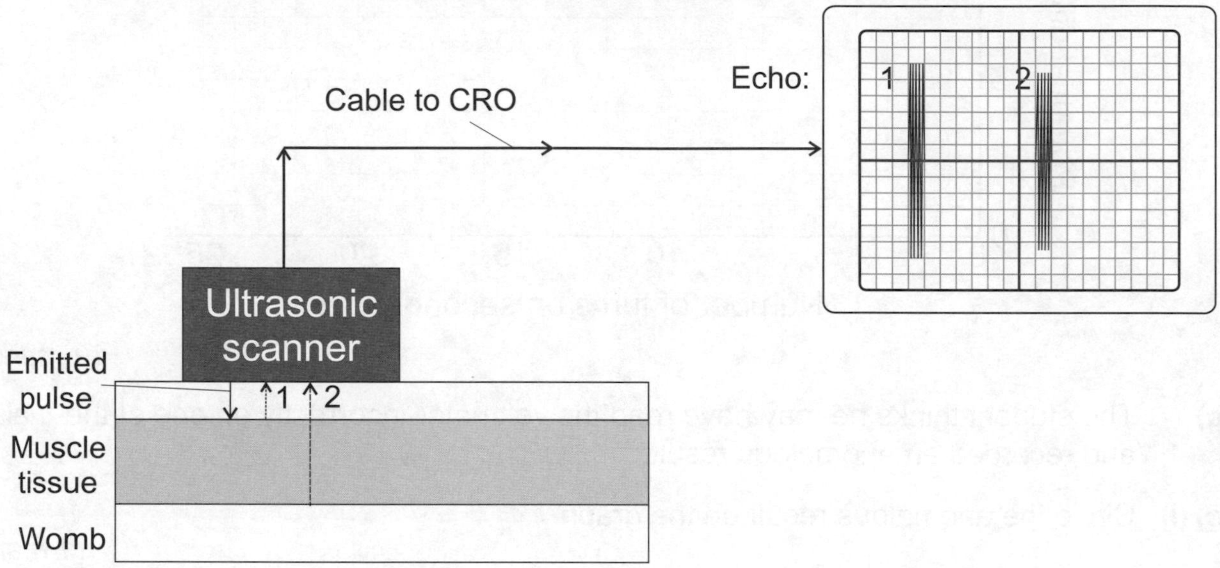

Cable to CRO

Echo:     1     2

Ultrasonic
scanner

Emitted
pulse          1  2

Muscle
tissue

Womb

The muscle tissue between the surface of the skin and the womb is 0.0024 m
thick.  The time interval between reflections 1 and 2 is $3 \times 10^{-6}$ s.
Calculate the speed of the ultrasound through the muscle tissue.

..................................................................................................................................

..................................................................................................................................

..................................................................................................................................

speed = .................................. m/s
*(3 marks)*

**8 (c)** X-rays are also used for medical imaging. Modern X-ray machines produce images using charge-coupled devices (CCDs).

Explain why CCDs are used in modern X-ray machines.

..................................................................................................................

..................................................................................................................

*(1 mark)*

**8 (d)** *In this question you will be assessed on the quality of your English, the organisation of your ideas and your use of appropriate specialist vocabulary.*

Outline the advantages and disadvantages of using ultrasound to create a medical image rather than using X-rays.

..................................................................................................................

..................................................................................................................

..................................................................................................................

..................................................................................................................

..................................................................................................................

..................................................................................................................

..................................................................................................................

..................................................................................................................

..................................................................................................................

..................................................................................................................

..................................................................................................................

*(6 marks)*

11

**END OF QUESTIONS**

## Page 22

### Warm-Up Questions

1) E.g. make the surface darker in colour, make the surface less shiny/more matt.

2) The particles in a gas have high (kinetic) energies, move in random directions at high speeds and are not arranged in any pattern — they are free to move.

3) Particles that vibrate faster than others pass on their extra kinetic energy to their neighbours.

4) Heated air expands, so it becomes less dense than the surrounding cooler air and rises.

### Exam Questions

1 (a) The temperature of the water would fall more quickly *(1 mark)* — the rate of heat transfer would be greater because the difference in temperature between the water and its surroundings is greater *(1 mark)*.

(b) The temperature of the water would fall more quickly *(1 mark)* — the rate of heat transfer would be greater because the cup is now made from metal, which is a better conductor than plastic *(1 mark)*.

2 (a) (i) by heat radiation *(1 mark)*

(ii) by conduction through the metal pipe *(1 mark)*

(iii) by convection currents in the water *(1 mark)*

(b) Because black surfaces are good absorbers of heat radiation *(1 mark)*.

## Page 27

### Warm-Up Questions

1) Condensation is when a gas changes state and becomes a liquid.

2) Coats help trap a layer of air around the body, which acts as an insulator and helps stop heat loss by conduction. (The coat itself will also usually be made of an insulating material.)

3) They reflect infrared radiation and so help reduce heat transfer by radiation.

4) E.g. any three from: lowering the temperature of the gas / decreasing the airflow/increasing the concentration of the gas / decreasing the temperature of the surface the gas is condensing on / increasing the density of the gas.

### Exam Questions

1 (a) Ears with a large surface area will allow a high rate of heat transfer away from the body *(1 mark)* which will help the animal to stay cool in hot conditions. *(1 mark)*

(b) The particles of sweat that evaporate *(1 mark)* have high energies *(1 mark)*. When they evaporate, the average energy of the remaining particles decreases and so the temperature of the sweat decreases, helping to cool the animal. *(1 mark)*

2 (a) The larger the surface area of an object, the higher the rate of heat transfer will be *(1 mark)*. The heat sink has fins which give it a large surface area *(1 mark)* so it will have a high rate of heat transfer. The heat sink is in direct contact with the whole of the processor *(1 mark)*, which will maximise the heat transfer by conduction between the processor and the heat sink *(1 mark)*.

(b) The heat sink is made from metal *(1 mark)* which is a good conductor, and so will be able to conduct heat away quickly from the processor *(1 mark)*.

(c) A fan will increase the difference in temperature between the heat sink and its surroundings *(1 mark)*, and so will increase the rate of heat transfer *(1 mark)*.

## Page 32

### Warm-Up Questions

1) E.g. any three of: loft insulation / cavity wall insulation / draught-proofing / double glazing / using thick curtains.

2) The amount of time it takes for the initial cost to equal the money saved.

3) convection

4) Specific heat capacity is the amount of energy needed to raise the temperature of 1 kg of a substance by 1 °C.

### Exam Questions

1 (a) $\theta = 100\ °C - 20\ °C = 80\ °C$
$E = m \times c \times \theta$, so $c = E \div (m \times \theta) = 36\ 000 \div (0.5 \times 80) = 900\ J/kg°C$

*(4 marks, allow 1 mark for correct rearrangement of the equation, 1 mark for using the correct temperature, and 1 mark for correct substitution into the equation.)*

(b) Concrete has a high specific heat capacity *(1 mark)* and so will be able to store a lot of heat *(1 mark)*.

2 (a) £300 × 0.25 = £75 *(1 mark)*

(b) (i) Insulation B — it has a lower U-value and is therefore a better insulator. *(1 mark)*

(ii) 300 − 255 = £45 saved per year *(1 mark)*.
Payback time = cost ÷ saving per year
= 350 ÷ 45 = 7.8 years *(1 mark)*

## Pages 41-43

### Warm-Up Questions

1) chemical energy

2) E.g. wind-up radio, clockwork toy.

3) More of the input energy is transformed into useful energy in modern appliances.

4) Some energy is always wasted and so all the input energy isn't transformed usefully.

5) kilowatt-hour (kWh)

6) No. of units (kWh) used = power (in kW) × time (in hours)

### Exam Questions

1 (a) Energy can be transferred usefully, stored or dissipated, but cannot be **created** or **destroyed**. *(1 mark)*

(b) (i) A loud speaker transfers electrical energy to sound and heat energy *(1 mark)*.

(ii) A television transfers electrical energy to light, heat and sound energy *(1 mark)*.

2 (a) A *(1 mark)*

*Each square represents 10 J. The bulb is 15% efficient, so when 100 J of energy are input, the useful output must be 1.5 squares wide.*

(b) E.g. Advantages: They are more efficient and generally last longer than traditional bulbs. *(2 marks, 1 mark for each advantage)*

Disadvantages: They are more expensive to buy and don't give out as much light as traditional bulbs. *(2 marks, 1 mark for each disadvantage)*

3 (a) Gravitational potential energy *(1 mark)*

(b) Efficiency = useful energy out ÷ total energy in
= 140 ÷ 200 = 0.7 (or 70%)
*(2 marks, allow 1 mark for correct substitution)*

4 (a) 1200 − 120 − 100 = 980 W *(1 mark)*

(b) Efficiency = useful power out ÷ total power in
= (980 + 100) ÷ 1200 = 1080 ÷ 1200 = 0.9 (or 90%)
*(2 marks, allow 1 mark for the correct substitution)*

(c) By reducing the amount of energy wasted as sound / by having a quieter motor *(1 mark)*.

*Only the energy converted to sound is wasted — kinetic and heat energy are what you want from a hairdryer.*

(d) 4 minutes = 4 × 60 = 240 s
Energy = power × time = 1200 W × 240 s
= 288 000 J
*(2 marks, allow 1 mark for the correct substitution)*

5 (a) Energy = final reading − initial reading = 10 612 − 10 582.5
= 29.5 kWh *(1 mark)*

(b) cost = number of kWh × cost per kWh
cost = 29.5 × 0.14 = £4.13. No, his bill is not correct.
*(2 marks for correct answer, otherwise 1 mark for correct substitution)*

5 (a) E.g.

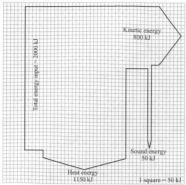

*(3 marks, allow 1 mark for each correctly drawn energy output)*

(b) Heat exchangers work by collecting heat energy and making it useful — so they reduce the amount of energy wasted *(1 mark)*.

7 How to grade your answer:

0 marks: There is no relevant information.

1-2 marks: There is a brief description of how access to mains electricity could improve the standard of living in Angola.

3-4 marks: There is a clear description of several ways access to mains electricity could improve the standard of living in Angola. The answer has a logical structure and spelling, punctuation and grammar are mostly correct.

5-6 marks: There is a clear and detailed description of how access to mains electricity could improve the standard of living in Angola. The answer has a logical structure and uses correct spelling, grammar and punctuation.

Here are some points your answer may include:

- Electric lighting could be used which is not only useful and convenient, but it can also help improve safety at night.
- Refrigerators could be used to help keep food fresh for longer and could also be used to keep vaccines cold.
- Giving hospitals access to mains electricity could increase the standard of health care in the country and could increase life expectancy.
- People could have access to the internet and phones, which would make it easier to send and receive news and information.

# Page 44

# Revision Summary for Physics 1a

15) 40 years

20) 90 000 J (90 kJ)

25) 70% or 0.7

26) a) 80 J

b) 20 J

c) 0.8 or 80%

28) 0.125 kWh

# Page 55

## Warm-Up Questions

1) Any three of: wind / waves / tides / hydroelectric / solar / geothermal / food / biofuels.

2) 'Spare' night-time electricity is used to pump water up to a reservoir. This can then be released quickly when extra electricity is needed.

3) E.g. any two of: it releases greenhouse gases/contributes to global warming / it causes acid rain / coal mining damages the landscape.

4) E.g. Nuclear fission results in the production of nuclear waste, which is very difficult and expensive to dispose of safely. / A nuclear power plant has high set-up/decommissioning costs and a long set up/decommissioning time. / With all nuclear power plants there is a risk of nuclear catastrophe.

5) Organic matter that can be burnt to release energy.

## Exam Questions

1 (a) Heat energy from inside the Earth *(1 mark)*.

(b) The source of energy will never run out *(1 mark)*.

(c) There are few suitable locations for geothermal power plants, since they can only be built in volcanic areas with hot rocks close to the surface *(1 mark)*. The cost to set up a geothermal power plant is high relative to the energy available *(1 mark)*.

2 (a) 2 000 000 ÷ 4000 = 500 *(1 mark)*

(b) If the wind isn't blowing strongly, the turbines will not generate as much as 4000 W each *(1 mark)*.

(c) E.g. any two of: they might think it would spoil the view (visual pollution) / cause noise pollution / kill or disturb local wildlife *(1 mark each)*.

(d) Step-up transformers step up the voltage of the electricity supply, allowing the electricity to be transmitted at high voltages (and low currents) *(1 mark)* to reduce the amount of energy lost as heat *(1 mark)*.

3 (a) E.g. any two of: wave / tidal / geothermal / biofuels *(1 mark for each)*.

(b) E.g. any two of: set-up time / set-up costs / running costs / impact on environment / social impact *(1 mark for each)*.

# Page 57

2375 m/s

# Page 61

## Warm-Up Questions

1) Transverse

2) wave speed = frequency × wavelength ($v = f \times \lambda$)

3) Diffraction occurs — the wave spreads out.

4) True

5) In a longitudinal wave, the vibrations are parallel to the direction of travel/energy transfer.

## Exam Questions

1 (a) Transverse *(1 mark)*

(b) 5 cm *(1 mark)*

(c) 1 complete wave would pass a point every 2 seconds, so f = 1 ÷ 2 = 0.5 Hz *(1 mark)*

(d) It will halve. *(1 mark)*

2 (a) Reflection *(1 mark)*

(b)

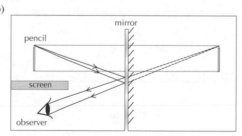

*(1 mark for correctly drawn virtual image, 1 mark for rays drawn from virtual image to observer, 1 mark for rays correctly drawn from pencil to mirror)*

# Page 65

## Warm-Up Questions

1) Gamma rays

2) Radio waves

3) E.g. They can pass through the Earth's watery atmosphere.

4) Radio waves

5) Visible light

## Exam Questions

1 (a) Infrared *(1 mark)*

(b) E.g. remote controls / optical fibre transmissions *(1 mark)*

(c) Some wavelengths of microwave are absorbed by water molecules and heat them up *(1 mark)*. It is this property of microwaves that allows them to be used to cook food, so some people might worry that the microwaves emitted by mobile phones could 'cook' the cells in your brain. *(1 mark)*

2 (a)

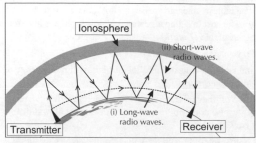

*(1 mark for each path drawn correctly)*

(b) Diffraction *(1 mark)*

(c) FM signals have very short wavelengths and so don't diffract like long wavelength radio waves *(1 mark)*. This means they are blocked by any barriers between the transmitter and receiver *(1 mark)*.

# Page 70

# Warm-Up Questions

1) False

2) The higher the frequency, the higher pitched the sound waves will be.

3) A reflected sound wave.

4) The Steady State theory says that the universe has always existed as it is now and it always will.

# Exam Questions

1 (a) (i) The observed wavelength of the sound waves from the ambulance will decrease as the ambulance approaches the observer *(1 mark)* and increase as it travels away from the observer *(1 mark)*.

   (ii) The Doppler effect *(1 mark)*.

   (iii) The observer will hear the pitch of the siren drop as the ambulance passes them. *(1 mark)*

   (b) They all appear to be moving away from us *(1 mark)*.

2 (a) All the matter and energy was in a very small space *(1 mark)*, then there was an explosion/a 'Big Bang' which caused it to expand. *(1 mark)*

   (b) (i) The further the galaxy, the greater the red shift *(1 mark)*. This shows that the more distant the galaxy, the faster it's moving away from us *(1 mark)*. This must mean that the universe is expanding. *(1 mark)*

   (ii) Cosmic microwave background radiation (CMBR) *(1 mark)*.

# Page 71

# Revision Summary for Physics 1b

15) 150 m/s

# Pages 76-77

# Warm-Up Questions

1) Speed

2) Acceleration — m/s², mass — kilograms (kg), weight — newtons (N)

3) $(30 - 0) \div 6 = 30 \div 6 = 5$ m/s²

4) Gravity

# Exam Questions

1 (a) Because its direction is constantly changing. *(1 mark)*

   (b) Acceleration = change in velocity ÷ time taken
   $= (59 - 45) \div 5$
   $= 14 \div 5 = 2.8$ m/s²
   *(2 marks, allow 1 mark for correct working)*

2 (a) (i) 200 m *(1 mark)*
       *Read the distance travelled from the graph.*

   (ii) $200 \div 15 = 13.3$ m/s (to 1 d.p.)
       *(2 marks, allow 1 mark for correct working)*

   (b) 13 s (allow answers from 11 s to 15 s) *(1 mark)*
       *The bus is stationary between about 33 and 46 seconds.*

(c) The bus is travelling at constant speed (10 m/s) back towards the point it started from. *(1 mark)*

(d) E.g.

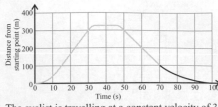

*(1 mark)*

3 (a) The cyclist is travelling at a constant velocity of 3 m/s. *(1 mark)*

   (b) The cyclist's speed is constantly decreasing. *(1 mark)*

   (c) $(3 - 0) \times (5 - 2) \div 2 = 4.5$ m *(1 mark)*
       *Remember, distance travelled is the area under the graph.*

4 (a) The value of g would be smaller *(1 mark)* and so the weight of the ball would be smaller *(1 mark)* and the force exerted on the spring would be smaller *(1 mark)*.

   (b) $3 \div 1.1 = 2.7$ (to 1 d.p.) So, the spring extends 2.7 times as far on Earth, so g on Earth must be 2.7 times bigger than on Mars. *(1 mark)*
   $10 \div 2.7 = 3.7$ m/s² (to 1 d.p.)
   *(2 marks, allow 1 mark for correct working)*

5 (a) Acceleration = change in velocity ÷ time taken
   $= (10 - 0) \div 1 = 10$ m/s² *(1 mark)*

   (b) Change in velocity = acceleration × time = $10 \times 3 = 30$ m/s
   *(2 marks, allow 1 mark for correct working)*

   (c) Assume g = 10 m/s².
   Weight = mass × g = $0.12 \times 10 = 1.2$ N
   *(2 marks, allow 1 mark for correct working)*

   (d) None — the stone's acceleration due to gravity is determined by the mass of the Earth, not the stone. *(1 mark)*

6 All of them — everything with mass exerts a gravitational force. *(1 mark)*

# Page 83

# Warm-Up Questions

1) $(30 + 30) - 10 = 50$ N towards the shore

2) 0 N

3) The acceleration also doubles.

4) Against motion.

# Exam Questions

1 (a) (i) 900 N – 900 N = 0 N *(1 mark)*

   (ii) Parachutist A is falling at a constant (terminal) velocity. *(1 mark)*

   (b) (i) Terminal velocity is reached when the force of air resistance equals the parachutist's weight. *(1 mark)*
   Weight = mass × g = $70 \times 10$ *(1 mark)* = 700 N *(1 mark)*

   (ii) Parachutist A would have a higher terminal velocity *(1 mark)* because he has a greater weight. *(1 mark)* This means the force of air resistance would need to be greater to balance his weight, and air resistance is greater at higher speeds. *(1 mark)*

   (c) Because the parachute increases their air resistance/drag. *(1 mark)*

2 (a) The upwards force must be greater *(1 mark)* because Stefan is accelerating upwards. *(1 mark)*

   (b) Assume g = 10 N/kg, Stefan's mass is $600 \div 10 = 60$ kg *(1 mark)*
   Force = mass × acceleration = $60 \times 2.5$ *(1 mark)* = 150 N *(1 mark)*

3 (a) -500 N. *(1 mark)* If the bat exerts a force of 500 N on the ball, the ball also exerts a force of 500 N on the bat, but in the opposite direction. *(1 mark)*

   (b) The ball's acceleration is greater *(1 mark)* because it has a smaller mass than the bat and receives the same force (F = ma). *(1 mark)*

# Pages 89-90

# Warm-Up Questions

1) The distance travelled in the time between a hazard appearing and the driver braking.

2) Braking distance

3) Because work done is a measure of energy transfer.

4) The energy an object has due to its vertical position in a gravitational field.

5) Friction as they enter the atmosphere transfers some of their kinetic energy to heat — the temperature gets so extreme that most burn up.

6) Elastic potential energy

7) The spring will be permanently stretched.

## Exam Questions

1 (a) (i) Accept answers between 12 and 13 m *(1 mark)*

(ii) 35 m *(1 mark)*

(iii) 35 m – 12 m = 23 m  or  35 m – 13 m = 22 m *(1 mark)*

(b) Braking distance *(1 mark)*
*Using the graph, thinking distance is about 15 m and braking distance about 38 m.*

(c) No, *(1 mark)* if stopping distance and speed were proportional the relationship between them would be shown by a straight line. *(1 mark)*

2 (a) $E_p = m \times g \times h = 2.5 \text{ kg} \times 10 \text{ N/kg} \times 1.3 \text{ m} = 32.5 \text{ J}$
*(2 marks, allow 1 mark for correct working)*

(b) $E_k = \frac{1}{2} \times m \times v^2$, so $v^2 = E_k \div (\frac{1}{2} \times m)$
$v^2 = 32.5 \text{ J} \div (\frac{1}{2} \times 2.5 \text{ kg})$
$v = 5.1 \text{ m/s}$ (to 1 d.p.)
*(3 marks, allow 1 mark for correctly rearranging the equation and 1 mark for correct substitution of values into the equation)*

(c) $F = k \times e$
$k = F \div e = 4 \text{ N} \div 0.035 \text{ m} = 114 \text{ N/m}$ (to 3 s.f.)
*(3 marks, allow 1 mark for correctly rearranging the equation and 1 mark for correct substitution of values into the equation)*

3 (a) $40\,000 \text{ kg} \times 1.05 \text{ m/s}^2 = 42\,000 \text{ N}$
*(2 marks, allow 1 mark for correct working)*

(b) $42\,000 \text{ N} \times 700 \text{ m} = 29\,400\,000 \text{ J}$
*(2 marks, allow 1 mark for correct working)*

(c) $29\,400\,000 \text{ J} \div 29\,400 \text{ N} = 1000 \text{ m}$ (1 km)
*(2 marks, allow 1 mark for correct working)*

(d) Heat/sound energy *(1 mark)*

4 (a) $\frac{1}{2} \times 2750 \text{ kg} \times (12 \text{ m/s})^2 = 198\,000 \text{ J}$
*(2 marks, allow 1 mark for correct working)*

(b) The van has more energy as it has a bigger mass. *(1 mark)*

(c) $550\,000 \text{ J} \div 25 \text{ m} = 22\,000 \text{ N}$
*(2 marks, allow 1 mark for correct working)*

## Pages 95-96

## Warm-Up Questions

1) Power is the rate at which work is done.

2) Momentum = mass × velocity ($p = m \times v$)

3) The total momentum before an event is the same as after the event.

4) Any two of, e.g. seat belts / air bags / crumple zones.

5) E.g. power of the engine, how aerodynamic the car is.

## Exam Questions

1 (a) They help direct the kinetic energy of the crash *(1 mark)* away from passengers to other areas of the car. *(1 mark)*

(b) To increase the time it takes for the person to stop moving *(1 mark)* which reduces the forces acting on the chest. *(1 mark)* They also absorb some of their kinetic energy. *(1 mark)*

(c) Air flows easily over aerodynamic cars so there is less air resistance. *(1 mark)*. Cars reach their top speed when the resistive force equals the driving force *(1 mark)*. With less air resistance to overcome, aerodynamic cars can reach a higher speed before this happens. *(1 mark)*

2 (a) (i) Momentum = mass × velocity = $100 \times 6 = 600$ kg m/s to the right
*(2 marks, allow 1 mark for correct working)*

(ii) $80 \times 9 = 720$ kg m/s to the left
*(2 marks, allow 1 mark for correct working)*

(b) (i) Take left as positive, then the momentum of the two players is
$720 - 600 = 120$ kg m/s. *(1 mark)*

The mass of the two players is 100 + 80 = 180 kg, so the speed is
$120 \div 180 = 0.67$ m/s
*(2 marks, allow 1 mark for correct working)*

(ii) Left *(1 mark)*
*The two players travel in the direction player B was going because player B had more momentum before the collision.*

3 (a) Energy transferred = power × time taken = $90\,000 \times 5$
$= 450\,000 \text{ J} = 450 \text{ kJ}$
*(2 marks, allow 1 mark for correct working)*

(b) (i) During braking, the vehicle's motor is put into reverse which slows the wheels. *(1 mark)* This motor acts as an electrical generator and converts kinetic energy into electrical energy *(1 mark)* which is stored as chemical energy in the vehicle's battery. *(1 mark)*

(ii) The energy transferred by braking is stored rather than wasted, e.g. as heat. *(1 mark)*

4 $E_p = m \times g \times h = 60 \times 10 \times 35 = 21\,000 \text{ J}$
*(2 marks, allow 1 mark for correct working)*
Power $= E \div t = 2100 \div 50 = 420$ W
*(2 marks, allow 1 mark for correct working)*

5 momentum before = momentum after *(1 mark)*
$(1 \times 14\,000) = (1 \times -13\,000) + (235 \times v_2)$ *(1 mark)*
$14\,000 = 235v_2 - 13\,000$
$v_2 = (14\,000 + 13\,000) \div 235$
$= 115$ km/s to the right (to 3 s.f.) *(1 mark)*

## Page 99

## Warm-Up Questions

1) Insulator

2) Positive and negative

3) Repel

4) Bad insulators

## Exam Questions

1 (a) A *(1 mark)* The rod is negatively charged so would repel the negative charges in the balloon, making them move away from the rod. *(1 mark)*

(b) The negative charges in the rod attract the positive charges in the balloon. *(1 mark)* As Jane brings the rod closer to the balloon this attraction gets stronger, causing the balloon to move. *(1 mark)*

2 (a) Electrons are scraped from the cloth onto the surface. *(1 mark)*

(b) -23 *(1 mark)*

(c) E.g. metal *(1 mark)*

## Page 105

## Warm-Up Questions

1) Ohms, $\Omega$

2) Potential difference = work done ÷ charge ($V = W \div Q$)

3)

4) E.g. automatic night lights / outdoor lighting / burglar detectors.

5) It decreases.

## Exam Questions

1 (a) (i) Resistance = potential difference ÷ current = $1.5 \div 0.3 = 5 \ \Omega$
*(2 marks, allow 1 mark for correct working)*

(ii) Charge = current × time = $0.3 \times 35 = 10.5$ C
*(2 marks, allow 1 mark for correct working)*

(b) The amount of current flowing will decrease. *(1 mark)*

(c) (i)

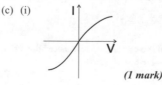

*(1 mark)*

(ii) As electrical charges flow through the filament some of the electrical energy is transferred into heat energy. *(1 mark)* This causes the ions in the filament to vibrate more *(1 mark)* which makes it harder for the charges to move through the filament, so the resistance increases. *(1 mark)*

2 (a) Diodes only allow current to flow in one direction. *(1 mark)*

(b) Resistance = potential difference ÷ current = 6 ÷ 3 = 2 Ω
*(2 marks, allow 1 mark for correct working)*
*Read the values from the graph, then use the formula R = V ÷ I.*

(c) E.g. They use a smaller current. *(1 mark)*

# Page 110
# Warm-Up Questions

1) E.g. If you remove or disconnect one component, then the whole circuit is broken. / You can't switch components on or off independently.

2) The total resistance is the sum of all the resistances.

3) Series

4) the same

5) Parallel

# Exam Questions

1 (a) Total resistance = $R_1 + R_2 + R_3$ = 2 + 3 + 5 = 10 Ω
*(2 marks, allow 1 mark for correct working)*

(b) The current will be 0.4 A *(1 mark)* because in a series circuit the same current flows through all parts of the circuit. *(1 mark)*

(c) $V_3 = V - V_1 - V_2$ = 4 – 0.8 – 1.2 = 2 V
*(2 marks, allow 1 mark for correct working)*

2 (a) 15 V *(1 mark)*
*Potential difference is the same across each branch in a parallel circuit.*

(b) Current = potential difference ÷ resistance = 15 ÷ 3 = 5 A
*(2 marks, allow 1 mark for correct working)*

(c) 5 + 3.75 = 8.75 A *(2 marks, allow 1 mark for correct working)*

# Page 111
# Revision Summary for Physics 2a

2) a = (v – u) ÷ t, a = (14 – 0) ÷ 0.4 = 35 m/s²

7) F = ma, a = F ÷ m = 30 ÷ 4 = 7.5 m/s²

8) Downward force of gravity on skydiver:
F = m × a = 75 × 10 = 750 N.
Resultant force at 80 mph:
F = 750 – 650 = 100 N downwards.
Resultant acceleration:
a = F ÷ m = 100 ÷ 75 = 1.33 m/s²

9) 120 N

12) Work done = force × distance.
W = 535 × 12 = 6420 J

13) $E_p$ = m × g × h = 4 × 10 × 30 = 1200 J

14) $E_k$ = ½ × m × v²
$E_k$ = ½ × 78 × 23² = 20 631 J

15) $E_k$ just as it hits the ground = $E_p$ at the top.   (g = 10 N/kg)
So $E_k$ = m × g × h = 78 × 10 × 20 = 15 600 J

16) $E_k$ transferred = work done by brakes
½ × m × v² = F × d
½ × 1000 × 2² = 395 × d
d = 2000 ÷ 395 = 5.1 m
The car would come to a stop in 5.1 m, so no, he can't avoid hitting the sheep.

18) P = (m × g × h) ÷ t  (g = 10 N/kg)
P = (78 × 10 × 20) ÷ 16.5 = 945.5 W

24) I = Q ÷ t, so   I = 240 ÷ (1 × 60) = 4 A

28) V = I × R, so V = 2 × 0.6 = 1.2 V

30)a) Current is the same everywhere in the circuit and resistance adds up in a series circuit. Total resistance = 4 + 6 = 10 Ω
I = V ÷ R = 12 ÷ 10 = 1.2 A

b) P.D. is shared between the bulbs. V = I × R = 1.2 × 6 = 7.2 V

c) In parallel, the P.D. is the same over each branch of the circuit and is equal to the supply P.D., therefore the P.D. over either bulb = 12 V.

# Page 120
# Warm-Up Questions

1) 50 Hz

2) The neutral wire (also accept the earth wire).

3) Plastic is a good insulator.

4) Earth wire

5) Electrical energy (to kinetic energy) to heat energy.

6) E (energy) = Q (charge) × V (voltage).

# Exam Questions

1 (a) (i) brown *(1 mark)*
(ii) blue *(1 mark)*
(iii) green and yellow stripes *(1 mark)*

(b) The live and neutral wires. *(1 mark)*

(c) A fuse. *(1 mark)*

2 How to grade your answer:

0 marks: There is no relevant information.

1-2 marks: There is a brief description of how the earth wire and fuse protect the appliance and prevent electric shocks.

3-4 marks: There is some description of how the earth wire and fuse protect the appliance and prevent electric shocks. The answer has a logical structure and spelling, punctuation and grammar are mostly correct.

5-6 marks: There is a clear and detailed description of how the earth wire and fuse protect the appliance and prevent electric shocks. The answer has a logical structure and uses correct spelling, grammar and punctuation.

Here are some points your answer may include:

The earth wire and fuse are used to protect the circuit from being damaged by current surges.

The metal case of the appliance is earthed using the earth wire. If the live wire touches the metal case, a huge current will flow through the live wire, through the case and then out through the earth wire.

This surge in current melts the fuse, which breaks the circuit and cuts off the electricity supply. This isolates the whole appliance and protects the circuits and wiring in the appliance from damage.

Isolating the appliance also makes it impossible to get an electric shock from the case.

Shutting off the live supply also prevents fires caused by the heating effect of a large current.

3 (a) Power = current × potential difference = 0.5 × 3 = 1.5 W
*(2 marks, allow 1 mark for correct working)*

(b) Energy transformed = charge × potential difference = 900 × 3 = 2700 J *(2 marks, allow 1 mark for correct working)*

4 (a) The trace shows an AC source so cannot be from a battery / must be from mains electricity. *(1 mark)*

(b) 20 ms *(1 mark)*
*The wave takes four divisions to repeat. 4 × 5 ms = 20 ms.*

(c) 20 ms = 0.02 s. Frequency = 1 ÷ time = 1 ÷ 0.02 = 50 Hz
*(2 marks, allow 1 mark for correct working)*

(d) The amplitude (vertical height) of the wave will be decreased so the peaks and troughs will be smaller. *(1 mark)*

# Page 127
# Warm-Up Questions

1) Electrons

2) E.g. fallout from nuclear weapons tests / nuclear accidents / dumped nuclear waste.

3) Alpha particles

4) E.g. location and job.

5) Cosmic rays

# Exam Questions

1 (a) (i) -1 *(1 mark)*

    (ii) +1 *(1 mark)*

    (iii) 0 *(1 mark)*

  (b) Protons *(1 mark)* and neutrons *(1 mark)*

  (c) It increases by one. *(1 mark)*

  (d) It decreases by four. *(1 mark)*

  (e) (i) The number of protons and neutrons in the atom. *(1 mark)*

    (ii) Atom A and atom B *(1 mark)* because isotopes of the same element have the same atomic number. *(1 mark)*

  (f) (i) They have opposite charge. *(1 mark)*

    (ii) Alpha particles have a much greater mass. *(1 mark)*

2 (a) Most of the alpha particles went straight through the foil. *(1 mark)* But a small number of alpha particles were deflected straight back at them. *(1 mark)*

  (b) E.g. Most of the atom is empty space. *(1 mark)* The nucleus of an atom is tiny *(1 mark)* and contains most of the mass *(1 mark)* and is positively charged. *(1 mark)*

# Page 133

## Warm-Up Questions

1) A weak alpha source is used to ionise the air between two electrodes so that a current can flow. If the alpha radiation is absorbed by smoke, the current stops and the alarm sounds.

2) Because it is ionising and can damage cells.

3) Alpha particles

4) Any two of, e.g. never look directly at the source / always handle a source with tongs / never allow the source to touch the skin / never have the source out of its lead-lined box for longer than necessary.

5) Any one of, e.g. wear lead aprons / work behind lead/concrete barriers.

## Exam Questions

1 Smoke detectors *(1 mark)*

2 (a) Alpha radiation is stopped by the body's tissues and so wouldn't be detected externally. *(1 mark)* It is also strongly ionising which makes it dangerous inside the body. *(1 mark)*

  (b) So that the device lasts a long time and therefore doesn't need to be replaced as often. *(1 mark)*

  (c) So that the dose to the rest of the body is minimised, to reduce damage to healthy cells. *(1 mark)*

3 (a) The radiation can collide with molecules in the body's cells, causing ionisation and damaging the cell. *(1 mark)* This can then result in mutant cells dividing uncontrollably, which is cancer. *(1 mark)*

  (b) It can kill cells, which causes radiation sickness if a large part of the body is affected. *(1 mark)*

4 (a) The average time taken for half of the unstable nuclei in a sample to decay / the time taken for the count rate or activity to halve. *(1 mark)*

  (b) one quarter / 25% *(1 mark)*

  (c) E.g. any two from: keep exposure time short / don't allow skin contact with sample / hold container at arm's length / wear protective lead clothing / put it in a lead container. *(1 mark for each)*

# Page 137

## Warm-Up Questions

1) E.g. uranium and plutonium.

2) It produces a lot of radioactive waste that must be carefully disposed of.

3) Clouds of dust and gas.

4) No — our Sun is a small star. Only big stars become black holes.

5) A red giant.

## Exam Questions

1 (a) U-235 is bombarded with slow-moving neutrons *(1 mark)*. A U-235 nucleus captures a neutron *(1 mark)* and splits into two smaller nuclei and releases 2 or 3 neutrons *(1 mark)*. These neutrons go on to start other fissions, and so on, creating a chain reaction *(1 mark)*.

  (b) The heat energy is used to heat water *(1 mark)* to drive a steam turbine and generator *(1 mark)*.

2 (a) Deuterium *(1 mark)* and hydrogen *(1 mark)*
*Fission uses heavy elements, whereas nuclear fusion uses light elements.*

  (b) Fusion power would allow a lot of electricity to be generated from a plentiful fuel *(1 mark)* without the large amounts of waste currently produced by fission. *(1 mark)*

  (c) Fusion only works at such high temperatures that it uses more energy than it can produce. *(1 mark)*

3 (a) Stars form from clouds of dust and gas which spiral in due to gravitational attraction. *(1 mark)* Gravity compresses the matter so much that intense heat develops. *(1 mark)* When the temperature gets hot enough, nuclear fusion happens and huge amounts of heat and light are emitted. *(1 mark)*

  (b) The forces acting on a main sequence star are balanced, so it doesn't collapse or explode. *(1 mark)* The heat caused by nuclear fusion provides an outward force to balance the force of gravity pulling everything inwards. *(1 mark)*

  (c) (i) They become unstable and eject their outer layer of dust and gases as a planetary nebula *(1 mark)* which leaves a hot, dense solid core known as a white dwarf. *(1 mark)* White dwarfs then cool to become black dwarfs. *(1 mark)*

    (ii) They start to glow brightly again and undergo more fusion, and expand and contract several times. *(1 mark)* Heavier elements are formed and the star eventually explodes in a supernova. *(1 mark)* The supernova leaves behind a neutron star or a black hole. *(1 mark)*

# Page 138

## Revision Summary for Physics 2b

1) f = 1 ÷ T, so f = 1 ÷ 0.08 = 12.5 Hz

6) E = P × t
Hair straighteners: E = 45 × (5 × 60) = 13 500 J
Hair dryer: E = 105 × (2 × 60) = 12 600 J
The hair straighteners use more energy.

7) P = I × V, I = P ÷ V
a) I = 1100 ÷ 230 = 4.8 A, so use a 5 A fuse.

b) I = 2000 ÷ 230 = 8.7 A, so use a 13 A fuse.

8) E = Q × V, E = 530 × 6 = 3180 J

# Page 144

## Warm-Up Questions

1) Broken bones and dental problems.

2) X-rays

3) They are ionising which means they can kill cells.

4) They can be shielded with lead.

5) Partial reflection occurs when a wave meets a boundary between media. Some of the wave travels into the new medium and is refracted, whilst some is reflected. It is important for ultrasound scanning as it allows ultrasound beams to be reflected by different boundaries at different depths.

6) Any two from: pre-natal scanning / breaking down kidney stones / checking blood flow in organs / imaging soft tissue / diagnosing heart problems.

## Exam Questions

1 (a) Because X-rays mostly pass straight through soft tissue, so the structure of soft tissues doesn't appear on X-ray images *(1 mark)*.

  (b) (i) CCDs are made of grids divided into millions of identical pixels *(1 mark)*. When an X-ray hits a pixel it produces an electronic signal *(1 mark)*. This can be used by a computer to form a digital image *(1 mark)*.

    (ii) E.g. CCDs can be used to produce high resolution images *(1 mark)*.

  (c) Any two from: leave the room while the X-ray image is being taken / wear a lead apron (if they need to remain in the room) / stand behind a lead screen. *(1 mark for each)*

2 (a) Advantage — any one from: can image soft tissue / is safe for the fetus *(1 mark)*.

Disadvantage — any one from: produces a fuzzy image / not as clear as other imaging techniques / poor resolution *(1 mark)*.

(b) $s = v \times t$
$v = 1550$ m/s, $t = 20{\times}10^{-6}$ s,
$s = 1550 \times 20{\times}10^{-6}$ *(1 mark)* $= 0.031$ m $(= 3.1$ cm$)$ *(1 mark)*
but this is the distance the ultrasound wave travels there and back, so distance between boundaries $= 0.032 \div 2 = 0.0155$ m $(= 1.55$ cm$)$ *(1 mark)*.

(c) X-rays are ionising *(1 mark)* so they could harm the developing fetus *(1 mark)*.

3 (a) The X-rays used in CT scans can pass through and image both soft and hard tissue *(1 mark)*. CT scans produce high resolution images, which are necessary when diagnosing head injuries *(1 mark)*.

(b) CT scans use a high intensity X-ray beam *(1 mark)*. This means they expose the patient to lots of ionising radiation which could be dangerous to the patient's health *(1 mark)*.

## Page 150

## Warm-Up Questions

1) Diverging/concave/and converging/convex.

2) Converging lenses bulge outwards, diverging lenses curve inwards.

3) Diverging/concave lenses always create virtual images.
Converging/convex lenses can create real or virtual images (depending on the position of the object).

4) diverging

5) Magnification = image height ÷ object height

## Exam Questions

1 (a) A diverging (concave) lens causes parallel rays of light to diverge (spread out) rather than converge (come together) *(1 mark)*. This means that Edward's lens cannot focus the sunlight to start a fire *(1 mark)*.

(b) (i)

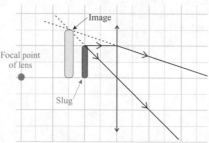

***(1 mark for showing a ray going to a correctly positioned focal point. 1 mark for showing a ray going through the centre of the lens. 1 mark for showing both rays extended backwards (dotted) and image drawn where they cross.)***

*You sometimes need to draw another focal point on the opposite side of lens, the same distance away from the centre line of the lens.*

(ii) Magnification = image height ÷ object height = $3 \div 2 = 1.5$
***(2 marks for answer between 1.4 and 1.6, otherwise 1 mark for correct substitution)***

*Draw diagrams like this as neatly as you can so that you can measure the image and the object accurately.*

2 (a) Power = 1 ÷ focal length
focal length = 0.3 m, so power = $1 \div 0.3$ *(1 mark)* = 3.33 D *(1 mark)*

(b) The focal length will be shorter *(1 mark)* and the lens will be more powerful *(1 mark)*.

## Page 155

## Warm-Up Questions

1) On the retina.

2) real

3) converging

4) E.g. eye surgery / treating skin conditions.

5) The wave must be travelling from a dense substance to a less dense substance. The angle of incidence must be greater than the critical angle.

## Exam Questions

1 (a)

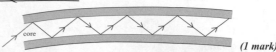
*(1 mark)*

(b) The light ray meets the core/outer boundary at an angle greater than the critical angle, so is totally internally reflected, and this happens repeatedly *(1 mark)*.

(c) refractive index = 1 ÷ sin C, refractive index = 1.65
sin C = $1 \div 1.65 = 0.606$
C = $\sin^{-1}(0.606)$ *(1 mark)*
C = 37.3° *(1 mark)*

2 (a) (i) retina = E          *(1 mark)*
(ii) lens = C          *(1 mark)*
(iii) iris = A          *(1 mark)*
(iv) pupil = B          *(1 mark)*
(v) ciliary muscle = D  *(1 mark)*

(b) The ciliary muscles contract or relax *(1 mark)* to change the shape of the lens *(1 mark)* to focus the images of objects at different distances on the retina *(1 mark)*.

(c) (i) short sight *(1 mark)*
(ii) E.g. put a diverging lens in front of the eye *(1 mark)*, remove corneal tissue using a laser *(1 mark)*.

(d) The near point is the closest distance that the eye can focus on *(1 mark)*.

## Page 156

## Revision Summary for Physics 3a

7) $s = v \times t$, $s = 1000 \times 0.00004 = 0.04$ m
so thickness of fat $= 0.04 \div 2 = 0.02$ m = 2 cm

12) Refractive index (n) = sin i ÷ sin r, $i = 27°$, $r = 18°$
n = sin 27 ÷ sin 18 = 1.47 (to 2 d.p.)

16) Magnification = image height ÷ object height
image height = 4.5, object height = 1.5
Magnification = $4.5 \div 1.5 = 3$

17) Power = 1 ÷ focal length, focal length = 10 cm = 0.1 m
Power = $1 \div 0.1 = 10$ D

## Page 162

## Warm-Up Questions

1) Multiply the force by the perpendicular distance from the line of action of the force to the pivot.

2) Nm (newton metres)

3) The point where the object's whole mass can be considered to be 'concentrated'.

4) There is a resultant moment so it turns.

5) Because there is a resultant moment (caused by the line of action of the weight lying outside the base of the object).

## Exam Questions

1 (a) (i) Moment = force × distance from pivot
= $15 \times 0.03 = 0.45$ Nm
***(2 marks, allow 1 mark for correct working)***
(ii) $15 \times 0.12 = 1.8$ Nm
***(2 marks, allow 1 mark for correct working)***

(b) End B should be put into the bolt *(1 mark)* because the same force exerts a larger moment (because it allows a larger distance between the pivot and the point where the force is applied) *(1 mark)*.

2 How to grade your answer:

| | |
|---|---|
| 0 marks: | There is no relevant information. |
| 1-2 marks: | There is a brief description of the method. |
| 3-4 marks: | There is some description of the method. The answer has a logical structure and spelling, punctuation and grammar are mostly correct. |
| 5-6 marks: | There is a clear and detailed description of the method. The answer has a logical structure and uses correct spelling, grammar and punctuation. |

Here are some points your answer may include:
- The decoration will need to be hung with its centre of mass directly below the point of suspension for the M to be the right way up. If Maurice knows where the centre of mass is, he can put the string directly above it.
- Maurice should suspend the decoration and a plumb line from the same point.
- When they stop moving, he should draw a line on the decoration where the plumb line lies.
- He should then repeat this, but with the shape suspended from a different pivot point.
- The centre of mass is where the two lines cross.

3 (a) No Robert is not correct *(1 mark)*. A seesaw will balance when the moments acting on each side of the pivot are equal (the masses only have to be equal when they are at the same distance from the pivot) *(1 mark)*.

(b) Clockwise moments = anticlockwise moments *(1 mark)*.
$50 \times 1 = T \times (1.4 + 1)$. $T = 50 \div 2.4 = 20.8$ N (to 1 d.p.)
*(2 marks, allow 1 mark for correct working)*

# Page 167

## Warm-Up Questions

1) Time period = 1 ÷ frequency
2) It would decrease.
3) Any one from: car braking systems / hydraulic car jacks / manufacturing / deployment of landing gear.
4) They use a small force to create a bigger force.
5) centripetal force

## Exam Questions

1 (a) Because its direction (and therefore velocity) is constantly changing *(1 mark)*.

(b) (i) bigger / increased *(1 mark)*
(ii) bigger / increased *(1 mark)*

2 (a) Pressure = force ÷ cross-sectional area
= 175 ÷ 0.25 = 700 Pa (or 700 N/m²)
*(2 marks, allow 1 mark for correct working)*

(b) Pressure at piston 1 = pressure at piston 2 *(1 mark)*
Force = pressure × cross-sectional area
= 700 × 1.3 = 910 N
*(2 marks, allow 1 mark for correct working)*

# Pages 172-173

## Warm-Up Questions

1) The direction of the magnetic field around a current carrying wire.
2) It's made up of concentric circles with the wire in the centre.
3) E.g. cranes use them to pick up iron and steel in scrap yards/steel works.
4) First finger — field, Second finger — current, Thumb — motion
5) E.g. any three from: CD players / food mixers / fan heaters / fans / printers / drills / hair dryers / cement mixers.

## Exam Questions

1 (a)

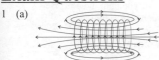

*(1 mark for correct field shape, 1 mark for direction)*

(b) E.g. soft iron *(1 mark)*

(c) (i) The electromagnet only works if a current is flowing *(1 mark)* because it is the current that creates the magnetic field *(1 mark)*.

(ii) They can be switched on and off so it makes it easier to pick up the iron and steel and drop it when you want to *(1 mark)*.

2 (a) It travels from the north pole to the south pole (from left to right) *(1 mark)*.

(b) *(1 mark)*

(c) The direction of the force would be reversed too *(1 mark.)*

(d) (i) The force would be less *(1 mark)*.

(ii) The would be no force on the wire *(1 mark)*.

3 (a) anticlockwise *(1 mark)*
*Use Fleming's left-hand rule on one of the arms of the coil.*

(b) The split-ring commutator keeps the motor turning in the same direction by swapping the contacts every half turn *(1 mark)*.

(c) E.g. increase the current flowing through the coil / use a stronger magnet / add an iron core to the coil *(1 mark)*.

(d) E.g. by reversing the direction of the current / the magnetic field *(1 mark)*.

# Page 179

## Warm-Up Questions

1) The creation of a potential difference across a conductor which is experiencing a change in magnetic field.

2) More turns on the secondary coil.

3) $V_p/V_s = n_p/n_s$ or $V_s/V_p = n_s/n_p$

4) E.g. they are lighter than ordinary transformers / they are more efficient than ordinary transformers when charging mobile phones / they don't use much power when they're switched on but have no load attached.

## Exam Questions

1 (a) As the wheel moves round it turns the cog wheel which is attached to a magnet *(1 mark)*. The magnet rotates near a coil of wire *(1 mark)*. This creates an alternating current in the wire which is used to power the light *(1 mark)*.

(b) (i) No potential difference is induced *(1 mark)*.

(ii) The lights would go out when the rider stops moving, e.g. at a junction *(1 mark)*.

2 (a) The transformer will have more turns on its primary coil because it is a step-down transformer *(1 mark)*.
*Step-down transformers have less turns on the secondary coil to reduce the voltage.*

(b) The primary coil produces a magnetic field within the iron core *(1 mark)*. Because the current in the coil is AC, the magnetic field in the core is constantly changing *(1 mark)*. This changing field induces an alternating potential difference across the secondary coil by electromagnetic induction *(1 mark)*.

3 (a) A voltage will not be induced in the secondary coil when using the DC supply from the battery *(1 mark)* because the magnetic field generated in the iron core is not changing *(1 mark)*.

(b) (i) Power = current × voltage = 2.5 × 12 = 30 W
*(2 marks, allow 1 mark for correct working)*

(ii) Assuming that the transformer is 100% efficient, the output power is 30 W *(1 mark)*.
Current = power ÷ voltage = 30 ÷ 4 = 7.5 A
*(2 marks, allow 1 mark for correct working)*

(iii) $V_s \div V_p = n_s \div n_p = 4 \div 12 = n_s \div 15 = 60 \div 12 = 5$ turns
*(2 marks, allow 1 mark for correct working)*

# Page 180

## Revision Summary for Physics 3b

3) $1.5 \times 600 = d \times 450$, so $d = 900 \div 450 = 2$ m

6) $T = 1 \div f$, $T = 1 \div 10 = 0.1$ s

7) $P = F \div A$, $P = 20 \div 0.25 = 80$ Pa (or 80 N/m²)

18) $V_s \div V_p = n_s \div n_p$ so $V_s = (600 \div 20) \times 9 = 30 \times 9 = 270$ V

19) $V_p \times I_p = V_s \times I_s$
so $I_s = (230 \times 2) \div 130 = 3.5$ A

# Exams

## Unit Physics 1

1 (a) Heat is conducted much more slowly through air than through solid materials like brick *(1 mark)*.

(b) Air near windows is cooled (by conduction) *(1 mark)* so it contracts / becomes denser and sinks which creates a convection current *(1 mark)*.

(c) He should choose brand B *(1 mark)* because materials with lower U-values are better insulators *(1 mark)*.

2 (a) The liquids are hotter than the surroundings and so transfer energy (to the surroundings) *(1 mark — reference to temperature difference or transfer to surroundings is required)*.

(b) oil *(1 mark)*
*The same amount of heating produces a larger temperature rise in oil — it needs less energy than water for a 1 °C rise.*

(c) Temperature change = 93 − 16 = 77 °C *(1 mark)*
Energy = mass × specific heat capacity × temperature change
126 = 1 × specific heat capacity × 77
Therefore specific heat capacity = 126 ÷ 77 = 1.64 kJ/kg°C
*(4 marks, allow 1 mark for correct temperature change, 1 mark for correctly rearranging the equation and 1 mark for correct substitution of values into the equation)*

(d) Water has a higher specific heat capacity than oil *(1 mark)* so it can store and then release more energy than oil *(1 mark)*.

3 (a) 4 *(1 mark)*
*It's the thickness of the arrows that matters — number 4 has the thinnest 'light energy' arrow.*

(b) efficiency = useful energy out ÷ total energy in
= 50 ÷ 200 = 0.25
0.25 × 100 = 25%
*(2 marks, allow 1 mark for correct working)*

(c) payback time = initial cost ÷ annual saving
= 375 ÷ 0.75 = 500 hours
*(2 marks, allow 1 mark for correct working)*

4 (a) The free electrons *(1 mark)* in the metal on the side nearest the hot soup will move faster *(1 mark)* and collide with other electrons transferring their extra energy to them and so on, through the metal. *(1 mark)*

(b) (i) Evaporation is when particles escape from a liquid and become gas particles *(1 mark)*.

(ii) The particles with the most kinetic energy are the ones that are most likely to escape from the liquid *(1 mark)*. When they do, the average speed and kinetic energy of the remaining particles decreases *(1 mark)*, which means that the temperature of the remaining liquid will fall and so the liquid will cool *(1 mark)*.

5 How to grade your answer:

0 marks: There is no relevant information.

1-2 marks: There is a brief explanation of how one feature of the fin's design helps it maximise energy transfer.

3-4 marks: There is some explanation of how at least two of the fin's design features help it maximise energy transfer.
The answer has a logical structure and spelling, punctuation and grammar are mostly correct.

5-6 marks: There is a clear and detailed explanation of how the fin's design helps it maximise energy transfer. The answer has a logical structure and uses correct spelling, grammar and punctuation.

Here are some points your answer may include:
- The cooling fin is shaped so that it has a large surface area — the larger the surface area, the higher the rate of energy transfer.
- More of the motorbike engine will be in contact with the surrounding air and so more heat will be radiated away.
- The fin has a black matt surface because dark matt surfaces are good emitters of heat radiation.
- The fin is made of metal, which is a good conductor, so the fin will transfer energy away quickly from the engine.

6 (a) (i) 2 and 3 *(1 mark)*

(ii) 1 because it has the longest wavelength and lowest frequency *(1 mark)*.

(b) Transmitted radio waves are reflected by the ionosphere and received by the receiver on the other side of the Earth *(1 mark)*.

(c) Long wavelength radio waves can be diffracted over the hill and into the house *(1 mark)*.

*(1 mark for waves correctly curving into the "shadow" of the hill to reach the house.)*

7 (a) (i) E.g. carbon dioxide *(1 mark)*.

(ii) E.g. any one from: fossil fuels are reliable, many renewables depend on the weather so can be unreliable / renewable resources often need larger power stations which means there are higher set-up costs / the amount of energy generated by fossil fuels is generally larger *(1 mark)*.

(iii) $CO_2$ is collected from power stations before it's released into the atmosphere and stored in empty gas and oil fields *(1 mark)*. This reduces the amount of $CO_2$ building up in the atmosphere and so reduces global warming *(1 mark)*.

(b) (i) 100 − 59.2 − 23.9 = 16.9% *(1 mark)*

(ii) Advantage — e.g. any one from: doesn't release harmful gases / fuel is relatively cheap. *(1 mark)*

Disadvantage — e.g. any one from: produces dangerous nuclear waste / waste is difficult to dispose of / cost of building power plant is high / cost of decommissioning is high / risk of major disaster / causes visual pollution. *(1 mark)*

8 (a) (i) time = 90 mins = 1.5 hours
energy transferred = power × time = 1.5 × 1.5 = 2.25 kWh
*(2 marks, allow 1 mark for correct working)*

(ii) cost = number of units × price per unit = 2.25 × 18 = 40.5p
*(2 marks for correct answer (allowing follow through from part (a), otherwise 1 mark for correctly rearranging the formula or a correct substitution))*

(b) The wind turns the blades of the wind turbine *(1 mark)* which drives a generator to generate electricity. *(1 mark)*

(c) Transformers are used to increase (step-up) the voltage and decrease the current before the electricity is distributed *(1 mark)*.
This reduces the amount of energy lost as heat *(1 mark)*.

9 (a) speed = frequency × wavelength
= $6.56 × 10^{-7} × 4.57 × 10^{14} = 3 × 10^8$ m/s
*(2 marks, allow 1 mark for correct working)*

(b) The universe began from a very small initial point that exploded and started expanding *(1 mark)*.

(c) How to grade your answer:

0 marks: There is no relevant information.

1-2 marks: There is a brief explanation of how they have led to the Big Bang theory being the currently accepted model of how the universe began.

3-4 marks: There is some explanation of how they have led to the Big Bang theory being the currently accepted model of how the universe began. The answer has a logical structure and spelling, punctuation and grammar are mostly correct.

5-6 marks: There is a clear and detailed explanation of how they have led to the Big Bang theory being the currently accepted model of how the universe began. The answer has a logical structure and uses correct spelling, grammar and punctuation.

Here are some points your answer may include:
- Red-shift shows that all distant galaxies are moving away from each other and that the furthest galaxies are moving away from us faster than nearer galaxies.
- This supports the Big Bang theory which says that the whole universe is expanding due to an initial explosion.
- The Big Bang theory explains the cosmic microwave background (CMBR) by saying that initially everything in the universe was hot and emitted very high frequency radiation.
- As the universe expanded this radiation cooled and dropped in frequency and is now seen as the CMBR that is detected from all parts of the universe.
- The Big Bang theory is the only theory that explains CMBR.

## Unit Physics 2

1 (a) (i) total momentum = 500 kg m/s + 200 kg m/s
= 700 kg m/s to the east *(1 mark)*

(ii) 700 kg m/s to the east
*(1 mark — must include units and direction)*

(b) Momentum of Car K is 700 − 200 = 500 kg m/s
Velocity = momentum ÷ mass = 500 ÷ 160 = 3.13 m/s to the east
*(3 marks for the correct speed, otherwise 1 mark for calculating the momentum of Car K, 1 mark for correct substitution. 1 mark for stating the correct direction.)*

2  (a)  acceleration = gradient of line = $-15 \div 7 = -2.14$ m/s$^2$ (to 2 d.p.)
*(2 marks for correct answer, otherwise 1 mark for correct substitution)*

(b)  It increases *(1 mark)*, as the brakes transfer the kinetic energy of wheels into heat energy *(1 mark)*.

(c)  E.g. they store some of the energy transferred by braking rather than wasting it *(1 mark)*.

(d)  E.g. driver tiredness *(1 mark)*, influence of alcohol or other drugs *(1 mark)*

3  (a)  work done = force × distance moved
= 20 N × 300 m
= 6000 J
*(2 marks for correct answer, otherwise 1 mark for correct substitution)*

(b)  power = work done ÷ time taken, so
time taken = work done ÷ power = 6000 J ÷ 15 W
= 400 s
*(2 marks for correct answer, allowing follow through from part (a), otherwise 1 mark for correctly rearranging the formula or a correct substitution)*

4  (a)  The air bag can change shape when a person hits it / slow a person down more gradually *(1 mark)*. This absorbs some of the energy of the impact / increases the time over which the change of momentum happens which reduces the forces acting *(1 mark)*.

(b)  force = spring constant × extension, so
extension = force ÷ spring constant
= 13 500 N ÷ 180 000 N/m
= 0.075 m
*(3 marks for correct answer with unit, otherwise 1 mark for correct rearrangement of the formula or substitution, 1 mark for the correct numerical answer)*

5  (a)  force = mass × acceleration, so
= 83 kg × 10 N/kg = 830 N
*(2 marks for correct answer, otherwise 1 mark for correct substitution)*

(b)  How to grade your answer:

0 marks:  There is no relevant information on the skydiver's motion.

1-2 marks:  There is a brief description of the skydiver's motion.

3-4 marks:  There is some description of the skydiver's motion, with brief reference to the forces acting on him. The answer has a logical structure and spelling, grammar and punctuation are mostly correct.

5-6 marks:  There is a clear and detailed description of the skydiver's motion, including details of the forces acting on him. The answer has a logical structure and uses correct spelling, grammar and punctuation.

Here are some points your answer may include:
•  At first, the slope of the graph is steep because he is accelerating as the force of gravity acting on him is much more than the frictional force slowing him down.
•  As his speed increases the friction builds up, so his acceleration is gradually reduced — shown on the graph by the gradient of the slope decreasing.
•  Eventually the frictional force is equal to the accelerating force and The skydiver no longer accelerates and travels at a constant velocity.
•  The constant velocity is shown by the flat line on the graph.
•  This shows that the skydiver has reached his terminal velocity.

6  (a)  Circuit B has greater resistance *(1 mark)* and a smaller current *(1 mark)*.

(b)  Power = 3 V × 0.5 A = 1.5 W
*(2 marks for correct value with unit, otherwise 1 mark for correct substitution)*

(c)  (i)  A — LDR / light dependent resistor *(1 mark)*
B — thermistor *(1 mark)*

(ii)  it decreases *(1 mark)*

7  (a)  Alpha, because some of the radiation is stopped by the sheet of paper *(1 mark)*.

(b)  (i)  E.g. alpha and beta radiation *(1 mark)*.

(ii)  The two types of radiation are deflected in opposite directions because they have opposite charges *(1 mark)*. Despite having a larger charge, the alpha particles (that follow path 2) have a larger mass *(1 mark)*, and so are deflected less by the electric field than the beta particles (that follow path 1) *(1 mark)*.

(c)  It detects background radiation *(1 mark)*.

8  (a)  The splitting of atomic nuclei *(1 mark)*.

(b)  Plutonium-239 / uranium-235 *(1 mark)*

(c)  The joining together of atomic/light nuclei to form larger/heavier ones *(1 mark)*.

(c)  How to grade your answer:

0 marks:  No advantages and disadvantages are given.

1-2 marks:  Brief description of one advantage and one disadvantage.

3-4 marks:  At least two advantages and two disadvantages are given. The answer has a logical structure and spelling, grammar and punctuation are mostly correct.

5-6 marks:  Answer gives at least three advantages and three disadvantages. The answer has a logical structure and uses correct spelling, grammar and punctuation.

Here are some points your answer may include:

Advantages:
•  Much more energy is released by nuclear fusion than by nuclear fission for an equivalent mass of starting material.
•  Nuclear fusion does not produce radioactive waste.
•  There's no risk of nuclear fallout with nuclear fusion.
•  Hydrogen can be used as fuel for nuclear fusion — so there's no problem of fuel shortage.

Disadvantages:
•  Scientists have not yet found a way of getting more energy out of nuclear fusion reactors than they put in.
•  Nuclear fusion can only happen at very high temperatures.
•  The nuclear fusion reaction would need to be held in a magnetic field as the temperature would be too high for a physical container to be used.

9  (a)

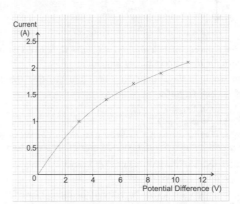

*(1 mark for correctly plotted points, 1 mark for good curve of best fit.)*

(b)  The resistance of the lamp increases as the current increases *(1 mark)*. The increased current causes the lamp to heat up, which makes the lattice ions of the metal filament vibrate more *(1 mark)*.
This leads to more collisions between lattice ions and charge-carrying electrons — increasing the electrical resistance *(1 mark)*.

(c)  2 A (accept 1.95 to 2.05 A) *(1 mark)*

(d)  Resistance = potential difference ÷ current
Resistance = 10 ÷ 2
Resistance = 5 Ω *(1 mark for value and 1 mark for unit. Allow follow-through from part (c))*

# Unit Physics 3

1  (a)  Moment = force × perpendicular distance = 100 × 0.2 = 20 Nm
*(3 marks for correct answer, otherwise 1 mark for correct substitution, 1 mark for correct numerical answer, 1 mark for correct unit.)*

(b)  The moment will decrease *(1 mark)* because the perpendicular distance between the line of action of the force and the axis of rotation/point A will decrease *(1 mark)*.

(c)  The stabilisers increase the width of the base of the bike *(1 mark)*. When the child is riding, the line of action of the weight of him and his bike is less likely to fall outside this wider base *(1 mark)*. Therefore there is no resultant moment/clockwise moment, so he is less likely to topple over *(1 mark)*.

2  (a)  friction *(1 mark)*

(b)  Because it is constantly changing direction *(1 mark)*.

(c)

*(1 mark for arrow A, pointing from motorbike to the centre of the circle)*

(d) Less than the force on the lorry *(1 mark)*.

*The force on the bike is equal to its mass × its acceleration. The lorry has the same acceleration but a greater mass, so the force on it is larger.*

(e) Yes. The force on the motorbike will be less because the radius of the circle it is turning in will be greater *(1 mark)*.

3 (a) rotate clockwise / left side moves upwards *(1 mark)*.

(b) (i) It would slow down *(1 mark)*.

(ii) It would speed up *(1 mark)*.

(iii) Nothing would change *(1 mark)*.

4 (a)

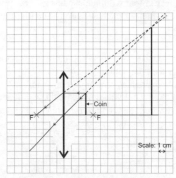

*(1 mark for correct construction lines, 1 mark for correct position and 1 mark for the correct size of image)*

(b) The image would be larger than the coin and further from the lens (but on the opposite side) *(1 mark)*.

(c) Power = 1 ÷ focal length
Power = 1 ÷ 0.04 m = 25 D
*(3 marks for correct answer, otherwise 1 mark for correct substitution, 1 mark for correct numerical answer, 1 mark for correct unit)*

(d) 1. Refractive index of the lens material *(1 mark)*
2. Shape/curvature of lens *(1 mark)*

5 (a) The force on piston A causes a pressure in the liquid *(1 mark)*. Liquids are virtually incompressible and the pressure in a liquid is transmitted equally in all directions *(1 mark)*. The pressure of the liquid at piston B causes a force on piston B (equal to $F = P_A \times A_B$ where $P_A$ is the pressure at piston A and $A_B$ is the area of piston B) *(1 mark)*.

(b) The pressure on piston A is equal to the pressure on piston B: $P_A = P_B$

$P_A$ = Force on piston A ÷ Area of piston A = 25 ÷ 0.01 = 2500 N/m²

so the pressure on piston B = $P_B$ = 2500 N/m²

Force on piston B = $F_B$ = $P_B$ × Area of piston B

$F_B$ = 2500 × 0.15 = 375 N

*(5 marks for correct answer, otherwise 1 mark for stating that $P_A = P_B$, 1 mark for correctly calculating the pressure on piston A, 1 mark for correct rearrangement of force-pressure equation, 1 mark for correct substitution.)*

6 (a) Light changes direction as it passes from one medium to another. *(1 mark)*

(b) (i) Only light that hits the boundary at an angle greater than the critical angle will totally internally reflected *(1 mark)*.

(ii) Total internal reflection can only happen when light travels from a medium with a higher refractive index into a medium with a lower refractive index *(1 mark)*. Light travels from air to diamond at the top, but from diamond to air at the bottom *(1 mark)*.

(c) The refractive index of diamond is greater than the refractive index of glass, so the critical angle of diamond is less than the critical angle of glass *(1 mark)*. More rays of light will be totally internally reflected by the diamond *(1 mark)*.

7 (a) The alternating current in the primary coil causes a rapidly changing magnetic field in the iron core *(1 mark)*. The changing magnetic field induces an alternating potential difference in the secondary coil *(1 mark)*.

(b)

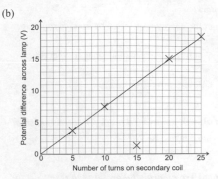

*(1 mark for all points correctly plotted, 1 mark for line of best fit)*

(c) (i) The result using 15 turns on the primary coil should be circled. *(1 mark)*

(ii) 11 V (Accept values between 10.5 and 11.5 V) *(1 mark)*

(d) Switch mode transformers are smaller than traditional transformers *(1 mark)*. This makes them lighter and so they are more suitable for devices that need to be portable *(1 mark)*. They are also much more efficient than traditional transformers./They don't use much power when there is no load *(1 mark)*.

8 (a) 'Sound' waves that have a higher frequency than the upper limit of hearing for humans. / Sound waves with a frequency greater than 20 000 Hz *(1 mark)*.

(b) Total distance travelled by pulse = 0.0048 m
Speed of ultrasound pulse = distance ÷ time = 0.0048 ÷ (3 × 10⁻⁶)
= 1600 m/s
*(3 marks for correct answer, otherwise 1 mark for correct substitution, 1 mark for correct total distance travelled by pulse.)*

(c) E.g. They create high resolution images. / They can help produce images that can be stored digitally. *(1 mark)*

(d) How to grade your answer:

0 marks: No advantages and disadvantages are given.

1-2 marks: Brief description of one advantage and one disadvantage.

3-4 marks: At least two advantages and two disadvantages are given. The answer has a logical structure and spelling, grammar and punctuation are mostly correct.

5-6 marks: Answer gives at least three advantages and three disadvantages. The answer has a logical structure and uses correct spelling, grammar and punctuation.

Here are some points your answer may include:

- Ultrasound waves are non-ionising and, as far as anyone can tell, safe.
- X-rays are ionising and can cause cancer if the patient is exposed to too high a dose.
- Ultrasound is safe to use for pre-natal scans of the developing fetus because of the lack of damaging ionising radiation.
- X-rays are definitely not safe for pre-natal scanning because they are ionising.
- The most suitable imaging technique to use depends on the type of tissue that you want to look at.
- X-rays penetrate soft tissue and can be used to image hard tissue such as bones and teeth.
- Ultrasound can be used to image soft tissue.
- Ultrasound can be used in the analysis of blood flow, which makes it useful in diagnosing heart problems.
- Ultrasound images are typically low resolution (fuzzy).
- X-ray images are typically clearer than ultrasound images and allow the doctor to see fine details that help diagnosis and treatment.

# Index

# Index